Don't Stick to Sports

DON'T STICK TO SPORTS

The American Athlete's Fight against Injustice

DEREK CHARLES CATSAM

ROWMAN & LITTLEFIELD
Lanham • Boulder • New York • London

Published by Rowman & Littlefield
An imprint of The Rowman & Littlefield Publishing Group, Inc.
4501 Forbes Boulevard, Suite 200, Lanham, Maryland 20706
www.rowman.com

86-90 Paul Street, London EC2A 4NE, United Kingdom

British Library Cataloguing in Publication Information Available

Library of Congress Cataloging-in-Publication Data

Names: Catsam, Derek author.
Title: Don't stick to sports: the American athlete's fight against injustice / Derek Charles Catsam.
Description: Lanham, MD: Rowman & Littlefield Publishing Group, [2023] |Includes
    bibliographical references and index. | Summary: "The intersection of sports and politics has
    been making headlines in the last few years, but the reality is that this clash has been going on
    for decades. This book examines the history of sports as a means to advance social change and
    connects that history to today's world"—Provided by publisher.
Identifiers: LCCN 2023006894 (print) | LCCN 2023006895 (ebook) | ISBN 9781538144718
    (cloth) | ISBN 9781538144725 (epub)
Subjects: LCSH: Sports—Social aspects—United States—History. | Racism in Sports—United
    States—History. | Sex discrimination in sports—United States—History. | Athletes—Political
    activity—United States—History. | Social change—United States.
Classification: LCC GV706.5 .C39 2023 (print) | LCC GV706.5 (ebook) | DDC306.4/830973—
    dc23/eng/20230310
LC record available at https://lccn.loc.gov/2023006894
LC ebook record available at https://lccn.loc.gov/2023006895

Dedicated to

Charles Dew and Alonzo Hamby,

teachers, mentors, friends

Contents

CONTENTS

Acknowledgments

No book is a true solo project. Although this one came together quite quickly, it is the product of being both a lifelong sports fan and a critic of so much of what sport represents.

Christen Karniski at Rowman & Littlefield conceived of this project before I did. While we were working on my previous book, *Flashpoint*, she suggested that I consider a book on American sports and politics. Her vision (and gentle prodding) made this book happen. The folks at R&L turned this from a manuscript into a book. In particular, Samantha Delwarte helped to make sure the sausage got made, and Nicole Carty proved a line editor extraordinaire who saved me from countless embarrassing mistakes.

I have the best agent in the biz. Amaryah Orenstein of GO Literary keeps me on my toes, is a world-class editor, and provides the kind of suggestions that make a book better. She's demanding when the situation calls for it but is always encouraging and is both an agent and a friend.

The bulk of this book fell into place in the summer of 2022. My friend Chris Frantz, who founded the Student Diplomacy Corps, offered me the chance to teach a college-level course on sports and civil rights in a summer program for gifted high school students at the Massachusetts College of Liberal Arts (MCLA). Chris does a fantastic job on a shoestring budget. His colleagues Tony Allen, John Meislin, and Madelaine Eulich made sure that the summer, still beleaguered by COVID, went off with as few hitches as possible. The folks at MCLA were always helpful to a visiting professor. Above all, the students in "(Don't) Stick to Sports: Sports and Civil Rights in the United States"—Caleb Lys, Daniel Smith, Gabriel Aofolajuwonlo, Jesus Cardon-Morales, Jordan Mensah-Boateng,

Julia Carmona, Mackenzie Young, Matyas Wagner, Sire Basse, and Yoselin Flores—made the summer a joy. Each one of them made me think more deeply and challenged me every day of the program. They are the future. The future is bright.

Over the course of the summer, my uncle and aunt, Nick and Sue Catsam, hosted me on multiple weekends, allowing me to clear my head and refresh. Rob and Janice Simler similarly opened their home to me. Rob is a fellow lifelong Boston sports fan off whom I have bounced many ideas, with me putting up with his nonsense in return. (Sorry about the plumbing.) Josh Pepin, another Boston fan, similarly hosted me during my time developing some of the ideas for this book. Rajiv Dwivedi secured the tickets to a gloriously catastrophic monstrosity of a Sox game and played host for a Boston night. Wesley McDowell: Stay Black.

My colleagues at UTPB have been endlessly supportive. Mike Frawley, Roland Spickermann, Jeff Washburn, and Jenny Paxton have been all that you can ask for in a history department. Graded on a curve, Bill Harlow and Todd Richardson have been perfectly cromulent. Raj Dakshinamurthy has been a fine interim provost and interim dean in trying times. I also should thank the Rhodes University history department, which hosts me as senior research associate, especially Head of Department Alan Kirkaldy.

Poppy Fry and the history department at the University of Puget Sound hosted me for a series of talks in the spring of 2022. Among these was a talk on sports in American history in one of Dr. Nancy Bristow's classes that forced me to clarify some of the major themes of this book.

To Mom and Dad, for letting me play and watch sports. And to Marcus, for reluctantly playing floor football and a million other games with me even though he could not have cared less about the outcomes.

As per convention, I am supposed to attribute all the good aspects of this book to others and claim any mistakes as my own. That is nonsense. Every typo and error, every infelicitous phrase and tortured sentence, every misattribution and certainly anything subject to litigation, is the sole province of Tom Bruscino and Steve Tootle. Tom and his better half, Terrie, hosted me while I was returning from Carlisle, so his share of the blame looms especially large. If you guys could stop making my books worse, I'd really appreciate it.

Ben Farmer: friend, confidante, bibliographer, indexer, researcher, idea-bouncer-offer, road trip partner, and summer roommate. We covered a giant swath from Odessa to Oklahoma City to St. Louis to Canton. We spent the better part of a summer in North Adams, Williamstown, and New Hampshire, then covered Carlisle to Louisville to Oxford to DFW. And, of course, Uranus.

And, as always, to Ana and George. I do this all for you and for us. I love you both beyond all measure.

Finally, I dedicate this book to Charles Dew and Alonzo Hamby. Charles took me, a rough-hewn working-class kid, under his wing at Williams College, introduced me to the complexities and wonder of Southern history, and showed me what a historian should be like. An outstanding teacher and scholar, Charles is truly one of the kindest men in the profession, and I have valued his support and encouragement and friendship over the years. In the summer of 2022, we were able to spend several hours together over dinners and lunches in Williamstown, and I will always cherish that time. Despite all of Charles's efforts, I was not much less rough around the edges when I arrived in Athens for my PhD program at Ohio University. Lon turned me into a historian. He provided encouragement and prodding, tough love and protection, mentorship and all the support that a graduate advisee needs. Without both these men I would not have become a historian, would never have written a book, would never have climbed high or climbed far, aiming for sky and star.

INTRODUCTION

THE BOUND AND THE PROTECTED

In early 2022, conservatives in the Florida legislature proposed a law that would require all professional sports teams in the state to play the national anthem before their events. This law was, of course, culture war dog whistling. For one thing, it was blatantly unconstitutional. Forcing anyone in Florida, never mind a private company, to engage in any kind of speech is a clear violation of the First Amendment.

But beyond that, in recent history, Florida's professional sports teams have always played "The Star-Spangled Banner" before games. In other words, Florida's legislation was not just dumb and repugnant to the Constitution, it was also superfluous. Sadly, it was also effective in rousing the ire of culture warriors against imaginary foes representing an undifferentiated, unpatriotic Other, because laws about patriotism in the United States are much less about laws per se than they are about enforcing laws for the strong against the weak.

At almost the same time, the same legislature, echoing those in more than a score of other states, put forth legislation, supported by Governor Ron DeSantis (as such legislation was supported by Republican governors in other states), that would ban so-called critical race theory (CRT) from being taught in schools. But beyond the fact that no real version of CRT was being taught in primary or secondary schools, this legislation went further, allowing for books to be banned from schools and libraries—not books that were based on any kind of critical theory, race or otherwise, but rather books that simply taught the sometimes messy history of race in the United States, including Florida. Books about race or by

Black authors were the target of this wide-ranging fearmongering—and, yes, racist law making, because laws about critical race theory, like laws about patriotism, are about reenforcing white supremacy and exercising power over the Other.

It did not matter whether this wave of patriotic or racist legislation reflected or responded to any kind of realities because symbolically the proposed legislation was pure gold. It allowed cynical politicians to propose cynical legislation that a cynical constituency would support wholeheartedly. But it also allowed for another American tradition to flourish: the Othering of entire groups of Americans.

This book is about how these processes manifest themselves in sports, an arena in which, in theory, merit is supposed to prevail above all else, but in which people have been excluded based on race, ethnicity, gender, or sexuality for virtually the entire history of the American sporting experience. The main premise of the book is that the common cry in public discussions that athletes, fans, and journalists should "stick to sports"—that sports and politics are somehow sealed off from one another—is not only faulty, it is absurd. But their cry does serve to perpetuate power dynamics, which is the real goal all along. If athletes or fans, coaches or journalists, choose to use their platforms to speak out against injustice, the desire for them to "stick to sports" is a desire to not address the underlying injustices. Demanding that athletes (and others) stick to the status quo is in effect demanding the perpetuation of injustice. The demand to "stick to sports," then, is cynical and indeed cruel.

But when it comes to the interaction between politics and sports, cynical and cruel has a remarkable winning percentage.

This monumental cynicism and cruelty is not new, for it comes from a basic branch of the American Experience: That there is a Them and there is an Us, a They and a We. They don't belong. We do, and We define that American Experience—and thus who belongs. In the words of Frank Wilhoit, a commenter at the blog *Crooked Timber* who has created one of the great truisms of the internet age, "Conservatism consists of exactly one proposition," which is that "there must be in-groups whom the law protects but does not bind, alongside out-groups whom the law binds but does not protect."[1] Or, as Sigmund Freud wrote in *Civilization and Its Discontents*, "It is always possible to bind a greater number of people together in love, if only some others remain against whom aggression can be expressed."[2] Indeed this book is about those bound out groups, the unloved targets of aggression—Black and brown, women and girls, gay and trans—or simply those political outsiders, cognizant that their own love of sport does not cover for the fact that they do not, or at least to some minds should not, belong. It is also about how sometimes, patriotism and nationalism have provided the pretext for either enforcing that outsider status or for binding those outsiders to prevent them any chance at the vaunted insider status.

This book, a collection of linked essays pursuing these themes, makes no claim at comprehensiveness. It does not tell the entire history of exclusion in sports in the United States, the whole story of the role of race and gender in sporting nationalism. Instead, it uses a series of case studies to illustrate the ways in which both exclusion and the fight against that exclusion have helped to define a sporting ecosystem that has often been anything but a meritocracy in an environment that has used politics as a weapon while forbidding political expression from athletes whose exclusion and restriction was wholly political.

"The Highest Point of the Game's Enthusiasm"

The National Anthem, Patriotism, and the 1918 World Series

THE GREAT WAR SEEMED TO HOVER OVER EVERY ASPECT OF AMERICAN society by 1918, and baseball was not immune. During the 1917 season, 76 major leaguers joined the armed services by spring training, and that number grew to 250 by the end of the season. Indeed, for the first half or so of the 1918 baseball season, baseball players (and other entertainers) were exempt from Secretary of War Newton Baker's "work or fight" policy, in which all healthy men were to either join the service or work in a war-related industry. In July, Baker changed his mind, declaring baseball inessential. Baseball players were now exempt through Labor Day but were then eligible for the draft. With the World Series in jeopardy, Baker exempted the players from World Series–eligible teams less than two weeks before the end of the regular season, justifying the move because of the intense fandom of American troops in France. After the 1917 season, Red Sox manager Jack Barry, who had spent just one year at the helm of the Sox, joined the naval reserve, just as 2 million other men volunteered for the service to go along with the 2.8 million men drafted under the new Selective Service Act. Meanwhile, the Red Sox won the 1918 American League pennant with a new manager. Ed Barrow, who had never played professional ball, led Boston to the pennant, which they had also won in 1903, 1904, 1912, 1915, and 1916.[1]

The United States was a vital difference-maker in what had been largely a protracted bloody European stalemate; it also emerged from the conflict as a major power and the only winner in any meaningful way. But the aftermath, though in sight, was far from clear from the vantage point of September 1918. The tens of thousands of dead Americans were not the only victims of war; large numbers of severely wounded and psychologically maimed Americans returned from Europe's killing fields as well. The war had created tensions at home; dissent against the war was effectively illegal as the administration of Woodrow Wilson, with the support of an acquiescent Congress, cracked down severely on opposition.

As if the stress of war, with its concomitant domestic crackdown, was not enough, on the day before the World Series was to commence—a day when a local newspaper headline read "Chicagoans on the List" of war dead—a bomb exploded in the Chicago Federal Building. The Industrial Workers of the World, the "Wobblies," were widely believed to be responsible for the attack, possibly as a response to several of the group's members being found guilty of federal sedition charges. Others simply blamed "anarchists" or "radicals." The judge in the case was Kenesaw Mountain Landis. A future commissioner of baseball, Landis would come to be known for his dour, authoritarian demeanor, which he had revealed in his career as a judge and would characterize his period as commissioner, in which he exercised absolute authority—including, in the minds of most observers, enforcing the color line that kept Black players out of the major leagues.

Furthering domestic tensions and anxieties was a global influenza pandemic that deeply divided society even as it proved monstrously deadly. Life expectancy heading into 1918 was fifty-four for women and forty-eight for men. By the end of the year, that number was reduced by a dozen years almost solely because of a pandemic that had not only proven deadly, but had also created debates about the line between personal freedom and public health. On the day the World Series began, the Massachusetts Department of Health declared that a new wave of influenza outbreak was likely to hit Boston and beyond, though officials initially downplayed the danger.

For these reasons, attendance at the opening game of the still relatively young Fall Classic on the afternoon of September 5 (delayed by a day because of rain) was underwhelming. Fewer than twenty thousand fans showed up to Comiskey Park, paying prices ranging from fifty cents to three dollars.[2] The game, perhaps ironically, was played at the home field of the American League Chicago White Sox rather than at the Cubs' own Wheegham Park (later to be rechristened Wrigley Field) because it held more fans. Game 1 of the 1917 World Series, which the White Sox hosted in the same stadium, had drawn thirty-two thousand patrons. High railroad rates probably discouraged many out-of-town fans from attending, and many fans (male and female) between the ages of eighteen and thirty were occupied with the war effort in one way or other.

Furthermore, some baseball fans did not see either the Cubs or the Red Sox as "legitimate champions," viewing them instead "as the two teams fortunate enough to have survived the attrition caused by the draft, enlistment, and shipyard dodgers."[3] Nonetheless, the two teams had emerged from their respective leagues and were prepared to compete for a championship. And while for myriad reasons fans did not show up in droves, the media in the two cities and beyond—in an era where newsprint was king—relished the World Series matchup. The Cubs were favored to win, but one individual hovered above all others: George Herman "Babe" Ruth, the Sox' ace pitcher and a burgeoning slugger who had been forced to spend time in the outfield in addition to his mound duties because of the depletion of players caused by the war.[4] "The mighty shadow of Babe Ruth falls athwart Chicago tonight like a menace," *Boston Herald and Journal* sportswriter Burt Whitman wrote on the eve of the scheduled first game. "Take him out of the way and the Cubs would have enough confidence to do harsh things to the men from Massachusetts. But there he is, a huge, horrifying prospect" for the Cubs' manager "and his men. He is the difference between defeat and victory." Ruth "absolutely lacks the nervousness which has hampered so many great pitchers" on the eve of a big series, asserting that he'd have been happy to pitch every game. Further, he maintained, "I hope not to sit on the bench a single inning of the series."[5]

During the seventh-inning stretch, fans stood for their "afternoon yawn, that has been the privilege and custom of baseball fans for many generations." It was during this interregnum that a twelve-piece military band "stationed in the outfield" broke into a spontaneous version of "The Star-Spangled Banner," and for the fans "the yawn was checked and heads were bared as the ball players turned quickly about and faced the music." It took some time for the fans to show similar respect as the players, but by the end of the band's rendition the performance was met with massive cheers "that marked the highest point of the game's enthusiasm." It was "the great moment of the game" and marked an event "far different from any incident that has ever occurred in the history of baseball."[6] The *Boston Globe* noted that "the left field bleacher space, usually given over to the virtues of a certain chewing gum"—Wrigley's, the namesake gum of the Cubs' owner—"admonished the crowd to 'Keep the Glow in Old Glory,' and the right field space commanded 'Buy War Savings Stamps, and Do It Now.'"[7] At least temporarily, patriotism had supplanted commerce.

Red Sox third baseman Fred Thomas was on furlough from the Navy. He was based at the Great Lakes Naval Training Station in Chicago, having managed to enlist in the Navy after the Army rejected him due to his diabetes.[8] The station's commander, Captain William Moffett, was a rabid baseball fan who seemed as committed to having a successful training center baseball team as he was to creating future seamen. Thomas, who had begun playing professionally out of high school in Wisconsin, later recalled, "I had it made at Great Lakes. All [I] had to do was play baseball."[9] The Red Sox, who had used nine journeyman third basemen throughout the 1918 season, asked if Thomas could play for them in the World Series. He thus was standing at third base when the band commenced a new version of "The Star-Spangled Banner" that John Philip Sousa, the leader of the Navy band (although he was not there that day) had written, and Thomas "immediately faced the flag and snapped to attention with a military salute. The other players on the field followed suit in 'civilian' fashion, meaning they stood and put their right hands over their hearts."[10] Fans joined in singing, growing in strength as the song reached its conclusion. Men in the stands tossed their caps in the air when the song was done, though Thomas kept his on and simply saluted.

The *New York Times* led off its story on the game not with the 1–0 Red Sox victory in one of the great pitching duels in World Series history but with the story of the playing of "The Star-Spangled Banner."[11] Indeed, fans seemed far more interested in watching a group of Army biplanes performing stunts within sight of the stadium than they were engrossed in most of the game. They even avoided "the usual umpire baiting."[12] The *Chicago Tribune*'s James Crusinberry also made note of the air display: "At one time there were six planes over the field. Occasionally one of them would do a nose dive or a tail spin just to let us know they were ready for a flight to Berlin."[13] Legendary Chicago sports writer Ring Lardner recognized the event in passing when he snidely mentioned that Thomas had thrice stood at attention—once during the anthem and twice watching called strike threes.[14]

In fact, for fans of pitchers' duels the game was tremendous. Babe Ruth (who may well have been hungover after imbibing with a motley crew the night before)[15] earned the shutout win for the Red Sox over Chicago starter Hippo Vaughn. First baseman Stuffy McInnis drove in the sole run on a hit-and-run single in the fourth that sent Dave Shean home, ensuring Ruth the victory and continuing his World Series scoreless streak, which stretched to twenty-two innings. As Nick Flatey of the *Boston American* described Ruth's performance on the mound, "Ruth had bewildering speed, a great curve and was as cool as a radiator in an apartment house. He worked the batters perfectly, and, on the three occasions when a hit meant a run, turned back the hostilities with consummate ease."[16]

Meanwhile the patriotic display of playing "The Star-Spangled Banner" was such a hit that the two team owners had a band play the song at each subsequent game. The Navy band played it during games 2 and 3 in Chicago, while at Fenway Park the Red Sox owners shifted the anthem from the seventh-inning stretch to the pregame, when they also honored veterans attending the game for free. People gave up their seats for wounded soldiers and in some cases helped them to their seats, even carrying them if need be. Fans donated to the Clark Griffith Bat and Ball Fund, which shipped baseball equipment to the men serving overseas. An anthem tradition for big games—Opening Day, the postseason, holidays—had begun. It would not be too long before the tradition extended to games of less significance. Sometime during World War II every Major League Baseball team but one—ironically enough, the Chicago Cubs—played it before every game, a tradition that continued after the war. Meanwhile, the Cubs would hold out for another two decades.[17]

* * *

And yet, as with many origin stories, the story of the spontaneous first sporting game national anthem at Chicago's Comiskey Park in Game 1 of the 1918 World Series, while embodying a perfect storm of earnest patriotism and America's pastime, is as much mythology as history. Yes, the anthem was played that series. Yes, it garnered a lot of attention, and yes, it is fairly well documented. The story is too good, too pure, too doused in 100 percent Americanism not to be the origin of the national anthem tradition at sporting events. This sort of mythmaking is actually common in sports. The origin myth of baseball itself has Abner Doubleday inventing the game in Cooperstown, New York, in 1839, even though he did no such thing and in fact the emergence of modern baseball took place over the course of decades, with varying rules in different places across the country. Similarly, and moving away from the United States, the game of rugby allegedly emerged during an 1823 game of football at England's Rugby School in which, according to a plaque erected at the school in 1895, William Webb Ellis "with a fine disregard for the rules of football, as played in his time, first took the ball in his arms and ran with it, thus originating the distinctive feature of the rugby game."[18] No such thing happened. But like the baseball origin myth, this story became a post facto justification to give a moment of birth to a game that changed, evolved, and adapted over the course of decades.

Similarly, while the playing of "The Star-Spangled Banner" during the 1918 World Series is acknowledged as a historic first, the real story is more complex. The earliest documented playing of "The Star-Spangled Banner" at a game took place decades before World War I, on May 15, 1862, when a band played the song during a game held at the Union Base Ball and Cricket Grounds in Brooklyn. Because the facility was the first enclosed stadium in the United States, the owners were able to charge attendees an admission fee; the music was part of a larger entertainment package, likely intended to entice patrons to a full day of entertainment with baseball at the center of it.[19] It is possible, of course, that the song was played even before that date, but we have no evidence showing as much.

By the mid-1890s, the playing of the song on professional baseball's Opening Day was commonplace. It was played at Opening Day in Philadelphia in 1897, for example. The linking of sport, patriotism, and "The Star-Spangled Banner" ratcheted up during times of war—on Opening Day in 1898, the Spanish-American War was raging, with the United States on its way to easy victory in what Secretary of State John Hay called a "splendid little war." Charles Ebbets, owner of the Brooklyn National League entry, held a flag raising, and both teams lined up for the 23rd Regiment band's playing of the song before an enraptured crowd waving small American flags.[20] By 1899, the song was played at the annual Army–Navy football game. By regulation, members of the military were to stand at attention and remove their hats for the playing of the song, which President Woodrow Wilson had named the national anthem by Executive Order. (Congress would not recognize it as such until 1931.) At the time, people lamented that spectators did not show the song proper respect, but the military decorum likely helped create the practices of standing at attention, removing hats, and fans generally mirroring the behavior of the military.[21] The song had also been played before a game in Boston around the turn of the century and was regularly played on Opening Day at Fenway Park and elsewhere, even before the Great War.[22]

If it makes little sense to play a national anthem before a professional sporting event, a college game, a high school contest, or a Little League game, it does make perfect sense to do so before national teams compete in international competition where players, coaches, and support staff are representing their countries. It appears that the first incidence of a national team playing their national anthem before a sporting event took place at Cardiff Arms Park in Wales on December 16, 1905, when, in response to the New Zealand All Blacks' performance of their traditional

Haka, the Welsh team sang their national anthem. Knowing the Haka was coming, the Welsh team planned their response in advance, but the home supporters joined them in the singing of "Hen Wlad Fy Nhadau." Wales pulled out a historic victory against a New Zealand side that had won twenty-seven straight, including all the games on a tour that established their "All Blacks" nickname. In one of the most controversial matches in rugby history, Wales emerged as 3–0 victors.

The tradition of playing the national anthem of gold medal winners at the Olympics did not begin until 1924, though at the Opening Ceremonies before that year each country's delegation in the parade of nations included a flag bearer, considered to be a high honor among Olympians. Even with this sporting tradition, U.S. Olympic athletes have carved out a jingoistic exception: Each team's delegation, when it reaches the place where the head of state of the host nation is seated, traditionally dips their flag as an honor to the host. In 1908, amid tension between the U.S. Olympic team and the British hosts in London—many of which seem to stem from petty behaviors on both sides—the American flag bearer, Ralph Rose, refused to lower the flag when he "presented" it to King Edward. Rose is supposed to have said, "This flag dips to no earthly king."[23] For the next generation, American flag bearers were not consistent in this stance, but since 1936, when the Americans understandably did not want to lower their flag before Adolf Hitler, the U.S. delegations have steadfastly refused to do so. This has caused a great deal of consternation among many who believe this smacks of arrogance and defied the Olympic ideal. Over the years, other countries have adopted the refusal to dip their flag.

For the rest of the world, this American hyperpatriotism, embedded in the ubiquitous playing of "The Star-Spangled Banner" and the refusal to adhere to Olympic tradition, is most often amusing, sometimes bemusing, and occasionally annoying. By now, the rest of the world can watch the Super Bowl, though American football cannot in any meaningful way be considered a global sport like basketball and, to some extent, baseball. But the jingoism, amusing though it is, also reveals a certain level of arrogance that for many across the globe serves as a reminder of the United States' standing as global hegemon. The very term "World Series" gets at the heart of a particularly noxious form of American exceptionalism driven by jingoistic patriotism. For the World Series in 1918 pitted two teams of Americans who were playing a game that especially at the time was almost exclusively played in the United States. (The Red Sox won that series in six games, by the way.)[24] As would become common in American sports, an American professional sports league was going to declare a "world's champion" without engaging in the rudimentary courtesy of inviting the rest of the world along. This continues to vex the rest of the world and is perhaps the quintessential example of what they see as American arrogance.

Nonetheless, baseball was certainly crucial in the popularizing of "The Star-Spangled Banner" as the de facto national anthem. Even if Congress had not yet officially legislated the song as the official national anthem in 1918, "thanks to a brass band, some fickle fans and a player who snapped to attention on a somber day in September, the old battle ballad was the national pastime's anthem more than a decade before it was the nation's."[25]

In the words of historian Jim Leeke, a Navy veteran, "In 1918, [the playing of the anthem and the response to it] was spontaneous. And today almost nothing about organized sports and the national anthem is spontaneous." Baseball historian John Thorne echoes Leeke's sentiment. For him, the spontaneity of 1918 "has been replaced by manufactured patriotism. The predictable, mandatory patriotism."[26] Indeed, perhaps Cubs owner Phillip Wrigley saw this coming all along. He did not hold out from playing the national anthem before every game because he was unpatriotic; he did so because he thought its frequent playing "cheapened the anthem." He relented on this stand only in 1967, during yet another war—this one in Vietnam—in which the flag became a tool for demanding blind patriotic fealty.[27]

But this "celebratory patriotism," as historian Ben Railton has called it, is often weaponized.[28] It is weaponized against dissent but also sometimes simply against the Other and especially weaponized against those Others who also dissent. For as we shall see, sport in America has historically been as much about exclusion as it has been about inclusion, and this exclusion has not only extended to ideology—excluding ideology has been central to this exclusion. Because exclusion of African Americans and other minorities and ethnic groups, exclusion of women, and exclusion of gay athletes has also been driven by ideologies of white supremacy, misogyny, and homophobia.

CHAPTER 2

Of "Dead Sparrows" and "Muscle Molls"

Gender Expectations and Women's Sport

THE 1928 OLYMPICS AND PATERNALISM

Baron de Coubertin, the founder of the modern Olympic Games, was no fan of women in sport, calling it the "most unaesthetic sight human eyes could contemplate." He argued in 1912 that "the Olympic Games must be reserved for men. . . . We must continue to try and achieve the following definition" of the Games: "the solemn and periodic exaltation of male athleticism, with internationalism as a base, loyalty as a means, art for its setting, and female applause as its reward."[1] As Coubertin's words make clear, from the outset of the Olympic movement, women's competition was deeply controversial, with many of the men who ran high-level sport globally believing women should be prevented from participating in events like the Olympics, or at least that their participation should be circumscribed.

As the century progressed, track and field would become the sport in which women were granted some of the greatest sporting opportunities, from which followed some of the greatest sporting pain. Yet even amid high-level competition, men could not help but impose gendered expectations and sexualize competitors. As we shall see, even after women had fought for and won the right to compete, they continued to be judged by their appearance.

* * *

In the early modern Olympics, women were confined to "women's sports": equestrianism, sailing, tennis, archery, swimming and diving, and—as an exhibition sport by 1924—gymnastics. But women's participation slowly grew with each succeeding Olympics. By 1928, 290 women competed—five times more than had taken part in the 1920 Antwerp Olympics—and gymnastics (now a full sport) and five track and field events had been added to the women's schedule, alongside fencing, which was newly added in 1924. The longest event on the program in track and field was the 800 meters, two laps around a regulation 400-meter track. It is perhaps not coincidence that these were the first Olympics in which Coubertin was not in charge.

Now keep in mind that the 800 is a grueling event. Although in many high school programs 800-meter runners train as distance runners (the 3200 meters is the longest event in almost every high school track meet), the fact is that at the elite level the 800, a middle distance event, can also be seen as the very outer limit of the sprints. When run at maximum capacity, the 800 is incredibly hard. It is a cardiovascular killer that simultaneously enlists the fast-twitch muscles activated in the sprinting events and requires speed, stamina, and strength in addition to race savvy. Runners often end up on their knees or lying on their backs gasping for air—even in the finals of an Olympic 800—because it is incredibly taxing.

Many people—Olympic organizers, international track officials, reporters, ordinary misogynists, and what we might today call concern trolls—had already built up a narrative that the 800 was too long, too difficult, and too challenging for women. It would create too much strain, leading to deleterious long-term effects. Reporters placed bets as to how many would be unable to finish and which competitors would be the first to succumb. Some made fun of the athletes preparing to run in the trials and finals in earshot of their teammates. In a sense, this set up an inevitable postrace response because these men were then invested not in a particular outcome on the track, but a particular kind of scenario as a result of the race being run at all.

Strip away the chauvinism that preceded the race and that would follow in its wake, and the 1928 women's track and field 800 meter competition was quite compelling. Twenty-six athletes from thirteen countries competed overall. Three heats were run on August 1, with the top three from each heat qualifying for the next day's finals. Three Americans competed in the trials, but only one, Florence MacDonald, advanced to the finals. There had been rain the night before the finals, and the race was held in humid conditions on the hottest day of the entire competition. In the finals, Germany's Lina Radke, running a world record time of 2:16.8, edged out Japan's Kinue Hitomi (2:17.6) for gold, with Sweden's Inga Gentzel (2:17.8) winning the bronze. MacDonald finished sixth.

In the wake of the compelling, hard-fought, tactical race that saw several lead changes, and in light of the facts of the grueling nature of the 800, a number of competitors dropped to their knees or otherwise struggled to regain their breath.[2] Most who did "moved to the infield to lie down since they were not only winded but also disappointed at not winning."[3] One woman, Canadian Jeannie Thomas, did fall to the ground at the end of the race after crossing the line and was helped up immediately; her "collapse" was the result of fighting through to finish the race despite an injury, the sort of thing that athletes are normally lauded for enduring.[4] This is hardly rare in elite track and field. Second-place finisher Hitomi was one of those who briefly fell to the infield, disappointed with defeat and having given her all, an understandable response given that Hitomi was a sprinter who "had never run an event of that distance" before.[5]

Though several men who competed in the same event ended their race in the same fashion, a number of male observers claimed that most of the women in the race collapsed from exhaustion and that this proved that women could not handle the 800 meters. A narrative swirled that most of the competitors could not even finish the race, collapsing before the finish line. In fact, all nine of the athletes finished the finals race, with the top six all breaking the former world record, the top seven all coming in at or under 2:23, and the eighth place finisher running a slower 2:28—not so slow that she could have collapsed, gotten up, and finished only five seconds behind the seventh place finisher. There is no time listed for the ninth place finisher, but she did finish the race; had she collapsed and been attended to before finishing, she would have been disqualified. What had occurred was simply the greatest 800-meter race in history up to that time.

The newspaper coverage was ruthless. Papers across the globe seemed to reach a near consensus. Rotterdam's *De Maasbode* proclaimed, "It was a pitiful spectacle: to see there girls tumble down after the finish line like so many dead sparrows. This distance is far too strenuous for women." According to a reporter from London's *Telegraph*, "The final of the 800m for women was a demonstration of what girls may do to suffer and win renown as athletes and made a deep impression on me. But it left me firmly convinced that it would have been better if it had not been done."[6] The *Times* of London called the 800 meters "dangerous" for women. The *Montreal Daily Star* called the race "a disgrace," asked for the 800 meters "to be taken off any future program," and claimed that the distance "is obviously beyond women's powers of endurance, and can only be injurious to them."[7] An Australian weekly, the *Bulletin*, concluded, "After the 800 metres race at the Olympiad knocked out and hysterical females were floundering all over the place. Competition in such events can serve no useful or aesthetic purpose in feminine existence."[8] One newspaper "actually used a primitive form of Photoshop to scare readers with the sight of the women's contorted faces."[9]

The American press was no better, and most of it was built on a foundation of untruths. William Shirer, writing in the *Chicago Tribune*, claimed that five women did not finish the race, that MacDonald had to be "worked over" after "falling into the grass unconscious," and that silver medalist Hitomi required fifteen minutes to be revived after collapsing.[10] Notre Dame football coach Knute Rockne, who was in Amsterdam and served as a reporter for a press syndicate, claimed that only six finished the race and that five collapsed: "It was not a very edifying spectacle to see a group of fine girls running themselves into a state of exhaustion."[11] None of this was true. Writing for the *New York Times*, Wythe Williams reported that six of the women "fell headlong on the ground" and repeated the alleged travails of MacDonald and Hitomi. Again, none of this was true. Nonetheless, he concluded, "The final of the 800-meter run plainly demonstrated that even this distance makes too great a call on feminine strength."[12]

Facts did not seem to be a major concern for the journalistic critics. Reflecting in *Harper's Monthly* a year later, in July 1929, John Tunis wrote that those who doubted that women's bodies were more vulnerable in the 1928 Olympics "should have stood beside me during the" 800 in Amsterdam: "Below us on the cinder track were eleven wretched women [only nine competed in the finals] five of whom dropped out before the finish [all nine finalists finished the race] while five collapsed after crossing the tape." This is not what the actual video shows, and it should be noted that there is a difference between "collapsing" because one has run a hard race and a medical emergency. "I was informed later," Tunis continued, "that the remaining starter fainted in the dressing room shortly afterward."[13] There is literally no evidence that this happened; of all the alleged facts in this narrative, almost all are provably false.

The hypocrisy was also clear, as "while men received praise for do-or-die determination, the same behavior by women was seen as completely inappropriate."[14]

After having won the inaugural Olympic women's 100-meter dash in a world record time, Betty Robinson, "the new queen of the track," did not help her teammates or other woman athletes, buying into reductionist arguments about what events were appropriate for women to run. "I believe that the 220-yard dash is long enough for any girl to run. Any distance beyond that taxes the strength of a girl, even though some of them might be built 'like an ox,' as they sometimes say," the teenager told a journalist. "Some of the scenes at the finish of various 800-meter races recently have been actually distressing. Imagine girls falling down before they hit the finish line or collapsing when the race is over! The laws of nature never provided a girl with the physical equipment to withstand the grueling pace of such a grind. . . . I do not profess to be an expert on heart and nerve reaction to the longer distances, but common sense will tell you that they must be quite severe."[15] Her analysis, like that of the male journalists and other critics, simply does not reflect the reality of what happened in the finals in Amsterdam.

One male Olympic track and field official, Dr. Fr. M. Messerli, who had worked with woman athletes for many years, wrote a report after the race: "When reaching the winning post, two Canadians and one Japanese competitors [*sic*] collapsed on the lawn, the public and journalists believed them to be in a state of exhaustion. I was judging this particular event and on the spot at the time, I can therefore certify that there was nothing wrong with them, they burst into tears betraying their disappointment at having lost the race, a very feminine trait!"[16] This last aside captured an attitude toward women that even putatively progressive men of the era surely felt, but it also revealed the honest contemporary opinion of a witness and participant in the Games that gave the lie to the media treatment that followed, an official response that was fueled by that reaction.

Another contemporary from the German Olympic Committee also saw no problem in the women's competitions in Amsterdam. In fact, they took seriously the importance of women's training and preparation, even if they presented it in gendered terms: "In almost every specific sporting nation there are women whose constitution and somatyping vary from extreme femininity to the boyish or young men's." The correspondent, writing in an overview titled "Die Olympischen Spiele [The Olympic Games]," continued, "There was, therefore, an unmistakable advantage from those nations where physical education for girls and boys differ very little. This boyish type with the obvious advantages in the areas of sprinting and jumping was seen in competitors mainly from the USA and Canada."[17] The author also confronted the perceived end of the women's 800: "The condition of exhaustion of several competitors after the race, which had caused some complaints, was certainly more of a psychological nature. A nervous reaction caused by the excitement of competition for the world championship." Therefore, "it would be regrettable if this competition would not appear again in the next Olympic program. As in the case of men, adaptation and preparation will exclude these images of exhaustion."[18]

Because this testimony convinced no one whose mind was not already made up, whether on their own or as a result of the media frenzy, authorities—all men—in the International Amateur Athletics

Federation (IAAF; the governing body for track and field) and the International Olympic Committee (IOC) decided they had to act. The initial IAAF vote to eliminate all women's track and field events from the Olympics failed by a count of 16–6. Instead, the IAAF decided—and the IOC agreed—to exclude women from the 800 meters, long jump, shot put, and 200 meters. The vote to eliminate the 800 was 12–9, closer than many might have suspected, and the other three events were also eliminated by slim majorities. The women's 200, long jump, and shot put would return in the 1948 Olympics. The conclusion made by the male barons of sport who forbid women from running distances of more than 100 meters cited vague "medical 'evidence.'"[19]

In the aftermath of the women's 800 and the tempest it caused, Coubertin's successor, Count Henri de Baillet-Latour proposed that women only be allowed to partake in "aesthetical" sporting events. In the debate that followed, it was established that "a vote would be taken separately as to whether women should be admitted in athletics and fencing, the vote for swimming, gymnastics, lawn tennis and swimming"—apparently the women's sports—"was passed by 26 votes to 1." In the separate vote regarding athletics, the vote was much closer, 17–9 in favor of allowing women's track and field, a vote that turned out as it did at least in part because the IAAF indicated it might withdraw from the Games entirely. Nonetheless, voices within the IAAF—including the United States' Olympic martinet, Avery Brundage—continued to pursue the exclusion of women. Brundage, who headed the U.S. Amateur Athletic Union (AAU), which was in charge of not just track and field but almost the entire range of Olympic sports, "was against women's participation in track and field events, and after the Los Angeles and Berlin Olympics he became an outspoken ally of the anti-Olympic movement in women's sports."[20] (Brundage, an anti-Semite and racist in addition to being a sexist, might be included in a conversation for the title of most horrible person in the history of American sports.)

The IOC reinstated the 800 (but not the 400, and nothing longer than 800) for the 1960 Games in Rome, but this whole sordid situation offers but one example of the challenges woman athletes have sought to overcome. In Europe, where track and field was and continues to be a major spectator sport, meets regularly featured the 800. In the words of track historian, longtime *Runner's World* editor, and 1968 Boston Marathon winner Amby Burfoot, the continued European competition in the event "didn't seem to kill anyone, and it gave women track runners a bigger stage on which to test their abilities."[21]

Much of the paternalism surrounding women in distance events culminates in an irony: In ultradistance events there is a point where women are better equipped to run those distances than their male counterparts. Yet for the bulk of the twentieth century, women were not allowed to run even middle-distance events, never mind longer races. In fact, until the 1970s, women who wanted to run elite races like the Boston or New York City marathons had to sneak onto the course, sometimes running the risk of being bodily removed from the course. Women could not run either race officially until 1972.

Women were not allowed to compete in the Olympic marathon, one of the marquee events of the Games, until 1984. Then—world record holder Joan Benoit (who had won the Boston Marathon in 1979 and 1983, the latter in a world record time of 2:22.43) won the race in sizzling conditions that August day in Los Angeles, finishing first of fifty entrants from twenty-eight countries, forty-four of whom finished. Benoit's time of 2:24:52, establishing the women's record in the event, would have won every men's Olympic marathon through the 1948 Games. It also would have won in 1956. Although often praised as a pioneer in women's track and field, Benoit rejects that label. "I consider myself part of the next generation," she has said. "I'm not in the same league as the pioneer women runners who came before me. They were part of the process of history changing. They brought progress to the sport. They are in a league of their own. They had guts, they had talent, and most of all, they had the passion to pursue the sport they loved."[22] Clearly, she was talking about the women who ran the 800 at the Amsterdam Olympics as well as all those who followed.

Naturally this Olympian narrative reinforced other sexist tropes about woman athletes: that they were unfeminine, that competitive sports undercut their ability to reproduce, that sports promoted homosexuality, and so forth. These narratives were about controlling women's bodies and controlling their options.

Women, incidentally, did not take this insult without a response. In the wake of continued exclusion from track events in the 1920 Antwerp Games, French athlete and activist Alice Millait started her own organization. In its first meeting on October 31, 1921, the Fédération Sportives Fémenine Internationale (FSFI) voted to establish the Women's Olympics as an alternative to the traditional Games. The organization went on to hold four Olympiads—in 1922 (Paris), 1926 (Gothenburg), 1930 (Prague), and 1934 (London)—with athletes coming predominantly from Western Europe, North America, and Japan. (Starting in Gothenburg the name of the competition became the Women's World Games.) This challenge caused the IAAF to wrest more control of women's track and field starting in 1923 and led to the inclusion of the track events for women in 1928, and though the FSFI folded in the mid-1930s, it helped to fuel greater inclusion for women in the Olympic Games. Despite the restrictions on women's events after Amsterdam, the groundswell of support for women's sport was clear.

This might seem an odd departure—a story about an Olympics in Amsterdam that is not truly an American story. Yet it tells us a great deal about the global trends in women's sport in which America became deeply embedded. Racism in American sport was not unique; South Africa, New Zealand, Australia, and many other countries perpetuated racism in sport and saw struggles against that racism, but in most of those cases, local circumstances provided the bulk of the impetus and the context. But when it came to women's sport, the global trends—paternalism, misogyny, and control by global entities—was far more extensive. Victorian Britain set the tone for women's sport as it had set the tone in sporting amateurism. As we shall see, the development of women's sport in America eventually took on its own contours. Black men participating in mixed sport was seen as a problem in the United States, but Black men's participation in segregated sports was not necessarily seen as problematic. Women's sport, on the other hand, was itself largely seen as problematic in the United States—a view shared by many women. In matters of both race and gender, white men wanted control. They wanted to control *how*

Black men participated in sport and under what circumstances, and they wanted to control *whether* women could participate and under what circumstances. The latter trend was global, or at least centered in Europe, thus for the women's sporting experience in the United States, the events in Amsterdam mattered.

Cutting back on track and field events for women is perhaps the most obvious example of bowdlerizing women's sporting opportunities. Other examples include six-player basketball for girls in the Midwest, the slow and uneven emergence of women's professional sports leagues in the United States, and even the uncomfortable in-between status of cheerleading, an overwhelmingly female sport that requires both athleticism and commitment but that first and foremost exists to support high school boys' and college and professional men's sports. In Texas, high school football games regularly hold halftime events celebrating boys' peewee and middle school football players and the little girls in cheerleading outfits whose job it is to support them.

BABE DIDRIKSON AND THE MALE GAZE

In the wake of achieving the vote in the United States, women's status in sport was still thoroughly third class at best. When discussing the golden age of sports in the 1920s, we need to think of it as we do all golden ages: as romanticized nostalgia, not as a reality. The twenties were a golden age for some, but for women and for Black and Brown athletes, it was anything but. For the overwhelming majority of sportswomen, even middle-class white women, sporting options were deeply circumscribed, with women protected "for their own good" (or for the good of their future offspring, the purpose for which most women were presumed to exist) or because some events simply were not—according to the men in power— appropriate for ladies. The 800 at the Amsterdam Olympics marks the most visible manifestation of these trends—the nadir—but girls and women continued to struggle for more than another half century. Nonetheless, some women would leap over and barge through the barriers the men who dominated sports hierarchies had erected.

Jim Thorpe, Jackie Robinson, and Jim Brown are remembered as athletes who could take on any sport and excel at an elite level. Add to that list Mildred "Babe" Didrikson, a native of Port Arthur, Texas, whom one historian has suggested was "perhaps the twentieth century's most gifted all-around athlete."[23] She was an all-American basketball player. She excelled in both softball and baseball, pitching four innings in major league spring training games. She was an expert diver. She roller-skated, was an outstanding bowler, and played pool competitively. She boxed and threw a fair punch. She was a crack shot with a rifle. And these were not even her best sports. In the 1932 Los Angeles Olympics, she won two gold medals—in the 80-meter hurdles and the javelin—and silver in the high jump after tying for the highest jump but falling to second on a controversial technicality. She broke or tied four world records and remains the only person ever to win medals in a running, jumping, and throwing event. She did not even start seriously playing golf—the sport in which she would gain her most sustained fame—until 1936, but she would go on to a Hall of Fame career in which she would win forty-eight events and ten women's golf majors. Didrikson long rejected the frilly things that girls were supposed to be interested in, including most traditional girls' pastimes, referring to those girls who followed that path as "sissies." Didrikson refused to let her gender set limits for what she could and could not do. Once, when asked by an amateur woman golfer how she hit the ball so hard, Didrikson responded, "It's not enough to swing at the ball. You've got to loosen your girdle and really let the ball have it." She later claimed that this was the most quoted thing she'd ever said.[24]

Heading into the 1932 Olympic Games there was some dispute as to Didrikson's amateur eligibility because she had appeared in an advertisement for milk. She was briefly suspended by the AAU but was quickly reinstated, simultaneously restoring her eligibility. Yet Avery Brundage used the minor (and utterly fabricated) controversy to revive the debate over women's very right to participate in sports at all. "You know," he said, feigning that his thoughts were emerging spontaneously, "the ancient Greeks kept women out of their athletic games. They wouldn't even let them on the sidelines. I'm not so sure but they were right."[25] Given Brundage's role as head of the AAU, he had considerable sway, but the fact that the body reinstated Didrikson's eligibility meant that enough of the AAU membership was both committed to women's sport and willing to defy the powerful Brundage.

As historian Allen Guttmann has pointed out, it was quite ironic that Didrikson proved to be "the most remarkable performer" of the Los Angeles Games.[26] She should have been an even bigger star. One of the adjustments officials had made to restrict women's participation was to limit female athletes to three events in the track and field competition, a restriction that would have curbed only a tiny number of athletes—indeed probably one: Didrikson, who had won five events at the U.S. Olympic Trials. In so doing, she had singlehandedly not only won those five events and tied for first in another, she won the team meet as an individual.

Brundage's opinions never really shifted. In 1949, when he was vice president of the IOC, he wrote, "I think it is quite well known that I am lukewarm on most of the events for women for a number of reasons which I will not bother to expound because I probably will be outvoted anyway." He nonetheless persisted in his increasingly anachronistic—but hardly rare—view: "I think that women's events should be confined to those appropriate for women: swimming, tennis, figure skating, and fencing but certainly not shot putting."[27]

Nearly a decade later, Brundage still had not relented, though he knew the time of his type was fading. In 1957, he wrote to members of the IOC. "Many still believe that events for women should be eliminated from the Games," he claimed, acknowledging that "this group is now a minority. There is still, however, a well grounded protest against events which are not truly feminine, like putting a shot, or those too strenuous for most of the opposite sex, such as distance runs." And indeed, in the April 1953 meeting of the IOC in Mexico City, there had been a discussion that women "not be excluded from the Games" but that their participation be limited to "'suitable' sports." The pretext for the argument was that the Games were growing too large and unwieldy and that cutting women's sports (and thus officials, support staff, and the like) would make the Olympics smaller.[28] The Games—Winter and Summer—would continue to grow, and with it, women's participation, and thus women's sporting opportunities, would likewise grow.

Yet Brundage, while increasingly isolated, was not alone. As historian David Goldblatt has shown, "many found" Didrikson's "physique, demeanor, and intensity worryingly masculine" with journalists pointing out her "doorstop jaw and piano-wire muscles," and expressed concern about her "Viking capacity for baser rage."[29] Arthur Daley, writing in the *New York Times* in 1953, echoed Brundage in his willingness to restrict women's participation in sport, including the Olympics, still the foremost venue for woman athletes: "There is just nothing feminine or enchanting about a girl with beads of perspiration on her alabaster brow, the result of grotesque contortions in events totally unsuited to female architecture." Once again, the arbitrary aesthetic perceptions of (some) men were presumed to have a voice in the right of women to compete in sports. "It's probably boorish to say it," Daley wrote, "but any self-respecting schoolboy can achieve superior performance to a woman champion." Yes, it was boorish, but also irrelevant. Women's performances were improving with training and opportunity so that the typical schoolboy was not exceeding these performances, but also, many of the same men who levied this argument then (and those who still do now) had no problem watching high school boys' sporting events that would be exceeded by even the most meager small college athletes, or men's college sports whose performers would be destroyed by even the worst professional teams. This argument—which is common today, particularly in discussions of the WNBA or elite women's soccer—is a justification for watching only the tiniest slice of elite sport. It is not a legitimate argument against women's sport. Daley echoed Brundage's evocation of ancient Olympics. "The Greeks knew exactly what they were doing when they invented the Olympics," he wrote. "Not only did they bar the damsels from competing but they wouldn't even admit them as spectators." Yet he returned to what amounted to his own sexual voyeurism: "Don't get me wrong please. Women are wonderful. But when those delightful creatures begin to toss the discus or put the shot—well, it does something to a guy. And it ain't love, Buster."[30] It is quite incredible how many middle-aged sportswriters and athletic officials who looked like, well, middle-aged sportswriters and athletic officials, felt the right—indeed the need—to insert their views on the sexual desirability of competitive woman athletes into the discussion.

Swimming competitions in particular evoked a creepy admiration from the era's male journalists and their publications. Magazines and newspapers suddenly found themselves drawn to women's swimming, festooning their pages with pictures from the pool. Helene Madison, winner of three Los Angeles gold medals, was "the beautiful New Yorker." Diver Georgia Coleman was "Gorgeous Georgia." The male gaze was strong in the coverage from the water events. "You get your money's worth from Olympic swim—in Loveliness" wrote the *Chicago Tribune*. Paul Gallico wrote of bronze medalist Jane Fauntz, "Her marvellous body flowed through the dives with the smoothness of running quicksilver."[31]

Gallico was one of the stars of what many perceive to be the golden age of sportswriting, and he shared the sentiments of many of the sexists of his era when it came to woman athletes. In his collection of sportswriting, *Farewell to Sport* (he abandoned the sports pages and went on to be a novelist and screenwriter), he made his biases clear. "For all her occasional beauty and unquestioned courage, there has always been something faintly ridiculous about the big-time lady athletes. They never manage entirely to escape a vague hint of burlesque about the entire business," he wrote, an assertion that perhaps reveals more about the observer than the observed. "A generation ago they were funny in a mild way because they tried to play competitive games and at the same time retain their maiden modesty," he finished with a ghastly flourish. "Today they manage to be amusing for exactly the opposite reason; they play with complete abandon and exposure, and as if that were not enough, the mores and morals of the times have made possible deliciously frank and biological discussions in the columns of the newspapers as to whether this or that famous woman athlete should be addressed as 'Miss,' 'Mrs.,' 'Mr.,' or 'It.'"[32] Other sportswriters and observers had gone so far as to "cruelly label her a member of the 'Third Sex.'"[33]

In 1933, Gallico published a fictional piece with a main character, Honey, a barely concealed stand-in for Didrikson. She is an athletic star—a hurdler and javelin thrower—"who is best known for being an oddity who is more man than woman, is more sexually agnostic than heterosexual, and, in the end, allows her self-hatred to get the best of her, despite winning a gold medal." Gallico's "most withering passages lament

Honey's ungainly looks," an "unsettling dichotomy between 'the most beautiful body that anyone saw on a woman because it happened to be a boy's body'" and her "face, which 'is something else again.'" It turned out that Honey's athletic triumphs "were attributable to her all-consuming desire for revenge against all the men in the world."[34]

Indicative of at least some of Gallico's wider views, in earlier versions of *Farewell to Sport* he posited why Jewish people excelled at basketball in his era: "The game places a premium on an alert scheming mind and flashy trickiness, artful dodging and general smart aleckness."[35] It would be hard to conjure up more overtly anti-Semitic tropes in one line. To be fair, he advocated for Black athletic participation, but even then, he could not resist the occasional racist trope. He referred to "the colored brother" who is "not nearly so sensible to pain as his white bother. He has a thick, hard skull and good hands." Gallico was a founder of the Golden Gloves, but "for all his big talk about how blacks were unfairly treated, he went along with the segregation of his black boxers on the road." His chapter on Black athletes in *Farewell to Sport* was not-so-cleverly titled "Eight-ball." He "reasoned that if black athletes were used and discarded . . . it was their own fault." Gallico "wished that the black athletes 'racial pride carried him a few steps further than it does. His greed for the white man's blessings and the white man's mode of living defeats him and makes him set up for exploitation.'" As Robert Lipsyte writes about this argument, "Today we call that 'blame the victim,' Paulie."[36]

But women come in for the worst treatment in Gallico's work, and Didrikson most often faced his poison pen. The irony is that Gallico's scorn for Didrikson likely stemmed in part from the fact that Didrikson had once bested him in a footrace—dealing a bit of a blow to the 6-foot-3, 190-pound Gallico's legitimacy on matters of male athletic supremacy. In what Didrikson would later claim was her first-ever attempt at playing golf, she went out with four journalists—her friend and admirer Grantland Rice, Westbrook Pegler, Braven Dyer, and Gallico. She took a quick lesson from the pro—putatively so that she would not look foolish, but since she had played in high school this was a classic effort at sandbagging—and the five went out on the course.[37] As often happened, they teamed up—Didrikson with Rice, whom she called "Granny"—and a little betting took place. And thus, so did some gamesmanship. On the first tee she out-drove all the men. As she later recalled in her memoir, at the sixteenth hole, "there was a big dip down from the tee, and then the green was way up on top of a hill." Gallico hit the best drive and "it looked like he was a cinch to win the hole." That's when "Granny whispered to me, 'Babe, why don't you challenge Paul to race you down and up that hill?'"[38] Gallico, who according to Rice took "no challenge from any women and few men,"[39] was "a good sport," Didrikson wrote, "and he took the dare. Of course I beat him, because I was in peak condition, but he raced me all the way."[40] Didrikson toyed with Gallico, "teasingly maintaining a two-foot gap between them" like, in Rice's turn of phrase, "Rusty the electric rabbit at a dog track."[41] By the end Gallico "was so winded he had to lie down on the ground and catch his breath." Perhaps the other journalists should have suggested that men ought to be banned from racing on golf courses in the future. "When he finally got up he four-putted the green," Didrikson recalled. "Granny and I won the hole and the match."[42] Gallico seemed at the time to handle the defeat with aplomb.

The odd thing is that Gallico's attacks on Didrikson (and perhaps other woman athletes) may well have been at least partially performative. He could be clear-eyed about Didrikson's excellence, though even his praise came with barbs. He acknowledged her greatness but argued that it represented an effort at "escape, compensation" for being an "ugly duckling" and that she thus excelled at sport because she was not able to compete "with women at their own best game," which was "man snatching."[43] This bizarre argument is undercut by the fact that Didrikson never really showed any interest in "man-snatching" other than the fact that she married the wrestler George Zaharias in 1938, taking his last name and spending much of her career as Babe Zaharias or Babe Didrikson Zaharias. George Zaharias was the era's great wrestling heel, but he eventually took on the task of being Babe's full-time manager. They had met when they were partnered up in a golf tournament—the Los Angeles Open, a true open tournament where amateurs and professionals met, and a PGA tour event in which Didrikson became the first woman ever to compete in a professional tournament. The two flirted from the outset and married at the end of the year. Because she had heard all the sneers, they often played up their domestic life and Babe's role as a housewife. There had long been whispers about Didrikson's sexuality, and while the marriage quelled those for many years, when she and Betty Dodd later became inseparable, the old rumors began recirculating. Dodd, a young, rough-around-the-edges golfer from Texas, may well have reminded Babe a bit of herself. Didrikson ignored the whispers, and some of her friends scoffed at the idea in an era long before any athlete, male or female, would ever even consider acknowledging being gay.

In one chapter in *Farewell to Sport*, "Farewell to Muscle Molls Too," Gallico manages to damn Didrikson with high praise. While acknowledging Didrikson as "the best all-around woman performer the country has ever known," he fell back on physical descriptions. As a teenager, Didrikson "was a hard-bitten, hawk-nose, thin-mouthed little hoyden from Texas." He ran through the list of sports at which she dominated, noting, "Actually, there was no sport at which she could not perform better than average for a girl. She was the muscle moll to end all muscle molls, the complete girl athlete." But "apparently she didn't have another thought in her head but sport. She was a tomboy who never wore make-up, who shingled her hair until it was as short as a boy's and never bothered to comb it, who didn't care about clothes and who despised silk underthings as being sissy. She had a boy's body, slim, straight, curveless, and she looked best in a track suit." He asserted, "She hated women and loved to beat them. She was not, at that time, pretty. Her lips were thin and bloodless, with down showing on the upper one, and she had a prominent Adam's apple. She had good, clear, gray-green eyes but she was what is commonly described as hatchet-faced" and "she looked and acted more like a boy than a girl, but she was in every respect a wholesome, normal female."[44] Lipsyte, in reassessing his onetime hero Gallico, acidly notes, "After that race" at the golf course, when Didrikson beat Gallico, who collapsed to the ground at the end, "Gallico suddenly noticed Babe's Adam's apple. Of course if a woman beats you, she can't really be a woman."[45] Gallico's implication is the slimiest of the many slimy things he wrote about Didrikson and other women.

Then came a transformation—perhaps in Didrikson, perhaps in Gallico, possibly a little of both. The last time Gallico saw Didrikson before he gave up sportswriting was at a golf tournament in Pittsburgh. "The tomboy had vanished," he wrote. "Her hair had grown out and it had a stylish permanent wave. There was a touch of rouge on her cheeks and red at her lips. She wore an attractive sports ensemble and had a purse to match, with her initials on it." The two spoke, Didrikson acknowledged the change, and Gallico claimed a sort of victory. "She had come into her woman's birthright by a curiously devious route, but she had got there, which, I imagine, is more than she ever expected." All of this was buildup to an astringent assertion: "With but few exceptions, lady athletes are wretched sports."[46] Didrikson, who had an enormous ego that could turn off friend and foe alike, responded to barbs about her look directly, and somewhat heartbreakingly: "I know I'm not pretty, but I do try to be graceful."[47] In the latter stages of her life and career, "when asked about her sporting talents, she often steered the conversation toward her skills in cooking and sewing."[48]

Didrikson died of cancer in 1956. That disease ravaged her, making her final months a painful hell. Gallico wrote a tribute to her in *Sports Illustrated* that year. The magazine described the article as an admiration from "a longtime friend," but even when describing this "splendid woman who was the greatest-ever female athlete," Gallico could not help himself, remembering eighteen-year-old Babe with "a short cut, sand-colored hair, a well-defined Adam's apple, and a faint down on her upper lip."[49] Even in tribute Gallico had to cast aspersions.

Dave Zirin argues that Didrikson's transformation tied into Cold War politics. "Part of McCarthyism's shock therapy," he writes, "involved getting Rosie the Riveter out of the factory, back in the kitchen, and once again making babies." Women who had served the war effort in factories—and gotten some sense of independence in the process—found themselves fired, as millions lost their jobs in the years after the end of the war. Eighty-two percent of the country opposed women being in the workforce if their husbands had jobs. Twenty-six states had laws prohibiting the hiring of married women. "While the 1940s presented the formidable" Rosie the Riveter "as the feminine ideal, the 1950s saw Marilyn

Monroe, June Cleaver, and Donna Reed take center stage. Unless you could do housework and raise kids while wearing pearls, you were something less than a woman." Thus, women were expected to perform servile roles not only because of their gender, but as an act of patriotism. In sports this meant that woman athletes were expected to live up to that ideal—and of course some sports remained more acceptable than others. Golf was one of these sports, lucky for Didrikson, now going by Zaharias to signal her performance of the role of wife, an act that provided "a mark in her favor."[50] It was a testament to her massive athletic talent that she came to dominate a sport she had never seriously played until she was an adult.

Didrikson did have her defenders. The legendary Grantland Rice thought Didrikson proved that "a woman does not have to look like a weightlifter or a piano mover" to excel in sports. Like Gallico, though, much of the praise for Didrikson came after she started adhering to gendered norms. Westbrook Pegler "soothed the brow of Main Street," according to Goldblatt, when he wrote of the star athlete, "The mouth can relax and the eyes smile, and the greatest girl athlete in the world right now, with a special liking for men's games, is as feminine as hairpins."[51]

Didrikson, at least, was unfazed by all this speculation about her or other women's participation in elite sport, about her femininity, about her gender, and about her sexuality. Ironically enough, when American women's track and field was struggling through a rough patch during the hottest years of the Cold War, Didrikson was posed as a model to which woman athetes should aspire. "Where are the Babe Didriksons . . . of yesteryear?" a *Washington Post and Times Herald* columnist lamented.[52] And to future generations, Didrikson would prove to be a model. Ann Baker Furrow, who in 1967 became the first woman to earn a sports scholarship at the University of Tennessee, cited Didrikson as an early role model in her teen years. The pioneering East Tennessee native was a trailblazer in Knoxville, playing on the men's golf team because there was no women's team, then returning in the 1990s to start the women's program there. In addition to her golfing achievements, she was also the first woman to serve on the UT Board of Trustees.[53]

The history of sport, globally and in the United States, is largely one of exclusion of women, or at least severely circumscribing women's participation, limiting them to sports where they could be "objects of desire" when perhaps they could have been, in the words of one historian, "objects of liberty."[54] Woman athletes found themselves objectified one way or the other, with their first responsibility seemingly being to serve men's libidos.

It would take another generation for Title IX to come to pass, for woman athletes to be objects of liberty. This likely would have been nearly unimaginable to Babe Didrikson. Yet it is because of the work she and her generation of women did in proving themselves in the sporting arena that future generations of girls and women would have real opportunities to play, to compete, to win.

CHAPTER 3

Jackie Robinson, the Army, and Sam Huston College

The Dilemma of the Black Athlete in 1940s America

PROFESSIONAL SPORTS AND THE COLOR LINE

There was something in the water of the athletics department—and especially the football team—at the University of California, Los Angeles in the late 1930s and early 1940s.[1] During a very short period of time, several Black All-Americans who would make their mark in—and beyond—sports helped place UCLA firmly within the national consciousness. In 1946, Woody Strode and Kenny Washington would become the first players to reintegrate the NFL, the first Black NFL players since the 1932 season. Strode would later go on to become an actor in Hollywood, often playing toughs and enforcers. Fellow football standout Ray Bartlett would become a prominent civic leader in Southern California. Bruins track star Tom Bradley would go on to become the first Black mayor of Los Angeles, holding that office during the 1984 Olympics that played out against the background of a tit-for-tat boycott by the Soviet Union and other countries in response to the Americans' (and their allies') boycott of the 1980 Moscow Games.

And then there was Jack Roosevelt Robinson, the brightest star in this brilliant West Coast constellation. A product of Pasadena's John Muir High and Pasadena Junior College, Robinson was the first four-sport letterman in UCLA history. He earned varsity status in football, in which he led the Bruins in rushing, passing, and scoring and led the country in punt return yards. In basketball, he led the Pacific Coast Conference in scoring for two consecutive years. He was the 1940 NCAA champion in the long jump and was outstanding in several other events. Ironically, baseball was by far his weakest sport; in his senior year he hit only .097, though his speed and athleticism still made him dangerous when he did get on the basepath. But he earned All-American status in basketball, football, and track and field. Robinson's brother Mack had been the silver medalist in the 200 meters at the 1936 Olympics in Berlin, and it is quite clear that had he been so inclined, Jackie Robinson likely could have followed suit in the long jump and possibly other events. But that's not all. Robinson also played golf, winning the Pacific Coast intercollegiate golf championship. He reached the semifinals of the national tournament for Black tennis players. Even in swimming, he won competitions at UCLA.

And yet after serving on the home front in the U.S. Army during World War II, Robinson found himself largely on the outside looking in at America's sporting landscape. He played some semipro football and eventually found his way to the Negro Leagues, but at one point in 1945 the man who could plausibly have been called America's finest athlete found himself as a coach and administrator at a tiny historically Black college (HBCU) in Austin, Texas.[2]

In 1945—the year that saw the end of World War II, a war supposedly fought for freedom and democracy—none of the major American professional sports leagues had a single Black athlete. The National Football League (which is today over 70 percent African American) had no Black players from 1933 to 1946, the year Robinson's UCLA football teammates Strode and Washington took the field for the Los Angeles Rams. That same season, the Cleveland Browns of the All-America Football Conference (AAFC) signed Bill Willis and Marion Motley.[3] Organized baseball, by far the most popular sport in the United States, had not had a Black player since Moses Fleetwood Walker played forty-two games for the Toledo Blue Stockings in 1884. Although professional basketball had been sporadically and intermittently played in the United States since the late nineteenth century, the Basketball Association of America was not founded until 1946; it merged with the National Basketball League in 1949 to become the National Basketball Association (which today is over 80 percent African American). The NBA would not see its first Black players until the Celtics and the Knicks each drafted and played one in 1950. And the National Hockey League would not see its first Black player strap on skates until Willie O'Ree took to the ice for the Boston Bruins in January 1958.

In the mid-1940s, then, Jackie Robinson should have had the opportunity to play professionally in two or three sports and potentially compete for a spot on the U.S. Olympic track and field team. That he did not earn a paycheck as a professional in America's top sporting leagues until 1947 tells us a great deal about the nature of professional sports in the United States—allegedly one of the true meritocracies in American life but, in fact, a reflection of the deeply entrenched systemic racism that has scarred American society.

WORLD WAR II AND ROBINSON'S COURT-MARTIAL

One of America's greatest football players, an All-American who averaged more than 12 yards a carry (still a UCLA record) in the same backfield as future NFL star Kenny Washington and had led the NCAA in punt return yardage in 1940, Jackie Robinson was playing semiprofessional football in Hawaii and working in construction to supplement his meager earnings when the Japanese attacked Pearl Harbor in December 1941.

In 1942, Robinson, like millions of American males who registered for the draft, was inducted into the U.S. Army. He and some Black colleagues applied for Officer Training School, for which they were clearly qualified, but it took some time; while the Army was nominally supposed to be race neutral with regard to its officers, the entire service was segregated, even as it prepared to fight imperialism and racism abroad. Initially based in a segregated unit at Fort Riley, Kansas, Robinson had a successful stint at OCS that resulted in his commission as a second lieutenant based at Fort Hood, in segregated Texas, in January 1943. There he joined the all–African American 761st Tank Battalion, known as the "Black Panthers."

The military was hardly free from discrimination, as its own enforced segregation as well as its acquiescence to local (and not always just Southern) Jim Crow customs showed. Robinson had wanted to join the base baseball team at Fort Riley, but he was refused. Furious as he was, he was further incensed when the officer who denied him the chance to play snidely referred him to a "colored" team he knew did not exist. When the base football coach, which did accept Black players, asked Robinson to play, he refused because he was angry about the double standard. Even when a colonel threatened to order him to play, the former All-American running back did not relent. And, as morale officer for the Black troops at Fort Riley, he pushed to expand the number of seats available to Black soldiers at the base PX. In the process he got into a shouting match over the phone with a white officer who asked him, "How would you like to have your wife sitting next to a n———?"[4] Not long after, the Army transferred Robinson to Fort Hood. They also added more seats for Black soldiers in the base PX.

Robinson, then twenty-five years old, did not fare as well. On July 6, 1944, he boarded a Southwestern Bus Companies bus for McCloskey Hospital in Temple, about thirty miles from the base, where he was being seen for a persistent injury—a floating bone chip in his right heel—that might prevent him from being deployed. He either got on the bus with Virginia Jones, who was, according to Robinson, the wife of another lieutenant, or he met her on the bus. She was returning to her home, which was between the Army post, where Robinson had just spent a few hours at the "colored officers' club," and the hospital, and either Robinson sat next to an already seated Jones or they sat down together on the bus. Jones was light skinned, but Black, though the bus driver, Milton N. Renegar, assumed that she was white. As Robinson biographer David Falkner put it, "A black man seated alongside a white woman on a bus in the South, no matter how innocent their relationship, would have touched off battle-station alarms from Baltimore to Biloxi"—and clearly, beyond.[5] In Robinson's own words, "The driver glanced into his rear-view mirror and saw what he thought was a white woman talking with a black second lieutenant. He became visibly upset, stopped the bus, and came back to order me to move to the rear."[6]

Robinson would have been aware of the controversies swirling around Jim Crow on buses. He would have known that in North Carolina a white bus driver had killed a Black GI who challenged segregated seating and mistreatment. He also would have known that the Army was eliminating segregation on all conveyances in no small part because of confrontations boxers Ray Robinson and Joe Louis had experienced related to buses. Louis had been "jostled by MPs after using a telephone in a white area of a bus station to call a cab."[7] And he also would have known that while the Army's decision did not apply to local buses (though in many cases the Army tried to provide buses in segregated areas to avoid the conflicts with Jim Crow), it was supposed to apply on military property.

But Robinson "didn't stop talking, didn't even look at" Renegar. He was aware of the new regulations, knew what he thought were his rights, and "had no intention of being intimidated into moving to the back of the bus."[8] A shouting match ensued between Robinson and Renegar as well as other passengers. The driver eventually returned the bus to the post, quickly ran from the bus, and came back with other drivers and a dispatcher. A white passenger on the bus, Elizabeth Poitevint, who worked in the camp kitchen, declared that she was going to press charges against him as well; for what was entirely unclear. But she was a white woman in the South, and her participation "brought the incident close to a flash point," in the words of Robinson biographer Arnold Rampersad.[9] Another shouting match commenced, racial epithets flew, and Robinson gave as good as he got until military police showed up.

In his autobiography, Robinson said that as enlisted men, the MPs treated him, an officer, with respect and asked him to accompany them, a request to which he acceded. Jones asked to accompany Robinson, fearful that he would be framed, but Robinson demurred. "I was confident that it would be easily established that I had acted well within my rights," Robinson would later write.[10] Once he got to the MP guard room, he ran into a sergeant and also a private, Ben W. Mucklerath, with whom he had clashed at the scene of the incident, when Robinson accused Mucklerath of calling him a "n——" and threatened to "break" the private "in two."[11] The scene in the guard room grew increasingly tense.[12]

Robinson later would admit, "I was naive about the elaborate lengths to which racists in the Armed Forces would go to put a vocal black man in his place." He immediately realized that things were askew when he was interviewed by Captain Gerald M. Bear, a conversation that began with Bear trying to assert his authority by chastising Robinson for following him into the interview room without being invited in. Robinson responded to Bear's overly authoritarian behavior with excessive obsequiousness, which riled Bear further. What riled Robinson was the white civilian woman named Wilson who was with Bear: "She was doing all the talking, asking all the questions. They were real, nice, objective questions like, 'Don't you know you've got no right sitting up there in the white part of the bus?'" Robinson found the questions offensive and the fact that she didn't give him much of a chance to answer even more so, and the exchange grew tense. In Robinson's telling, Bear, apparently motivated by "traditional Southern chivalry for wounded white womanhood[,] took over," calling him an "uppity n——." The confrontation escalated. Bear ultimately denied racism and said "all the rest of the stuff that bigots talk when confronted with the charge of being bigots."[13] Robinson could only laugh despite the gravity of the situation as he realized that he was "up against one of those white supremacy characters."[14] Eventually Bear ordered Robinson to be returned (against his will) to the hospital, where he was met by a colonel and several military police who had been told that Robinson, a teetotaler, was drunk and disorderly—a charge that was clearly absurd, as a voluntary blood test later proved.

Even more sobering, when he returned to duty, Robinson faced a court-martial consisting of two charges connected to the contentious interview with Bear. Robinson knew the system was "loaded mostly in favor of those bringing the charges." Despite the "obvious smell of a frame-up in my case, it would have been an easy matter for me to be railroaded into some kind of punishment for simply insisting on my rights."[15] Robinson reached out to the National Association for the Advancement of Colored People (NAACP) in hopes that they would provide an attorney for an increasingly fraught situation, but the organization was late in responding, eventually telling him (after the court-martial had taken place) that they could not provide a lawyer but would provide support if he were convicted.

Robinson also "made calls and wrote letters" to a number of influential figures as well as to the media and those who could influence the media. He contacted Joe Louis and members of the Black press. He wrote to Truman Gibson, civilian aid to the Secretary of War Henry L. Stimson, told his story, and "not so subtly" reminded him, and thus the Pentagon, "that because he was a prominent athlete, his case was almost certain to be well publicized."[16]

Higher-ups in the Army understood that the situation was delicate. In a phone call, Colonel E. A. Kimball, commander of the 5th Armored Group, warned Colonel Walter D. Buie, chief of staff of the XXIII Corps, "This is a very serious case, and it is full of dynamite. It requires very delicate handling.... This bus situation here is not at all good, and I'm afraid that any officer in charge of troops at this post might be prejudiced."[17]

Robinson also caught a few breaks, and he knew it. The first legal officer assigned to defend him was from the South, acknowledged that he could not give a suitable defense, and recommended "a young Michigan officer who did a great job on [Robinson's] behalf." Prosecution witnesses had clearly been coached, badly, and Robinson's lawyer took advantage of that.[18] Bear was repeatedly made to look like a "petty authoritarian."[19] Throughout the testimony, witnesses freely used racial epithets. The defense also was able to get a number of character witnesses to testify on Robinson's behalf, including one senior officer, who claimed that "Robinson was an officer he would like to have under his command in combat," and "several times the prosecution and the court itself reprimanded the colonel for volunteering unsolicited praise of Robinson."[20]

Robinson's own appearance on the stand, a potentially risky decision, proved to be perhaps his main saving grace. One interaction particularly stands out. It addresses Mucklerath's usage of what even then was the most explosive racial slur one could use, especially directly in the face of a Black person. Robinson's response was, in the words of the most thorough chronicler of the court-martial, Major Adam Kama, "arguably the most poetic response ever captured in a U.S. military court-martial":

Defense Counsel: Let me interrupt you, Lieutenant—do you know what a n——is?

Robinson: I looked it up once, but my Grandmother gave me a good definition, she was a slave, and she said the definition of the word was a low, uncouth person and pertains to no one in particular; but I don't consider that I am low and uncouth. I looked it up in the dictionary afterwards and it says the word n——pertains to the negroid or negro. . . . I objected to being called a n——by this private or by anyone else. When I made the statement that I did not like to be called n——, I told the Captain, I said, "If you call me a n——, I might have to say the same thing to you, I don't mean to incriminate anybody, but I just don't like it. I do not consider myself a n——at all, I am a negro, but not a n——."[21]

Kama concludes that this "extemporaneous" response "captures the mind-set of this future American icon." The rest of Robinson's testimony went well: "He had conducted himself well on the stand under both direct and cross-examination. His answers were respectful and poised. He never contradicted himself nor allowed his emotions to get the better of him."[22]

Robinson later reflected, "Luckily there were some members of that court martial board who had the honesty to realize what was going on." The panel consisted of nine men, at least seven of whom were white. One who can be identified, Captain Thomas M. Campbell, a medical doctor, was Black. Evidence indicates that there was one other Black member on the panel, though the record is vague. One of the white panelists, Major Charles O. Mowder, had attended UCLA. Six votes were needed for acquittal. After a relatively brief trial lasting a little more than four hours, the panel acquitted Robinson of all charges on August 2, 1944.[23]

Robinson believed there was something else that helped his cause—a number of his "black brother officers were determined to help [him] beat the attempted injustice," writing letters to the Black press, including the *Pittsburgh Courier*, which "gave the matter important publicity." Robinson later noted that the Army was "sensitive to this kind of spotlight" and "knew that if I was unfairly treated, it would not be a secret."[24] And indeed, Robinson's "encounter with a cracker bus driver" had become a "racial cause célèbre," especially among Black soldiers in the Southwest. They were understandably deeply suspicious of the military's motives and doubted that Robinson would receive a fair trial. An underground network of news, innuendo, and support quickly emerged.[25]

In the end, as the defense summed up their case, the court-martial "involved no violations of the Articles of War, as charged, 'but simply a situation in which a few individuals sought to vent their bigotry on a Negro they considered "uppity" because he had the audacity to seek to exercise the rights that belonged to him as an American and as a soldier.'"[26]

Robinson's unit had been shipped overseas during the court-martial, and he decided he was "pretty much fed up with the service." So he violated the standard procedures of following through appropriate channels and respecting the chain of command and wrote a letter directly to the Adjutant General's Office in Washington, DC, requesting to be released from duty. In November 1944, Robinson received a transfer to Fort Breckenridge and an honorable discharge.[27] But it was not quite the honorable discharge it ought to have been. He was released from his service duties due to "physical disqualification"—allegedly connected to his pre-wartime injuries—and received no veterans' benefits. The whole situation "rankled Robinson for years,"[28] and, in the words of Kama, "the irony that a future hall of famer and Rookie of the Year was physically disqualified from the Army before his entry into professional baseball should not be lost on anyone."[29]

Robinson's case, and many others like it, "called into question the very ideals the Army and the nation said it stood for."[30] It also showed Robinson to be a courageous freedom fighter, someone willing to stand up against injustice no matter the cost and no matter who was in the way. Yet when he finally integrated Organized Baseball, he had to spend two years submerging his innate tendency to fight back, to resist, and sometimes to lash out. And after this period of seeming acquiescence, when Robinson did fight back and resist and sometimes lash out, many white fans, sportswriters, opponents, and even teammates suddenly found him less likeable. They liked a compliant Robinson, not a combative one. They also expected Robinson to avoid aggression, despite many white players being lauded for theirs. They wanted a Robinson who made them feel good and virtuous about themselves, not a real flesh-and-blood Jack Robinson willing to challenge the status quo—especially when he showed that the status quo still very much needed challenging.

HUSTON COLLEGE

The next stage in Robinson's strange career both set the scene for his future baseball triumphs and led to a bizarre detour that reveals just how entrenched Jim Crow was across the American sporting landscape. Following his discharge, Robinson remained in Kentucky, where, walking by a baseball field at Fort Breckenridge one day in November 1944, he "ran into a brother"[31] who was "snapping off some impressive curves."[32] Ted Alexander, then a soldier, had previously played for the Kansas City Monarchs in the Negro Leagues, and he and Robinson got involved in a game of catch. Alexander told him "there was good money in black baseball." According to Robinson, "He said the Monarchs were looking for players. I was looking for a decent postwar job. So I wrote the Monarchs."[33]

The timing of Robinson's letter to Monarchs founder J. L. Wilkinson and owner Thomas Y. Baird could not have been better. Even as the Negro Leagues were drawing some of the largest crowds in their history, the war depleted the player pool. Baird responded quickly, offering Robinson a monthly salary of $300. Robinson countered with a request of $400 a month, to which Baird assented. The pay was indeed "a bonanza" for Robinson. But Alexander had told him that he "would enjoy the life of a baseball pro"; Robinson encountered a different reality: "For me, it turned out to be a pretty miserable way to make a buck."[34]

Meanwhile, Robinson's minister, mentor, and friend, Texas native Reverend Karl Downs, had been named president of Samuel Huston College in Austin (now Huston-Tillotson University, located on what was Tillotson's campus).[35] When Robinson was a boy and teenager in Pasadena, he occasionally found himself in trouble and could easily have taken another path. He was the leader of the mixed-race Pepper Street gang, which was more mischievous than criminal but might have sent him on a bad trajectory. Indeed, as Ray Bartlett, Robinson's friend and

UCLA teammate, later said, "I'm not sure what would have happened to Jack if he had never met Reverend Downs."[36] In an interview in 2013, Rachel Robinson said, "Karl was the father that Jack didn't have. Jack was so close to him. He kept saying that Karl changed his life."[37]

Downs had been a young minister at the church Robinson's family attended. Before long, Robinson came to trust Downs, going to him for advice. Robinson found that under Downs's leadership, "participation in church life became a pleasure instead of a duty." Downs "was both stubborn and courageous. He believed in setting up programs and sticking to them, regardless of criticism," and he engaged in changes in his church, many opposed by some of the older, more conservative parishioners.[38] Downs was committed to young people, willing to reach out to troubled kids who had left the church and to recruit those who might have never attended services at all. Downs "had the ability to communicate with you spiritually" while still being "fun to be with." "He participated with us in our sports," Robinson said, and he "helped ease some of my tensions. It wasn't so much what he did to help as the fact that he was interested and concerned enough to offer the best advice he could."[39]

Downs's counsel and influence continued while Robinson was at UCLA. Robinson volunteered to teach Sunday school even as he maintained "a heavy athletic schedule at UCLA." He'd get up on Sundays even if he was sore after competing and would have preferred to stay in bed largely because "it was impossible to shirk duty when Karl Downs was involved." Downs was also young and competitive enough to try to compete with Robinson in sports such as golf. The young minister nonetheless "never forgot he was a minister," and he could usually "find a way of applying a story in the Bible to something that happened in real life." But "he didn't preach and he didn't talk down like so many adults or view you from some holy distance. He was in there with you."[40] No wonder Robinson eventually chose to work for Downs. He "wanted to repay Downs for all the help he had been given."[41]

Downs, just thirty-one years old, was likely the youngest college president in America at the time of his appointment. In early December 1944, Downs had sent Robinson a telegram inviting him to teach physical education and coach basketball at the college. The college's athletic director had abruptly quit his position sometime in the fall, and Downs hoped Robinson would fill that role as well. With the Monarchs training camp still months away, and needing money, Robinson was happy to help his old friend who had done so much for him. Downs had provided counsel to Robinson as he faced his court-martial. Downs's daughter Karleen believed her father had even visited Robinson at Camp Hood. Downs and his wife "had such great respect and affection" for Robinson.[42]

Although often described as "frail," Downs was passionate about sports. When he was a student at Gammon Theological Seminary in Atlanta in 1938, he played in an exhibition basketball game; a newspaper described his exploits. His play that day was "outstanding" as he put up "some twenty points to lead the scoring of the day." He had set up an athletic program at his church in Pasadena, and in 1940 he was one of the founders of the Pasadena Athletic Club. That organization's first president? A multisport UCLA athlete named Jack Robinson.[43]

Robinson had visited Downs regularly whenever he got leave from Fort Hood, and seeing his potential as a leader, Downs was thrilled to offer Robinson the three-headed position at Sam Huston. This would not be Robinson's first foray into coaching. When he was transferred to Fort Breckenridge after his acquittal in August 1944, he served as a coach for Army athletics until his honorable discharge in November. Nonetheless, Robinson ought to have been playing sports for a living, not coaching teams that nearly represented a peer group.

And although Robinson needed money to hold him over until his Monarchs career started, the job was not exactly highly remunerative. Samuel Huston, which was affiliated with the United Methodist Church, "was an institution in deep financial distress," with a tiny student body growing smaller in no small part because of the war. There were about three hundred students, the vast majority women. (Only about three dozen were men.) Downs, a 1933 graduate of the college, was charged with reversing this ugly trend, which had turned his alma mater into a "ghost," in the words of one observer.[44] Employee salaries "mirrored the very limited resources available to run the school" and "hardly provided a career opportunity for a young man hoping to marry and raise a family."[45]

Downs appeared up to the task. He enlisted his local congressman, a former teacher and rising political star who had shown himself willing to do anything it took to win. His name was Lyndon Baines Johnson. Johnson proved willing to support the little institution, in no small part because supporting Black colleges sustained the segregationist cause that, at least in 1946, the towering Hill Country representative still embraced. However, Johnson also seemed to sincerely support broad-based educational opportunities, no doubt as a result of some of the things he had seen teaching poor Mexican and Mexican American children in South Texas.

Downs proved indefatigable. He pursued a campaign that resulted in five new buildings on campus, doubling the number there when he arrived. He recruited faculty and staff. He became the lead cheerleader for a growing student body. Inviting Jackie Robinson to campus thus fit into a larger pattern. In the words of one of Downs's friends, "Bringing Jackie Robinson to campus was vintage Karl Downs. It was the same spirit that led him to put in a visiting artists program that brought in all sorts of celebrated musicians, and that in turn made some very influential local whites to take note of our little college. Nothing like that had ever happened before Karl came."[46] In 1944, Downs started a Sunday artists series at the college-connected Wesley Methodist Church that included such luminaries as sociologist, historian, NAACP founder, and Pan-Africanist W. E. B. Du Bois; poet Langston Hughes; New York politician Adam Clayton Powell; and renowned tenor Roland Hayes. Downs mixed vision with the ability to get those visions accomplished, and the college's academic reputation rose as a consequence.

Robinson spent the remainder of 1944 and the first part of 1945 as an administrator, coach, and teacher in Austin. But for all his ambition and clear vision for leadership, Downs did not micromanage Robinson. Indeed, the athletic superstar had carte blanche in all his capacities. Whatever the previous athletic director had done, he had not created much of an athletic program. Robinson was starting basically from scratch. He established the first physical training regimen for the college. He displayed his medals and trophies "to inspire the students."[47] And the students were inspired.

But the enthusiasm the students showed did not extend to a passion for his basketball team—at least not at first. When he made a campuswide announcement for players for his men's basketball team—there was no women's intercollegiate program—only seven responded, and some of them seemed to have been drawn more by Robinson's charisma than any passion about or even knowledge of the game. Somehow Robinson cobbled together a team, which played an intermittent schedule in the rugged HBCU Southwestern Conference. Robinson had to recruit players from the student body and in East Austin. One such player was Roland Harden, then a 6-foot, 150-pound freshman. "I was watching him practice, and I said, 'I can play as well as these guys,'" he recalled years later. "Well, put on some shoes and come out," Robinson replied.[48] "He started working me out and he put me on the team and gave me a scholarship. Tuition only, but my mother was elated."[49] Harden had not been involved in any sports at college up to that time: "That's how I got started. He took me out and took me under his wings and started teaching me the fundamentals."[50] When the SHC graduate later told people about this experience, the response tended to be incredulity: "You played basketball for Jackie Robinson? THE Jackie Robinson?" In a 2014 interview, he said, "I told someone a few weeks ago and they just laughed."[51]

Robinson also recruited at least one player who did not appear during his coaching tenure but would be a contributor in future seasons. Lonnie Jackson was a high school student getting a malt soda at Yeates Drug Store sometime in the spring of 1944 when Robinson walked in the door. This was before he had taken the job at the college, but Robinson was a bit of a local legend—his sporting exploits had been national news, especially in the Black community; his arrest at Fort Hood had come to be a story of resistance to Jim Crow; and his visits to see Downs made him almost an adopted local. Robinson commented on the sneakers Jackson had hanging over his shoulders, and Jackson recognized the star immediately. Robinson was dressed in his military uniform. "He looked like one of those Aggie officers," Jackson recalled many years later, referring to Texas A&M's corps of cadets, students who were aspiring military officers. Robinson decided he wanted to play some basketball, so he and Jackson went to a nearby gym and scrounged up a pair of sneakers for

Robinson; the two played for an hour or so.[52] "All I could think of was, I'm taking Jackie Robinson to the gym!" Jackson later recalled, though it is likely that Robinson's later fame influenced his recollection.[53]

Jackson probably would have been left with little but a memory and a party anecdote about a brush with minor celebrity, but a couple of months later, Downs "knocked on Jackson's door." The young college president "had been sent to wake this teenager in the summer because Jackie Robinson had asked him to do just that"; in order to build a competitive team, "his first order of business as coach would be to recruit athletes like Ronnie Jackson." Jackson did enroll at Sam Huston, but only after spending a year in the military, matriculating in the fall of 1945, when Robinson was with the Monarchs.[54] And apparently Robinson organized other games at local gyms as well in order to allow him to recruit as widely as possible from the local talent pool.

Robinson was an enthusiastic and committed coach and teacher, and the tiny, overmatched Sam Huston team did their best against even relative giants like Grambling and Southern, both Louisiana schools that today play in NCAA Division I. Other conference foes included Arkansas A&M and fellow Texas schools Prairie View, Wiley, and Bishop. No photographs appear to exist of Robinson or the team, and the local newspapers did not cover the team's games. Somehow Robinson had cobbled together "a fairly good team," according to Harden. "He worked us hard and taught us a lot about the fundamentals of basketball" while also showing a commitment to his players' educations. "He was stern as far as the sport was concerned, and otherwise a good, friendly guy—and supremely talented. He'd get out and work with us, and bump us around. He was a much better player than anyone on our squad."[55] Harden also remembered that Robinson was ahead of his time in terms of strategy and tactics: "We were one of the few teams that ran at that time." He also notes that Robinson was a gentleman: "He required us to wear suits and ties when we got off the bus" for away games.[56] Another former player, D. C. Clements, echoed some of Harden's sentiments about Robinson's expectations: "He was a disciplinarian coach. He believed we should be students first and athletes second. If you cut a class or anything like that, he would put you off the team or give you some laps. He was a great coach and a great teacher. He was way ahead of his time."[57] But Robinson also displayed his more aggressive, competitive side when coaching. "I saw him go after officials when we were playing," Harden later remembered. "He didn't get ejected, but he would go to the breaking point."[58]

Alas, Robinson was only able to practice, scrimmage, and occasionally suit up in exhibitions against military teams and the like. On their own, the team struggled. In a tournament, Southern "humiliated" an "outmanned" Sam Huston team. Marques Haynes, a future Harlem Globetrotter who was then a star for Langston University in Oklahoma, was "repulsed" by what he saw as Southern's unsportsmanlike and bullying behavior. His team was to play Southern in the next round, and he decided to teach them a lesson. With two minutes remaining in a game Langston led, Haynes went into a dribbling routine the likes of which would eventually draw the attention of Globetrotters scouts, denying Southern any chance at the ball and running out the clock in a pre–shot clock era.[59]

A game against Bishop, the defending conference champions, proved to be the highlight of the season, as Robinson's charges pulled out a nail-biter, 61–59, for their lone victory of the season. This proved a wonderful win for Robinson's program. But his time at Sam Huston was, in the words of Robinson biographer David Falkner, "little more than a stopgap."[60] Soon after, he left for Houston and spring training with the Monarchs, then on to Kansas City for the regular season. Sam Huston trainer Harold "Pea Vine" Adanandus later recalled a conversation he had with Robinson after he broke the news to the team that he was leaving for his new baseball gig: "'Well, Jackie, I didn't even know you played any baseball.' And he said, 'Yeah, I play a little.'"[61] Within a year he would be making history. But in the winter of 1944–1945 he was doing fine, noble work in an environment that, in a better America, he would have visited only to see his old friend, rather than staying there to wear three hats for little money.

Downs presided over Jackie and Rachel (Isum) Robinson's wedding in 1946 and proudly watched Robinson integrate Major League Baseball when he joined the Brooklyn Dodgers in 1947. He visited the Robinsons, whom he continued to advise and counsel, at the end of the 1947 season, before the World Series pitting the Dodgers against the New York Yankees. The Dodgers were hosting Jackie Robinson Day at Ebbets Field, and Downs was proud of his protégé.

However, while in Brooklyn, Downs fell ill with a stomach ailment and had to fly back to Texas. His health took a turn for the worse, and in February 1948, he died in Austin's segregated Brackenridge Hospital after a white doctor refused to allow him to remain in a recovery room in the white part of the hospital after an operation. Instead, he was sent back to a segregated ward with inferior care. "When we learned the circumstances, Rae and I experienced the bitter feeling that Karl Downs had died a victim of racism," Robinson later wrote. "We believe Karl would not have died had he received proper care, and there are a number of whites who evidently shared this belief. After Karl's death the doctor who performed the operation was put under such pressure that he was forced to leave town."[62]

Robinson was effusive about the kind of man he thought Downs was—and would have become had he lived: "Karl Downs ranked with Roy Wilkins, Whitney Young, and Martin Luther King, Jr., in ability and dedication, and had he lived he would have developed into one of the front line leaders on the national scene. He was able to communicate with people of all colors because he was endowed with the ability to inspire confidence. It was hard to believe that God had taken the life of a man with such a promising future."[63]

During Downs's tragically brief tenure at Sam Huston, he put the college on stable footing. Enrollment more than doubled, to seven hundred students, as did the number of buildings on campus. Both the baseball facility, Downs Field, and the Downs-Jones Library and Communication Center at Huston-Tillotson University bear his name. And, of course, he left an indelible mark on one of the century's most important athletes, indeed, one of its most important figures. As one historian has written, "Perhaps the best testimonial of Downs' influence on Robinson came from the way Robinson understood sports in the broader context of life." Robinson's career, including his post-baseball life, showed that "for as much as he had accomplished in his athletic career, as much fame and celebrity as he had achieved, Robinson refused to see himself as a man set apart from the broader realities facing Black people in the United States."[64]

Meanwhile Lonnie Jackson, Robinson's pickup basketball partner from the drugstore whom Downs had recruited at Robinson's behest, would run into Robinson in person two more times. Their second meeting came in the late 1940s when Robinson participated in a barnstorming tour, common in those days, where professional baseball players joined forces and toured the country playing exhibitions against local teams. One of the games on that tour brought to Austin a team with Robinson and other notable stars—Larry Doby, the second player to integrate Major League Baseball (and the first in the American League) when he joined the Cleveland Indians; Bob Feller, a white fire-balling pitcher who was the first big star to sign up for military service after Pearl Harbor; and Robinson's Black Dodgers teammate Don Newcombe. They played at Disch Field, then a minor-league stadium on the site of what is now a major performing arts center on Lady Bird Lake near downtown Austin. (Part of the old Sam Huston campus is now occupied by the Lucky Lady bingo parlor.)

Their third encounter came as a surprise to Jackson, who, after graduating from Sam Huston, had left Austin for a few years but returned to his hometown to teach at L. C. Anderson High School. One day, perhaps in the late 1960s or early 1970s, the school secretary "came over the intercom and said there was someone in the office for me, so I had to get somebody to watch my class. I took off, going to the principal's office, wondering, 'What have I done now?' When I get up there, one of the secretaries led me into the office." Waiting for him "was Jackie Robinson. . . . He had come back to see how I was doing, and what was happening with me." The encounter came out of the blue, "but I remember that day well."[65] It is possible that Robinson's visit coincided with a return to Huston-Tillotson, for from 1969 until his death in 1972, Robinson sat on the Board of Trustees of the university with which, because of Jim Crow but also because of his vital relationship with Karl Downs, he had been briefly affiliated a quarter century earlier. He would have been required to attend the two board meetings a year that were held on campus.

* * *

This strange career detour is bizarre and fascinating, a seeming trivia question in a major figure's life. But it is also appalling to consider how constrained his options, and the options of hundreds of elite athletes, were at the time. Only in retrospect do we know how this story turns out, but at the time one of the greatest athletes in history had shockingly few opportunities simply because of his country's racism, racism that had already nearly railroaded him when he was trying to serve his country.

Think about the implications of this odd interlude in Robinson's life. One of the greatest athletes of his or any time, and a military veteran to boot, finds that his best option for a career in sports is to serve as a jack-of-all-trades at a tiny unknown college in Texas, while white peers with a fraction of his skills lived the lives of professional athletes. This flies in the face of all the high-flown rhetoric that Americans used in World War II and made a mockery of the idea of America as a land of opportunity.

Over the years we have seen the sanitization of Jackie Robinson similar to that of Martin Luther King Jr. Just as Americans generally and conservatives in particular have mischaracterized and decontextualized King's "content of their character" line from his "I Have a Dream" speech—a speech that was neither conciliatory on race nor blind to very real color differences created by white supremacy—so, too, has Robinson become a friendly face of American success. In this telling, Robinson's narrative becomes a triumphalist one rather than what it really ought to be: a fundamentally shameful story that illustrates an important victory and nonetheless reveals American shortcomings not American virtues.

Jackie Robinson indeed made history when he took the field for the Brooklyn Dodgers in April 1947. But this was just a beginning. The struggle to desegregate—never mind integrate—professional sports would take well more than a generation to play out, each incident proving the resilience of white supremacy as much as the triumph of American opportunity.

A Tale of Two Cities

The Integration of Professional Sports in Boston and Cleveland

STRANGERS IN THEIR OWN COUNTRY

Jesse Owens and Joe Louis were elite athletes who reached the absolute pinnacle of accomplishment in track and field and boxing, respectively. Born not far from one another in Alabama, they met at their athletic and public peak, and would remain friends for more than forty-five years. Both were used as patriotic symbols of American greatness and open-mindedness: Owens after he put a metaphorical thumb in the eye of white supremacy when he won four gold medals to put paid to German conceptions of racial superiority in the 1936 Berlin Olympics, Louis after he defeated the German Max Schmeling in a summer 1938 rematch after he had lost to the seeming Teutonic superman just two years earlier.

Yet after their sterling careers in sport ended, they found that their usefulness to white America faded. Owens was reduced to stunts like racing horses; Louis, to opening nightclubs. At one point, just two weeks after Louis demolished Schmeling and two years after Owens had been banned for life from American track and field for refusing to run in a series of post-Olympic barnstorming events, they raced one another. In no small part because of American racism, the financial bounty that their fame should have garnered them proved elusive. Both had troubles with the Internal Revenue Service. Both tried and failed to run businesses capitalizing on their names. Both found themselves derided as "Uncle Toms" during the 1960s when their approach to race relations came to be seen as too conciliatory and out of step with the aggressive nature of the times. They had become, as the title of a joint biography described them, "heroes without a country."[1]

Their experience serves as an object lesson about the state of things even for American sporting heroes if they did not have the "right" skin color. Yet they had been able to scratch their way to fame before American team sports opened their doors even a crack for Black athletes. As we've seen, when World War II ended, with the United States claiming victory—a victory that would not have happened without the help of a number of allies, including the Soviet Union, which took gleeful note of American racial inequities—none of the major professional team sports in the United States had a single Black athlete.

The United States had waged war for ideals it came far from living up to, and professional sports reflected this state of play. Owens and Louis had been used by white America as totems of American democracy's superiority and then effectively shunned. Meanwhile, many servicemen returned from fighting for ideals of freedom and democracy and the American Way, only to be responsible for enforcing and maintaining Jim Crow and fighting off challenges to it. Among those challenges were demands to integrate professional sports.

Over the next decade and a half, American professional sports leagues would all achieve at least minimal desegregation as the result of athletes and a few leaders who were willing to challenge the racist status quo. Integration was still a long time coming, and well into the 1960s and even the 1970s the college sporting landscape in particular would still follow a map that took on Jim Crow's geographic contours. Meanwhile, a wide range of courageous Black athletes provided a human face to what journalist Howard Bryant has called the "heritage"—a legacy of activist athletes forcing doors open and holding them open for generations to follow.[2]

Leadership Politics, Race, and Sports in Boston and Cleveland

It is easy but not especially useful to brand any given American city as racist. Certainly, some cities earned their reputations through a depth and depravity of racism and racial violence, especially during Jim Crow and in their reactions to the Civil Rights Movement. Jackson, Montgomery, and perhaps most notoriously Birmingham, which earned the nickname "Bombingham" because of the city's violent responses to the movement, all had well-earned reputations for savage white supremacy. But when it comes to racism, there is a Tolstoyan element to American cities: Every American city is racist in its own way.

Boston—the cradle of American liberty, the first city that rolls off the tongue of Southern conservatives who want to cite an example of a Godless liberal hellscape, an epicenter of elite education—has a tortured history when it comes to race. Communities like South Boston and Charlestown have come to be identified with white working-class grievance, largely (though not solely) because of their responses to attempts to address segregated and unequal schools through busing in the 1970s. Boston is well-known as a complex city that contains contradictory multitudes when it comes to race—pious liberal ideals and blatant hypocrisy, ruthless racism amid the shining city on the hill.

Cleveland's story is perhaps less well known. The city has never lacked racial animus, but also developed a reputation for racial progressivism. On the one hand, Black Clevelanders experienced segregation in education, employment opportunity, and housing, and they faced significant discrimination in the legal system, from police to the courts. When Cleveland's manufacturers went down South during World War I to recruit workers to replace the flow of immigrants that had been halted by the war, they were successful in selling the city to potential migrants. The recruiters did not mention that the recruits would be used as strikebreakers. "Fresh off the train," according to one chronicler of Cleveland's racial history, "new Black Clevelanders arrived for their first day of work crossing a picket line they didn't know anything about."[3] The city became inflamed in racial violence in the spring and summer of 1919, echoing events in cities across the North that year.

Four decades later, during the tumultuous 1960s, race once again became a flashpoint amid the civil rights era. Cleveland's Black population had exploded, becoming 34 percent of the city's total, most occupying a small swath of the city east of downtown and west of the city's unwelcoming suburbs. The city saw protests and violence, with white mobs often attacking Black protesters, as happened in Murray Hill, Cleveland's "Little Italy," when Black protesters ran into a mob of some fourteen hundred whites who set upon them with knives and clubs, bats and chains. They chased the activists away, attacking several while police watched and did nothing. The months and years to come saw many other incidents and the emergence of a vibrant and aggressive group of Black nationalists who took on the mantle of Black Power and ultimately developed into or worked with the city's emerging Black Panther Party. Integrationists and Black Power advocates consistently encountered white supremacists and even Nazi and neo-Nazi organizations, and by the end of the 1960s—and particularly chaotic 1968, which hit Cleveland as it did so many cities—increasingly radicalized Black Clevelanders weren't going to put up with it anymore.[4]

Yet, in the wake of all this turmoil, Cleveland was the first major American city to elect a Black mayor when Carl Stokes won the November 1967 election and took office on New Year's Day in 1968. And Cleveland's sports teams developed a reputation for being well ahead of the curve on racial issues.

Sports both reflected these trends but also complicated them, especially in Boston, where racial progress went arm in arm with white supremacy. Cleveland more often than not reinforced its reputation for racial progress, but behind the scenes there were a few indicators that all was not as it seemed. The key factor was not something as amorphous and impressionistic as either city's reputation. What mattered more than anything was leadership in any given sport at any given time, the incredible courage of the athletes tasked with forcing their way into professional sports, and their capacity to endure the slights that allowed them to remain there.

Browning the Browns: Cleveland Football, the NFL, and the AAFC

The Rams played in Cleveland from 1936 to 1945. They never fielded a Black player. Their ownership never seemed so inclined. Not many in the city of Cleveland seem to have applied particular pressure to the team to change their ways and bring in Black talent, so the Rams found themselves under pressure to integrate only when they moved to the West Coast for the 1946 season, despite having won the 1945 NFL title. Los Angeles city officials refused to grant the Rams the right to use the Los Angeles Coliseum, the grand stadium that hosted the opening and closing ceremonies and track and field events in the 1932 Olympics, unless the team signed Black players and retained them on their squad. This little bit of political arm-twisting would reintegrate the NFL after a thirteen-year interregnum, with Jackie Robinson's LA teammates Kenny Washington and Woody Strode making this lesser-known history.

Rams general manager Charles F. ("Chile") Walsh gave Washington the chance to "strut his stuff" for the NFL's defending champs after purchasing his contract from the Hollywood Bears of the Pacific Coast Professional League, a professional minor league that operated from 1940 to 1948.[5] Unconscionably, Washington, who had dominated college football for UCLA, went unselected in the 1940 NFL draft, seeing dozens of demonstrably inferior white players chosen over the twenty-two rounds of the draft. Observers at the time compared Washington to his former UCLA teammate Robinson, who at that point had signed with and played exhibition games for the International League Montreal Royals, integrating the top minor league but had not yet played for the Dodgers. But reports recognized that the NFL had fielded Black players in the past, before drawing an unofficial but very real color line in 1933. Washington was a strong candidate for the NFL in no small part because on top of his sterling record at UCLA, he was dominant in the Pacific Coast League, leading it in scoring in 1945, a season in which he also completed three passes of 60 or more yards. Interestingly, on the same day Washington's signing was announced, officials in Jacksonville, Florida, barred Robinson and another Black teammate, John Wright, from playing in an exhibition against Jersey City as part of their Florida spring training.

But Washington's (and soon after, Strode's) signing did not occur in a vacuum. Even as Robinson was taking what would be his lonely walk into the maw of American sporting white supremacy, integration in pro football was taking place on two fronts. In 1946, a rival league formed to challenge the NFL when the All-America Football Conference emerged with franchises in Buffalo, Chicago, Los Angeles, New York, San Francisco, Brooklyn, Miami, and Cleveland.

Paul Brown, the coach and cofounder of the new Cleveland franchise, came to the position as an Ohio wunderkind, having won six state championships in nine years as head coach of Canton's Massillon High School before moving on to win the national championship as head coach of the Ohio State University (Jesse Owens's alma mater) in 1942 and coaching a military team during the later war years. From its inception, the team carried Brown's stamp so thoroughly that Cleveland even named the team after him, calling them the Browns. His innovations would extend to nearly all aspects of the sport, from creative tactics and strategies on the field to taking the college draft seriously, utilizing new technologies, and mastering the rules to gain even the smallest advantage.

Brown was central to his franchise's signing of not one, but two Black players for that first AAFC season—Bill Willis and Marion Motley. Willis had starred on Brown's 1942 national champion Ohio State team as a dominant lineman. When he graduated in 1945 there were no NFL doors open to him, and so he spent a year as a coach at Kentucky State University, an HBCU, and was about to head to play for the Montreal Alouettes (in a league that would be the precursor to the Canadian Football League) when Brown scooped him up.[6]

Motley had also played for Brown before; while he was in training for the U.S. Navy in 1944, Brown coached Motley's armed services team and wanted him for his new Browns squad. Brown's eye for talent would be confirmed again and again, as both Motley and Willis would have Hall of Fame careers in the AAFC and, after the NFL absorbed some of the AAFC teams in a 1950 merger, in the NFL. Brown would continue to draft, sign, and otherwise acquire great Black players, culminating in

Jim Brown, arguably the greatest football player of all time as well as a vocal and prominent advocate for civil rights. In the words of one white sportswriter, Hy Turkin, Paul Brown was a "hero," a "Brown man who is a white man" and a "rabid foe of racial discrimination."[7]

The Browns had enormous success in their time in the AAFC, and that success in part forced the NFL to accept a merger in which some AAFC teams joined the senior league. The Browns won four straight titles from 1946 to 1949, largely due to Black stars, and Paul Brown became known as "Football's Branch Rickey," after the Dodgers general manager who signed Jackie Robinson, because of his willingness to integrate professional football. While integration may not have been his primary motivation, he recognized its importance: "I wanted to get the best possible players for our team. That [Marion] Motley, [Horace] Gillon, and [Bill] Willis are Negroes is incidental. But honestly now, if people of different colors can fight together to win a war, why shouldn't they play football together?"[8] Or in the words of one Black sportswriter, "The Cleveland Browns are not only the all-time champions in the victory column"—that was, suffice it to say, a very different era in Browns football—but they also "qualify as a hall of fame choice in professional football's democracy league."[9] It is no coincidence that Brown was successful on the field, allowing him latitude that others might not have gotten with regard to his team's personnel.

Two teams—both with Cleveland connections—desegregated professional football in 1946. The Rams did so under duress; the Browns did so voluntarily. Or, as one historian put it, "Two owners of football teams—one racist and the other not" signed Black players to contracts.[10] Leadership—from the city of Los Angeles in the one case, from Paul Brown and others in the other—mattered in these situations. Of course, it required the four players—Washington and Strode, Willis and Motley, men former NFL star wide receiver Keyshawn Johnson has called "the Forgotten First" for their pioneering role that has been overshadowed by events in baseball—to make this effort successful.[11]

LARRY DOBY AND THE INDIANS: AMERICAN LEAGUE PIONEERS

Larry Doby is the answer to a trivia question: Who was the second Black player to join the Major Leagues after Jackie Robinson (and the first in the American League)? But he deserves to be much more. In an era before interleague play, Doby was every bit the trailblazer Jackie Robinson was, enduring the same struggle in American League cities that Robinson had to fight in the National League. Doby was a Hall of Famer in his own right, a man whose inspirational role has been overshadowed by the Robinson story. Relative to Jackie Robinson, "the memory of Larry Doby and what he accomplished is forgotten, or at least has faded away, much like an iceberg drifting into more temperate waters and melting to nothing."[12] People remember, and history records, those who climb a mountain first, even if those who reach the peak second achieve equal heights.

Like Robinson, Doby was a multisport star. Born in South Carolina, he went to high school in Paterson, New Jersey, where he excelled in three sports. He attended Long Island University on a basketball scholarship, but he also played for the Newark Eagles in the Negro National League. He joined the Navy when World War II broke out, and when his stint ended (honorably and with no explosive incidents) he rejoined the Eagles, leading them to the Negro League World Series title in 1946 alongside his fellow star teammate Monte Irvin. Doby signed with the Cleveland Indians, making his debut three months after Robinson, in July 1947. Skipping the minor leagues, Doby was the first player to go straight from the Negro Leagues to the majors.

Like Robinson, Doby met with hostility from fans, opposing players, and even teammates. When the Indians' owner, the colorful and sometimes controversial Bill Veeck, gave a statement announcing the purchase of Doby from the Newark Eagles, he reportedly received twenty-thousand hate letters, all of which he responded to. Upon Doby's signing, Veeck declared, "I don't think any man who has the ability should be barred from major league baseball on account of color." In his mind, "The entrance of Negroes into both major leagues is not only inevitable . . . it is here. I am operating under the belief that the war advanced us in regard to racial tolerance."[13] However, as historian Louis

Moore argues, this was "language characteristic of post–World War II American democracy that tried to wipe away a racist past and instead focus on character and not color."[14]

In fact, Veeck, whom Moore identifies as one of the many important "white allies" who helped support, advocate for, and act on the behalf of Black athletes, had long shown an inclination toward breaking baseball's color line.[15] Legend has it that he had once tried to buy the Philadelphia Phillies. His plan was to seek a competitive advantage by stocking the team with Black players, but in some tellings of what might be an apocryphal tale, as Veeck was traveling to Philadelphia to finalize the deal, Commissioner Kenesaw Mountain Landis, who had gotten wind of Veeck's intentions, arranged for another group to buy the team, thwarting Veeck's plans.[16]

In 1946, Veeck, who would become a serial owner of major league franchises, purchased the Indians. He immediately put all the team's games on the radio—something many owners had been loath to do, wrongly believing that providing the game for free would diminish their live attendance—and moved the team permanently to Cleveland Municipal Stadium, where the team had previously played some of their games each season. Soon, the Black press and civic organizations began to push Veeck to integrate the Indians, demands that accelerated after Robinson made his debut with the Dodgers in April 1947. Although Veeck had primed the pump to integrate the Indians by hiring promoter Louis Jones, "a black press release man," to lay the groundwork for integration, Cleveland's Black community, led by *Cleveland Call and Post* columnist Cleveland Jackson, feared that Veeck wanted the benefit of seeming open-minded without having to act on those alleged inclinations.[17]

But Veeck did sign Doby, and truly believed in him, predicting the young infielder (who converted to center field when he joined the Indians) "would become a bigger star than any guy in this room."[18] Doby was nearly as important, symbolically and in very real terms, to African Americans as Robinson. As Jackson wrote in the *Cleveland Call and Post* after Doby's debut, "For Larry Doby it took but a few short minutes to walk up to that plate. But for 13 million American Negroes that simple action was the successful climax of a long uphill fight whose annals are like the saga of the race."[19]

The Indians' acquisition of Doby—and the Dodgers continuing to lead the way by signing other Black players after Robinson made his debut in April—sent a clear message. In the words of a writer for the *Chicago Star*, a leftist, trade union–affiliated weekly, "The signing of Larry Doby, brilliant Negro infielder, by the Cleveland Indians last week and the announcement by the Brooklyn Dodgers of signing Sammy Gee, 18-year-old schoolboy wonder, eliminates any doubt that Jim Crow has been shattered as far as big league baseball is concerned."[20] In fact, the question for the Chicago writer was, when would Chicago's White Sox follow suit? Integrating baseball would be a slow process, to be sure. But it would also not be reversed in the generation to come. (The White Sox, incidentally, would sign Sam Hairston, who made his debut as the first Black White Sox player in July 1951. Hairston would be followed by Bob Boyd that September.)

Although Veeck generally received praise from the Black press for his signing of Doby, some saw it as a publicity stunt, something for which Veeck would come to be known over the course of his career. But Veeck followed through, signing more Black players to the Indians and continuing to do so on the teams he subsequently owned. Anticipating integration, he moved Cleveland's spring training from Florida to Arizona and convinced Giants owner Horace Stoneham to do the same, effectively meaning Veeck "pioneered the Cactus League."[21] To be fair, Paul Brown's actions the year before surely paved the way for Veeck's work with the Indians, but Veeck probably deserves to be mentioned in the same breath as Branch Rickey when it comes to baseball integration—and Rickey warrants scrutiny equal to that Veeck received.

Cleveland had clearly set the pace for racial integration in American professional sports. In the words of *Cleveland Plain Dealer* sportswriter Gordon Cobbledick, Bill Veeck and Paul Brown did "more to break down the ancient racial barriers than any of the social groups that pay lip service to tolerance but do nothing about it."[22] Doby helped lead Cleveland to a championship in 1948, alongside fellow legend Satchel Paige, who broke into the majors that year at forty-two years of age. Paige was possibly the greatest pitcher of all time, in addition to being one of the game's most quotable and idiosyncratic characters, and had been denied his opportunity too long, including his entire otherworldly prime. He made a brief appearance in the 1948 Fall Classic. Doby, meanwhile, became the first Black player to hit a home run in the World Series when he smashed a 410-foot bomb in a 2–0 victory against the Boston Braves.[23] In September both the Braves and Red Sox led their respective leagues, with the Red Sox displaying one of the most formidable offenses in the history of the league, and "World Series fever captured" Boston, but it was not to be, with destiny smiling on Cleveland baseball (for the last time, it must be noted).[24]

The Indians, whose nickname (and later their cartoon mascot, Chief Wahoo, which would first be used in 1951) was not yet a source of controversy, continued to lead the sport in racial progress. They were the first major league team to hire a Black manager when they named former Hall of Fame player Frank Robinson to that position in the shockingly late year of 1975.

The second Black manager in the major leagues was Larry Doby, who took over the top job of the Chicago White Sox from his former teammate Bob Lemon at the end of June 1978. That would be his only managerial post; the White Sox did not retain him for 1979. In 1998, the Veterans Committee elected Doby to the Hall of Fame.

Larry Doby died of cancer in 2003. In an obituary of the underappreciated pioneer, former commissioner of baseball Fay Vincent lauded Doby, the man and his legacy: "In an age in which we struggle to identify true heroes, Larry Doby is one of mine. His decency, quiet courage, remarkable achievements, and lasting contribution to racial progress are permanent legacies. Well done, old friend. May you rest in peace."[25] Doby has never gotten the attention Robinson has received as a pioneer, but he is surely nearly as important in the history of the game and the history of American sports.

BLACK IRISH: THE CURIOUS CASE OF THE BOSTON CELTICS
If Boston's racial history in sports is, like the city's racial history, mixed, the Celtics stand as the outlier. They were the first NBA team to draft a

Black player when they selected Chuck Cooper of Duquesne University in the 1950 draft "in a closed-door meeting of power brokers at the Bismarck Hotel in Chicago."[26] When another owner at the draft challenged Celtics owner Walter Brown over his decision to select a Black player, Brown's response allegedly was, "I don't give a damn if he's striped or plaid or polka dot, Boston takes Charles Cooper of Duquesne."[27]

Cooper credited the Celtics, their leadership, and especially Walter Brown, for their willingness to take a chance on Black athletes. "I'm convinced that no NBA team would have made the move on blacks in 1950 if the Celtics hadn't drafted me early, taking me in the second round," he said. "Seven rounds later the Washington Caps took Earl Lloyd and a couple of months later the New York Knicks bought Sweetwater Clifton's contract from the Harlem Globetrotters. But it was a case of the Caps and Knicks following the Celtics' lead. Walter Brown was the man who put his neck on the line."[28]

The Celtics were also the first team to have a Black superstar in William Felton Russell, who had starred for the University of San Francisco Dons, leading the team to consecutive NCAA championships in 1955 and 1956. He also led the U.S. Olympic basketball team to a gold medal in the 1956 Melbourne Games. The St. Louis Hawks, a budding dynasty, originally drafted Russell but traded him to the Celtics—either because they decided they did not want or their fans would not abide a Black player or, more likely, because Red Auerbach, always ahead of the curve with personnel matters, managed to wrangle what would prove to be an advantageous trade for his Celtics. Russell, fellow rookie Tom Heinsohn (whom the Celtics drafted first, ahead of Russell, as a territorial pick from Holy Cross), and veteran point guard Bob Cousy led Boston to the NBA championship as a rookie, winning the crown by defeating those same Hawks in an epic seven-game series.[29] Russell was the league's first Black star, and the Celtics were the first team to have five Black starters amid their run of eleven NBA championships in thirteen years. Russell won five Most Valuable Player awards and spent his last years in the NBA as a player-coach, making him the first Black head coach in the NBA—and indeed, the first Black head coach of a major American professional sport—leading the Celtics to two more championships. He was elected to the Basketball Hall of Fame in 1974, becoming the first individual Black player to be elected, and in 1980, basketball writers across the country voted him the greatest player in NBA history.

It would be reductionist to credit one man other than Russell, of course, for all these real, concrete accomplishments not only in sports but in American race relations. Nonetheless, Auerbach deserves credit for his vision as an ally and a participant in these events. One of the great coaches in the history of American sport, Auerbach led the Celtics through the bulk of their early dynasty, taking the team to nine titles before handing things off to Russell and moving up to the front office—though during his tenure as coach he was effectively the team's general manager, with control over personnel that was, and remains, exceedingly rare. Tactically brilliant, he would infuriate his opponents by lighting a "victory cigar" while still on the sidelines when the Celtics had secured victory—something they did regularly during their stretch of championships. (Auerbach led the C's to titles in 1957 and every season from 1959 to 1966; he also helped the Celtics earn seven more championships in the front office.)

There is no question that Auerbach believed deeply in racial equality. But he also believed in winning, and he knew that the quickest way to gain an advantage in the early years of the NBA was to tap the Black talent pool. In other words, if Auerbach was a crusader for racial justice, it was because racial justice offered a logical path to victory. If this sounds cynical, keep in mind that virtually no other coaches or sporting officials were willing to take these same steps—their bigotry overwhelmed even their desire to win. Russell once described Auerbach as "a middle-of-the-roader" when it came to racial matters.[30] Yet the men would remain close, maintaining a profound friendship for "our whole adult lives—almost fifty years."[31] And Russell would come to understand that Red—a Jew who had faced discrimination and who took several of his Celtics players, including Russell, on an eye-opening tour of Auschwitz when they were doing a playing tour of Europe—cared deeply about fairness. But he did so within the sporting context of winning and losing, first and foremost, and with a gruff exterior that covered a softness, a kindness.

Meanwhile, Russell transcended his sport. On the court he was an otherworldly talent who changed the game with his rebounding and especially his play on the defensive end of the floor. In an era when the big man reigned supreme in basketball, the 6-foot-9 Russell was smaller than his main rival, Wilt Chamberlain, who may well have been more talented but whose teams Russell bested time after time. Russell's timing was exquisite and his understanding of the game unsurpassed—something that made his transition to coaching nearly seamless. He practically invented blocking an opponent's shot, but even then he further innovated—rather than swatting the shooter's attempt into the second row, he would block the shot in such a way that he could keep it in bounds, corral it, and send it up court so the offense could quickly capitalize on the turnover.

Russell's impact on the game was real. He changed the game—and, in very real ways, he changed the NBA. As Russell biographer Adam Goudsouzian argues, "By 1969 the NBA had a black majority, and fifteen of the twenty-four All-Stars were black. Basketball had incorporated an African American aesthetic, a grace, a swagger, a flourish of individuality and physicality. Young black men embraced the sport as an arena of cultural expression. Basketball and blackness had established links in the American imagination." But Russell had enormous impact beyond the court as well: "He transmitted messages of black equality. He protested when he faced segregation, and he became an international symbol of American democracy, earning admiration from Australia to Europe to Africa."[32]

Russell was a civil rights icon. He stood for racial progress. Even as a young player in the league he refused to countenance bigotry and discrimination. In 1958, he and his Black Celtics teammates were forced to stay in a Jim Crow hotel, separate from their white teammates, when the team was in Charlotte for an exhibition game. The Celtics had assured the players that this kind of segregation of the team would not happen, and Russell in particular felt that Auerbach had fallen short in his promises and his willingness to stand up for his Black players.[33] But Russell, Sam Jones, and K. C. Jones also knew that the pressure point was not on the Celtics, who had generally shown good faith on matters of race, but rather on the league, which had considerable muscle to flex. So the Celtics stars joined the Lakers' Elgin Baylor in publicly announcing that they would refuse ever again to play or stay under Jim Crow. They had the support of the Celtics and the NBA, and the league soon passed a resolution that teams would sign nondiscrimination assurances any time they traveled down South.

Nonetheless, in 1961, a Lexington, Kentucky, coffee shop refused to serve four of Russell's Black teammates. Incensed, Russell stood up and announced that the Black players on both the Celtics and their opposing team, the St. Louis Hawks, would not play in the game. Russell's leadership among the league's Black players was increasingly clear, and soon his work combating white supremacy would extend beyond matters connected to basketball. When *Sports Illustrated* named Russell its 1968 "Sportsman of the Year," it was as much for his persona and his off-court efforts as for his work as a player-coach, though that was obviously front and center as well.

And he certainly encountered white supremacy even in liberal eastern Massachusetts. In one of his memoirs, Russell tells the story of how after his third championship, a man walked up to him when "I was sitting in a new Lincoln at a traffic light. 'Hey, n——, how many crap games did it take you to win that car?' the man shouted."[34] And despite his status and resources as the star of the Celtics, Russell and his family had difficulty successfully purchasing a home in the Boston area, continuously getting turned down or finding houses mysteriously coming off the market as soon as he visited them. Eventually he did find a home in Reading, a suburb north of Boston, though when he tried to move across town, some community members started a petition and tried to buy the home Russell was eyeing so his family couldn't move in.

But the most horrifying story of Russell's time in Boston was when he and his family returned home from a three-day weekend and found they had been robbed. Not only did the perpetrators spray-paint racial slurs on the walls, but, as Russell's daughter Karen, a Harvard-educated lawyer, later wrote in the *New York Times*, "the burglars had poured beer on the pool table and ripped up the felt. They had broken into my father's trophy case and smashed most of the trophies." After the police, who were not especially helpful, left, "my parents pulled back their bedcovers to discover that the burglars had defecated in their bed." Vandals routinely smashed and knocked over the Russells' garbage cans. The police blamed raccoons, though after Russell asked about applying for a gun permit, "the raccoons never came back."[35] No wonder Russell, who moved to Seattle after his career with the Celtics ended, described Boston as "the most racist city in America."[36]

Sadly, the family grew accustomed to these sorts of incidents. But, Karen Russell recalled, "the only time we were really scared was after my father wrote an article about racism in professional basketball for the *Saturday Evening Post*. He earned the nickname Felton X," referring to Malcolm X and the general trend of members of the politically radicalized Nation of Islam (NOI) choosing new names to eradicate what they saw as their slave names. "We received threatening letters, and my parents notified the Federal Bureau of Investigation," she wrote. What was "most telling about this episode is that years later, after Congress had passed the Freedom of Information Act, my father requested his F.B.I. file and found that he was repeatedly referred to therein as 'an arrogant Negro who won't sign autographs for white children.'"[37] The FBI, as they so often did, had turned terrorist threats against Black persons into an opportunity to attack the victims of those threats.

Nor did fans appreciate what they had in those Russell-led Celtics teams. Despite them winning eleven championships in thirteen years, the Celtics averaged only 8,406 fans during Russell's tenure—in a Boston Garden that held thousands more. Russell teammate Satch Sanders, another Black star of the era who played his entire career for the Celtics from 1960 to 1973, remembered, "We always sold out on the road, but rarely when we played at home."[38] Just a generation later, during and beyond the Larry Bird era, the Celtics sold out 14,890-seat Boston Garden 662 straight times. It's true that basketball had become far more popular by the 1980s—in no small part because of the presence of Bird and Earvin "Magic" Johnson of the Lakers—but those numbers are nonetheless telling.

Russell was blunt about these realities: "From my very first year I thought of myself as playing for the Celtics, not for Boston."[39] He called the city a "Flea Market of racism."[40] He experienced the indignity of harassment from police for the age-old "crime" of "driving while black," or what he colorfully called, during one interaction with the Boston police, "stop-the-n———-in-the-expensive-car time."[41] As the years passed, Russell at least somewhat tempered his feelings toward Boston, which in turn showered Russell with affection, even as the hard edges of racism in many parts of the city were barely sanded down.

In between the Russell-led Celtics run of the 1950s and 1960s and the next great Celtics dynasty led by Bird in the 1980s came perhaps Boston's most shameful period. In the mid-1970s, the courts forced the city to rectify its geographically driven racial divides. The solution was one that other cities and metropolitan areas had attempted: busing students across district lines, in particular bringing Black students from their overwhelmingly minority-population schools into the overwhelmingly white schools elsewhere in the city. Geographically tiny, Boston nonetheless had rigid de facto segregation. Immediately the response to busing—especially in closed, provincial enclaves like white ethnic South Boston and Charlestown—was explosively violent. And the violence spread from these neighborhoods, culminating in the ugliest incident in a long stretch of ugliness: When he was walking to a meeting at Boston's architecturally ghastly city hall, Black lawyer Ted Landsmark was beset upon by snarling, screaming whites who targeted him as a representative of his race and of the perceived indignities of busing. Wielding an American flag on a pole, one young man speared Landsmark, a moment captured in a Pulitzer Prize–winning photograph that horrified the world. America's Athens, the (admittedly self-proclaimed) "Hub of the Universe," the quintessentially liberal city, had become a symbol of the ongoing scourge of racism in the United States.

An irony of the Celtics and their successful 1980s run, with Larry Bird in the superstar role, is that in their great rivalry with the Lakers during that decade, the Celtics became identified as a white team appealing to white fans, whereas the "Showtime" Lakers, led by Johnson and Kareem Abdul-Jabbar, carried the mantle as the Black team with a mixed-race fan base. The events of the 1970s almost certainly crystallized these stereotypes. There is little dispute about the demographics of the teams' respective fan bases, though the bulk of supporters at the Forum in LA were white, if not as overwhelmingly so as in Boston. Los Angeles was and is a more diverse city than Boston, but the city has also had its own tortured history with race, one at least as explosive as Boston's. And it is true that the '80s Celtics had more white players, including the otherworldly Bird and fellow future Hall of Famer Kevin McHale, than the Lakers. But the Celtics had plenty of Black players as well, including Robert "Chief" Parrish (the center who rounded out the Celtics' "Big Three" with Bird and McHale), Cedric "Cornbread" Maxwell, Tiny Archibald, Dennis Johnson, and others. K. C. Jones, one of the Black stars of the 1960s Celtics, was their coach. And while the Lakers under white coach Pat Riley played an up-tempo fast-break style with Johnson at the helm that seemed more "Black" in the eyes of observers, the architect of the Celtics of the 1980s was Red Auerbach, who did not have to sell his résumé on race and basketball to anyone. Furthermore, there was not a team in the NBA of that era that would not have built their team around Larry Bird, whose athleticism was always underestimated, as even the briefest perusal of his career highlights reveals. The 1980s Celtics did not "redeem" Boston. They did not, as one author asserts, "lead the city from division to harmony," though they did "galvanize" fans around the team—as successful teams tend to do, at least superficially.[42]

More racial controversy arose in 1987 when Isaiah Thomas of the Detroit Pistons asserted, "If Bird was black, he'd be just another" good player. Thomas was pilloried, not least by other Black players like Johnson, who always acknowledged Bird as the greatest player he ever played against, at least until the ascent of Michael Jordan. Yet Thomas had a larger point that got lost. As he later explained, "When Bird makes a great play it's due to his thinking and his work habits. It's not the case for blacks." For Thomas, the perception was that "all we do is run and jump. We never practice or give a thought to how we play. It's like I came dribbling out of my mother's womb."[43] Through no fault of his own, Bird had become the Great White Hope for millions of white fans—just as boxing fans dreamed of a white champion who could emerge to defeat Jack Johnson, the first Black heavyweight champion, in the 1910s. For many fans in Los Angeles and elsewhere, Bird and McHale and pesty

Danny Ainge embodied the hope among white fans that the Celtics and white players could restore white claims in an increasingly Black-dominated league. In a city intoxicated by racism, the Celtics of the 1980s had become an uncomfortable but real cultural talisman—a team for racists, even if there was nothing racist about those Celtics, even if Larry Bird truly was an all-time talent, and even if Red Auerbach had helped create the modern NBA because his desire to win included an understanding of how Black players could help him do so.

Of course, leadership mattered. Red Auerbach showed that leadership, his owner Walter Brown backed him, and Bill Russell proved to be the right man at the right time, along with some special teammates to make it all work. By the end of Russell's career, as one of his biographers notes, "The Boston Celtics served as professional sport's finest model of racial integration, and Russell led this athletic crusade."[44]

Yet, even then, the racists could not help but shit all over the star of a team that should have offered them nothing but joy. If nothing else, we learn from Russell's story, and his struggles even as a Hall of Famer and the greatest winner in the history of American professional team sports, that for white supremacists, it is never about the merits of the argument. It is about self-insulated ideas of white supremacy itself.

In a 2020 essay that Russell wrote for *SLAM* magazine, he reflected on current racism in American society: "Racism cannot just be shaken out of the fabric of society because, like dust from a rug, it dissipates into the air for a bit and then settles right back where it was, growing thicker with time." Writing when athletes were kneeling during the national anthem and Black Lives Matter marches and protests were ubiquitous, Russell argued that "police reform is a start, but it is not enough. We need to dismantle broken systems and start over. We need to make our voices heard, through multiple organizations, using many different tactics. We need to demand that America gets a new rug."[45] By the time of his death in July 2022, he was hailed as one of the great sports figures of all time, as a true hero in a world that overuses that word. Yet white supremacy continues after his death, the battle he so courageously waged not yet won.

BLACK, IRISH: WILLIE O'REE AND THE EVEN MORE CURIOUS CASE OF THE BOSTON BRUINS

The Boston Bruins sent the first Black player onto the ice in the National Hockey League when Willie O'Ree, a forward from Fredericton, New Brunswick, made his debut at the tail end of the 1957–1958 season, appearing in two games. He tells the story of his rise to the Bruins matter-of-factly: "In January 1958 the Quebec Aces [O'Ree's minor-league professional team at the time] got a phone call from the Boston Bruins: one of their forwards had been injured and they needed a player for a back-to-back series against the Montreal Canadiens. And the player they needed was me."[46] Compared to, say, Robinson's debut for the Dodgers or Doby's first appearance for Cleveland, O'Ree's debut was not treated as an especially historic moment. Canadian media largely ignored it, and where it warranted commentary at all, it was mostly as a novelty or curiosity. On the eve of his debut, the *New York Times* made passing mention of the fact that O'Ree would be "the first Negro to play in a National Hockey League Game" in a single-paragraph wire service piece titled "Negro Star Will Debut as Bruins' Wing." O'Ree notes, "My name had been forever etched in the story of the National Hockey League. Even if they hadn't quite registered it yet."[47]

In Canada, the *Globe and Mail* acknowledged O'Ree's pending debut with a headline that read, "First Negro to Perform in the NHL, Willie O'Ree Thrilled, Nervous." The article "gave me pause," according to O'Ree, because it asserted that "most hockey observers point out that the only reason a 'color line' existed was the fact that there hasn't been a Negro player qualified to make the National Hockey League." Even more bluntly, a couple of weeks later Len Bramson wrote in the *Hockey News*, "The fact that there has never been a Negro player in the NHL before O'Ree must be blamed on the Negro race itself." O'Ree strenuously disagrees, pointing out a list of Black Canadian greats who never got their chance.[48]

O'Ree returned to the Bruins, appearing in forty-three games in the 1960–1961 season and scoring 14 points on 4 goals and 10 assists, but never again played in the NHL. He did, however, continue as a pro in a number of leagues, including the upstart World Hockey League, through the 1977–1978 season. His rise is especially compelling because during the 1955–1956 season, while he was playing in the top of Canada's junior leagues, he suffered a severe injury from being hit in the right eye with a puck, permanently costing him 95 percent of the vision in that eye for the remainder of his life. A lesser player would have been deterred, but O'Ree's desire, talent, and commitment won out.

O'Ree's Bruins coach Milt Schmidt "had a standard line" about O'Ree's status, which was, "He isn't black, he's a Bruin." As O'Ree observes, however, "Nice to hear, but I was still one of the few black people at Boston Garden—and I was playing! Not many black people went to games in those days." But the Bruins were happy to provide tickets for players, so he "was able to increase the Garden's black attendance by giving tickets to my cousin and her friends."[49]

Meanwhile, the fact that the Bruins had integrated was a bit of a mark of shame in the eyes of some Americans, who were "embarrassed that the 'un-American' sport of hockey had integrated and, baseball, our 'national pastime,' still had a team clinging to segregationist practices." Perhaps even more awkward, that one team in baseball was the Red Sox: "At a time when Boston and the entire country was in a tug-of-war with how it portrayed itself externally and the internal realities of the significance of race, bringing attention to hockey's progressive step would only have heightened the already intense pressure to remedy America's racial ills."[50] Of course, hockey was also a minor sport in much of the country and a complete nonentity in much of it. Until 1967, there were only six franchises in the league, with four in the United States: in Boston, New York, Detroit, and Chicago. These cities certainly had passionate fans, but by and large that passion did not extend to vast swaths of the country, including where the majority of African Americans resided. Nonetheless, Boston could hardly brag given that the Red Sox, by far the city's defining sports team even as the Celtics were beginning their dynasty, remained an embarrassing holdout in desegregating baseball.

Not at all surprisingly, O'Ree experienced more than his share of racism on the ice. He heard constant racial epithets, with some players being worse than others, though some embraced him as well. "Maybe he'd thought using the N-word against me was just good old fashioned trash talking," O'Ree reflected several years later, after a civil off-ice encounter with one of his worst on-ice antagonists. "It's not. Trash talking aims to needle an opponent by casting doubt on his strength or his intelligence or his girlfriend, but within the context of the game. Racism aims to diminish the humanity of a person, period. It's not about a game, it's about your life. There's a huge difference, as anyone who's ever been racially abused will tell you."[51]

Perhaps shockingly, the next Black NHL player would not take to the ice until 1974, even though there was no shortage of talented Black players in Canada and the United States. One of them, Herb Carnegie, who almost certainly had enough talent to play in the NHL in the 1930s and 1940s, compared himself to a "fly in a pail of milk."[52] The first Black player signed at any professional level in North America was Canadian Art Darrington, who appeared for Washington's entry in the Eastern League in 1952.[53] O'Ree thus represented a rarity, and for nearly a generation the Bruins remained the only NHL team to have had a Black player. Jarome Iginla, a Black Canadian NHL All-Star who won two Olympic gold medals playing for Team Canada and had a more than two-decade NHL career, wrote about O'Ree, "There is one blessing every black hockey player has had since 1958 that Willie did not. We all had footsteps to follow in. But Willie never did. Willie O'Ree is the only one who made it without anyone showing him the way. I know what a trail-blazer like Willie means to those kids, because I was that kid."[54]

In 2018, Willie O'Ree was elected to the Hockey Hall of Fame in its "builder" category, with the support of large numbers of present and former Black players and others involved in the game. That same year, the NHL established the Willie O'Ree Community Hero Award "to recognise the individual who has worked to make a positive impact on his community, culture or society to make people better through hockey."[55] In his Hall of Fame induction speech, O'Ree entreated, "Tonight I am here to tell you that we are not done because the work is not done. We have barriers to break and knock down, opportunities to give." O'Ree, who since 1998 has been the NHL's Diversity Ambassador, met Jackie Robinson as a thirteen-year-old in 1949 when his baseball team won a trip to New York after winning their city's bantam league championship and has himself become an inspirational hero. He concluded his induction speech: "I leave this with you: When you return to your communities, take a look around, find a young boy or girl who needs the opportunity to play hockey and give it to them. You never know, they may make us dream."[56]

Today the NHL remains overwhelmingly white, albeit with lots of national representation from across Europe, even as Canada still provides the league with a majority of its players. As a result of this demographic reality, the few Black players—overwhelmingly Black Canadians and Americans—to this day tell stories of racism from fellow players, from the sport's administration, and especially from retrograde fans. It is perhaps not surprising that many NHL fans like to compare their sport favorably with the NBA for amorphous reasons that tread treacherously close to and often cross the line of outright racism. And the sport continues to be plagued with racist events on the ice from youth leagues through the pros, often from racist fans and sometimes even from parents at the youth and school ranks. Nearly every Black player has a story of a banana being thrown in their direction from the stands.

"GET THOSE N——S OFF THE FIELD!"

The Boston Red Sox were the last team to integrate baseball when Pumpsie Green made his debut for the team in 1959. There is a long-standing legend about the Red Sox suffering from "The Curse of the Bambino," which set in after Sox owner Harry Frazee sold Babe Ruth to the hated New York Yankees for $125,000 early in 1920.[57] Allegedly, and largely apocryphally, Frazee did so to finance his Broadway musical *No, No, Nanette*, and while theater fans said, "No, no" to Nanette, Babe Ruth, already a star who had led the Red Sox to three World Series championships in 1915, 1916, and 1918, went on to become, well, Babe Ruth. Meanwhile, the Red Sox would not win another championship until 2004, conquering the Yankees in epic fashion along the way.[58] The reality is a lot less romantic, a lot less whimsical, and a lot less wrapped in gauzy woe-is-me nostalgia. Almost certainly, the reason the Red Sox failed to win championships after 1919, and especially after the World War II era when the rest of the league slowly started to integrate, was simple: racism.

This racism manifested both in an unwillingness to sign Black players and in subsequent mistreatment and mishandling of Black players.[59]

If the Celtics and even the Bruins were pioneers in their sports, the Red Sox were shamefully retrograde in their racial attitudes. And that attitude started from the top. If longtime Red Sox owner Tom Yawkey was not a racist, he was racist-adjacent enough to render any differentiation irrelevant.[60] And there were a number of overt racists in the team's upper-level leadership.

Former federal judge Kenesaw Mountain Landis agreed to become commissioner of baseball in the wake of the notorious "Black Sox" scandal of 1919, when members of the Chicago White Sox teamed with gamblers to throw the World Series against the Cincinnati Reds. Landis conditioned his acceptance of the job on his having absolute authority, something league owners were willing to grant in light of the severe challenge to the game's integrity in the wake of the Black Sox scandal. Part of that authority included a clear directive that the league would remain all-white, as it had since the 1890s. Landis, then, further formalized the informal (but still unwritten) agreement that had prevailed since Chester Arthur's presidential administration. It was only after Landis's death in 1944, and nearly three years into the tenure of Commissioner Albert "Happy" Chandler, that Branch Rickey and the Dodgers tested the unwritten agreement by signing Jackie Robinson.

In 1945, the Red Sox—under pressure from Black journalists Sam Lacy and Wendell Smith, local white columnist Dave Egan, and Jewish Boston City Council member Isadore Muchnick—gave a tryout to three Black ballplayers: Sam Jethroe, Marvin Williams, and Jackie Robinson. Egan wrote in the *Boston Record*, "Could we, by chance, spare a thought for the Negro here in the United States? Do we, by any chance, feel disgust at the thought that Negro players, solely because of their color are barred from playing baseball?"[61]

Muchnick had long supported integration of the local nines.[62] In 1944, he wrote the Red Sox a scolding, cajoling letter in which he asserted, "I cannot understand how baseball, which claims to be the national sport, and which . . . receives special favors and dispensation from the federal government because of alleged moral value can continue a pre–Civil War attitude toward American citizens because of the color of their skin." In 1945, Muchnick used power politics to force the hand of Sox officials. Because of Boston's stringent blue laws, baseball was banned in the city on Sundays, but that restriction could be waived for both the Red Sox and the Braves through a unanimous vote of the city council. Muchnick was none too subtle—the Red Sox would hold tryouts for some Black players or they would not get his vote for the lucrative Sunday games.[63]

Their tryout was delayed a couple of days because of the death of President Franklin Delano Roosevelt, but Robinson, Jethroe, and Williams finally took the field in Fenway Park on the morning of April 16, 1945.[64] And it might have been the single most infamous moment in the history of a franchise lousy with infamous moments. Clif Keane, a reporter and columnist for the *Boston Globe*, long asserted that someone screamed from the stands, "Get those n———s off the field!" There is much debate as to whether this specific incident actually happened. If it did, no one else witnessed it, or at least acknowledged it, including the three players. And if it did happen, no one knows who did it, though some have speculated that it may have been Joe Cronin, others thought it was Eddie Collins, and still others—perhaps the largest number, including Keane himself—believed it was Red Sox owner Tom Yawkey who screamed the words that would come to define the franchise in the minds of many Black and liberal baseball fans, whether they supported the Red Sox or hated them. Even if the story was apocryphal, it had legs because it seemed to reflect racist beliefs among the Red Sox hierarchy. Whether anyone actually shouted the ugly command, it was something that any number of people associated with the Red Sox at the highest ranks absolutely could and even would have said.

Robinson believed from nearly the first moment at Fenway that his tryout was a farce, an exercise in window dressing the get the Red Sox credit for conducting the workout without burdening the team with actually following through, and that the Red Sox never intended to sign him or his colleagues. The Red Sox realistically could have signed a bevy of Black stars had they acted quickly enough, but here was a clear case of shoddy, racist leadership choosing to maintain white supremacy at the clear expense of the success of the team on the field. The team had the chance to scout Willie Mays, but a racist Southern scout scoffed at the prospect, believing it beneath his dignity to have to scout a Black player. As historian Louis Moore points out, "Racism kept the team away from having a stellar lineup with Jackie Robinson, Willie Mays, and Ted Williams."[65] For that matter, any Red Sox fan can simply look over the list of Black players from the era between 1945 and 1960 or so—African American, but also Caribbean and dark-skinned Latino players—and wonder at the prospects of what might have been. Great players and pioneers like Don Newcombe, Roy Campanella, Larry Doby, Willard Brown, Satchel Paige, Minnie Miñoso, Roberto Clemente, Monte Irvin, Sam Jethroe, and so many more all could have been Red Sox players.

Even in the wake of the disastrous 1945 tryout, the Red Sox still could have been among the first teams to integrate as early as 1950, the year they signed their first Black player to a contract. Lorenzo "Piper" Davis played for Birmingham's all-Black American Cast Iron Pipe Company baseball club in the early 1940s. Born in Piper, Alabama (from where he got his nickname), Davis drew the attention of the Birmingham Black Barons Negro League team, which signed him in 1942. The talented infielder quickly became a star, making multiple Negro League All-Star teams, and had several near-misses with major league scouts as desegregation accelerated. When the Red Sox moved their Double A Southern League affiliate from New Orleans to Birmingham, they caught wind of Davis, who by then had become player-manager for the Black Barons. Given that Davis was in his thirties at the time, it was somewhat curious that they signed him, especially after (intentionally) missing out on Robinson, Jethroe, Mays and others.

Davis appeared in fifteen games for Boston's Scranton, Pennsylvania, affiliate in the Eastern League. Davis played well, but whether because the experiment was a sham, because the Red Sox would have had to pay his Birmingham Negro League club a lot of money had they kept him, because he was too old, or maybe for other reasons that are lost to history, they released him before giving him a legitimate chance.

Davis continued a peripatetic career, including some time working as a coach and bus driver for the Harlem Globetrotters. But mostly he was involved in baseball as a player (including several seasons as a minor leaguer in the Giants' and Cubs' systems), as a coach, as a manager, and eventually as major league scout for Alabama and Mississippi for the Detroit Tigers, St. Louis Cardinals, and Montreal Expos.[66] It would be unfair, given his scant amount of time in Scranton, to say that Davis had a legitimate shot to be the first Black Red Sox player, but his very signing indicates a road not taken in terms of cultivating Black talent.

It would be another decade before the Red Sox finally promoted Elijah Jerry Green, whose mother called him "Pumpsie" from a young age, becoming the last team in Major League Baseball to field a Black player.[67] Other holdouts had been the Detroit Tigers, for whom Ozzie Virgil (who had already played for the New York Giants) became the first Black player in 1958, the Philadelphia Phillies (John Kennedy, 1957), and the New York Yankees (Elston Howard, 1955). The Red Sox had purchased Green's contract from the Oakland Oaks in 1955 and he had worked his way through the team's minor-league system, with the senior squad leadership in no particular haste to promote him to the big leagues.

Green had a great spring training in Arizona in 1959, on merit clearly earning a spot on the big-league club. The Red Sox instead sent him back to their Minneapolis Triple A affiliate. This decision drew the ire of Black activists and journalists in Boston and beyond. The Boston chapter of the NAACP filed discrimination charges against the team with the Massachusetts Commission Against Discrimination. Marvin E. Tucker, head of the Boston NAACP chapter, claimed, "What happened to Mr. Green is purely symbolic of a history of discriminatory employment policies by the Red Sox club." The Red Sox were in no position to argue the merits of the case. In the history of the franchise they had hired four Black men to work concessions and had only two Black men on the payroll in 1959. The team's business manager, Richard H. O'Connell, simply prevaricated and distracted in the face of reality, arguing before the commission, "The Boston Red Sox are entirely American. We have no discrimination against race, color, or creed." He argued that the Red Sox "think these charges have been unfair" and declared "a right to manage our own ball club. People from City Hall and the State House don't hire people for us. We hire them." Tucker had made the NAACP's position clear: "We are opposed to the hiring of any persons because they are Negro. If Pumpsie

Green cannot play well enough, don't hire him. But give the Negroes a fair opportunity, the same chance that anyone else would receive."[68]

That chance went wanting. In Arizona, the Red Sox segregated Green, not housing him with the rest of the white players on the team. The Red Sox traveled with the Chicago Cubs frequently during that spring training, sometimes playing one another at various stops, and Green traveled with Black players from the Cubs rather than his own teammates. Meanwhile, in June, the Discrimination Commission somehow found in favor of the Red Sox, despite their demonstrable history of discrimination.

Green excelled in Minneapolis, collecting a stunning 112 hits, 26 of them for extra bases, including seven home runs. He effectively forced his way onto the Red Sox, who called him up in July. More than a dozen years after Jackie Robinson's debut, every team in Major League Baseball finally had Black players. Years later, Green reflected on his experience in desegregating the Sox: "It was the hardest thing I've ever done in my life. The baseball part was the easiest, the rest was hard. I stayed by myself unless I was at the ballpark. I stayed by myself living and eating. You learn to live with it. It's not like you're on the Earth by yourself."[69]

Let there be no mistake—shoddy leadership in the Red Sox' front office and dugout provides all the explanation anyone needs for the team's shortcomings—not a curse from 1920, not a lack of qualified Black players, not the racism of an entire city or region. For until 1953, Boston had been a city with two baseball teams; the Red Sox shared Boston with the National League Braves (who, over their history, went by a number of names). While the Red Sox dragged their feet considerably, the Braves were only modest foot draggers. They signed their first Black player, Sam Jethroe—one of the players in the farcical Fenway Park tryout—in April 1950. The Braves were the fifth team to have a Black player represent them on the field, though because several of the teams that preceded them had by that point signed multiple players, Jethroe was the twelfth Black player to appear in a game in the twentieth century.

Jethroe, a center fielder whose nickname was "The Jet," had legendary speed—he once ran an unofficial time in the 60-yard sprint that was two-tenths of a second faster than the world record. He had been a star

78

in the Negro American League, playing for the Buckeyes, who in 1942 were based in Cincinnati but for the remainder of Jethroe's time were in Cleveland. In his April 18 debut, he had two hits, including a home run. He won Rookie of the Year in 1950, becoming the oldest player ever to claim the award, and twice led the National League in steals. Because he made his debut when he was thirty-three, he played for the Braves only from 1950 to 1952, then played one last year for the Pittsburgh Pirates in 1954. Like so many, his was both a career that so many worthy predecessors never got to have but also a far shorter career than it should have been. The Braves were fifth in a fifteen-team league to integrate. They do not deserve excessive credit, but they also show that the Red Sox could have integrated far earlier than they did. Only team leadership prevented it from happening, to the eternal shame of the franchise.

For more than a generation after Green's debut, the Red Sox seemed bedeviled with allegations of racism, seemingly confirming that the long-alleged Curse of the Bambino really may have been the Curse of Jackie Robinson. When Earl Wilson, the second Black player on the Sox, encountered racism during spring training in 1966, Red Sox officials effectively told him to endure it. Reggie Smith, a star for the Sox and the Dodgers in the 1960s and 1970s, called Boston racist. Tommy Harper, a former Sox player and then a coach, ran into racism during spring training in the 1980s; once again, Red Sox management was slow to react. Jim Rice felt racially isolated even as he was one of the game's dominant forces, forging a Hall of Fame career in the 1970s and 1980s as a left fielder and designated hitter. Outfielder Ellis Burks felt similarly isolated in the late 1980s and 1990s.

And the team's reputation extended well beyond the Boston clubhouse. Dave Justice, Albert Belle, Tim Raines, Gary Sheffield, Dave Winfield, Willie Randolph, and Barry Bonds are among the many players who expressed concerns about the prospect of playing in Boston. Some refused to entertain signing with or (if they had the power) being traded to Boston, expressing extra satisfaction at beating the Red Sox, especially in front of the fans in Fenway Park. And those fans have most often been the reason for accusations of racism. Adam Jones and Torii Hunter both asserted that fans shouted a barrage of racial slurs and expletives at them during the last decade. In 2020, the Red Sox finally acknowledged a real and ongoing problem with racism among the fan base.

After the 1950 season, Red Sox general manager Eddie Collins, one of the biggest forces against integrating his team, sat next to Sam Jethroe at the Boston Baseball Writers annual dinner. He congratulated Jethroe for winning Rookie of the Year. Jethroe "thanked him and without bitterness" responded, "You had your chance, Mr. Collins. You had your chance."[70] The Red Sox had their chance time after time after time, and they refused to take it.

OF REDSKINS AND PATRIOTS: BOSTON AND INTEGRATION IN THE NFL

Boston's short-lived entry in the NFL in 1946 was the Boston Yanks. It would be clever to say that their tenure in the city represented a time when Boston loved the Yankees, but frankly their tenure in the city was one that saw more empty seats than fans. The Yanks had no Black players. Boston got a foothold for good in professional football when the Boston (later New England) Patriots joined another group of upstarts in forming the American Football League (AFL), which began play in 1960. In their early years the Patriots were nomads in Boston, playing in a number of venues, including Fenway Park, before they moved to Foxborough, thirty miles from Boston. The forward-looking AFL—which, like the AAFC would merge with the NFL when it proved more than worthy competition—was integrated from the start. Indeed, the league embraced Black talent far more than did the NFL, drawing players not only from traditional powerhouses, but also from smaller colleges and from HBCUs.[71] The very first pick of the Boston Patriots in the very first AFL draft was Northwestern University All-American Ron Burton, a Black running back who was also chosen by the Philadelphia Eagles in the NFL draft. Burton chose to play for the Patriots.[72]

But the last team to integrate the NFL—indeed, the only segregated American professional sports team outside of the NHL after Pumpsie Green joined the Red Sox—had Boston connections as well. And once again poor, racist leadership provides nearly all the explanation. George Preston Marshall, who had inherited laundromats from his parents, joined with two other men and received an NFL franchise for Boston in 1932. In its first year they shared a playing facility with baseball's Boston Braves, so the team also was known as the Braves. A year later, after the team struggled to draw fans in its first season, his two co-owners sold Marshall their shares. He moved the team to Fenway Park and renamed it the Redskins, an uncontroversial choice at the time, especially because the coach he hired that year, William Henry "Lone Star" Dietz, claimed to be part Sioux.

The year 1933 marked the return to segregation for the NFL, which remained the status quo until the Rams' signings of Washington and Strode. In 1936, Boston won the NFL's Eastern division despite poor support from the home fans. That fan base was so sparse, in fact, that Marshall, whose team was to host the NFL championship game, moved the game from Boston to New York. He then moved the franchise from Boston to Washington, DC, for the 1937 season.

Though Marshall was an innovator in many ways—he treated his franchise more like a college team than a professional one in an era when the college game was more popular, introducing halftime shows, a marching band, and the like, and he was central to modernizing the passing game in the NFL—he was absolutely resistant to integration.[73] He "remained steadfastly mired in pre–World War II ways of segregation."[74] Because his was the southernmost team in the NFL for the vast majority of his ownership, he feared alienating Southern fans by signing Black players, though he revealed his true feelings when he said, "We'll start signing negroes when the Harlem Globetrotters start signing whites," a flabbergasting example of false equivalence.[75]

In 1961, through Secretary of the Interior Stewart Udall, the new presidential administration of John F. Kennedy began to pressure Marshall to integrate his team. Amid simmering—indeed, nearly boiling over—Cold War tensions, Marshall responded, "I am surprised that with the world on the brink of another war they are worried about whether or not a Negro is going to play for the Redskins." He also insisted that "the government" did not have "the right to tell the showman how to cast the play."[76] But the government did have control of one valuable commodity—a newly built facility that was then known as DC Stadium. Marshall had signed a thirty-year lease to use the new stadium, but it was located on federally owned land on the Anacostia Flats that was part of the National Capital Parks system and had been funded by the government. So in 1962, Udall and Attorney General Robert Kennedy gave Marshall an ultimatum: Integrate or find another place to play. Udall stood up to Marshall, a boorish man with the tendencies of a tyrant in his own little fiefdom. If Marshall "wants an argument, he is going to have a moral argument with the President and with the administration," Udall warned, in language that made national news.[77]

After much bluster, Marshall relented, drafting Syracuse All-American running back Ernie Davis in 1962. Davis, who had been the first Black player to win the Heisman Trophy in 1961, refused to play for Marshall and the Redskins, who traded him for another Black player, Bobby Mitchell. Marshall's trade partner? Cleveland's Paul Brown and his eponymous team.

Tragically, Davis would never play a snap for the Browns, who might have fielded a mighty backfield combination with Davis and Jim Brown. Davis died of leukemia in May 1963. But his stand against Marshall's racism, coupled with Jim Brown's own vocal and at times militant civil rights activism, might have provided a mighty one-two punch on and off the field.

Marshall allegedly grew fond of Bobby Mitchell, who would forge a Hall of Fame career of his own. Already an All-Pro for the Browns at the time of his trade to the nation's capital, Mitchell was an outstanding halfback, receiver, and kick returner who loved track and field as much as football. After his 1958 graduation from the University of Illinois, Mitchell almost chose to pursue a place as a sprinter on the 1960 U.S. Olympic team rather than a career in professional football.

Whatever Marshall's personal feelings about one outstanding player, his legacy of racism remained. Though a statue of the owner, who died in 1969, remained at what came to be known as RFK Memorial Stadium after Robert Kennedy's assassination in 1968, in the wake of the Black Lives Matter protests that followed George Floyd's murder at the hands of Minneapolis police officers in 2020, the statue was defaced. Officials removed it in June of that year. Washington's professional football team also removed Marshall from the team's Ring of Honor at FedEx Field, their new stadium in Maryland's DC suburbs, and scrubbed references to him from both the team's website and historical tributes to the team at their training facility in Ashburn, Virginia. These belated efforts to address the team's racist past may well have been an effort to distract from a series of controversies in the present—about the team's increasingly controversial name (which would eventually be changed, first to "Washington Football Club" and then to Washington Commanders) and also a spate of allegations of sexual harassment and a generally hostile work environment—but they also serve as an acknowledgment that the past and present are not as far removed as many of us might wish.

BILL RUSSELL, #6

In August 2022, less than two weeks after Bill Russell's death on July 31 at the age of eighty-eight, the NBA announced that effective immediately Russell's number 6 would be permanently retired. Players who still wore the number would be grandfathered in, able to wear the number, if they so chose, until they retired, were released, or changed teams. This was only the second time that a professional sports league in the United States permanently retired a jersey number—the first was Major League Baseball's 1997 retirement of Robinson's number 42. There is one exception to this rule: Every April 15th, the anniversary of Robinson's debut, MLB celebrates Jackie Robinson Day, and every player in the league wears a jersey bearing the number 42. In tribute to Russell, the NBA placed a shamrock (honoring Russell's association with the Celtics) with the number 6 on it on every NBA court during the 2022–2023 season. The Celtics also engaged in a number of gestures to honor Russell, including featuring a special Bill Russell tribute uniform, hosting two tribute games, and updating their famous parquet court by adding the number 6 to both of the lanes, the area of the court where Russell especially established his dominance as a player.

As transcendental a player as Russell was, as much as he was the greatest winner in the history of American team sports, it is clear that the NBA would not and could not separate Russell's excellence as a player from his monumental importance as a civil rights leader. Every tribute from the NBA connected Russell the player with Russell the activist. Russell was ambivalent in so many ways about Boston. But perhaps ironically, and certainly belatedly, the city embraced him. Leadership matters. And for his entire life, as a player and as a coach and as a civil rights spokesman and as a man, there was no doubt: William Felton Russell was a leader, and though the word is vastly overused, he was a hero.

CHAPTER 5

The 1960s and the Limits of "Integration" in American College Sports

ENTERING THE 1960S

There was nothing magical about January 1, 1960. The number-one song on the radio was Marty Robbins's "El Paso." Other hits of the day included songs from Frankie Avalon, Connie Francis, Paul Anka, and Bobby Darin. The number-one film for all of January 1960 was the World War II submarine-set comedy *Operation Petticoat.* The best-selling novel entering January was Allen Drury's Cold War anticommunist political thriller *Advise and Consent.* None of these popular culture hits foreshadowed the 1960s of sex, drugs, or even rock and roll. In fact, January 1960 looked an awful lot like the 1950s. So, too, did the team pictures of professional sports teams. High-and-tight haircuts ruled; there was no facial hair, jewelry, or tattoos; and rosters were overwhelmingly white even as the majority of teams in the big three professional sports—baseball, football, and basketball—had engaged in at least token integration. The decade to come would be characterized by radical change, volcanic social disruptions, and challenges to the status quo. Sports would not be immune to the decade's tumult, but racism and sexism would also not easily give way to change.

OF REBELS AND LONGHORNS: DISCRIMINATION AND COMPETITION IN SOUTHERN COLLEGE FOOTBALL

Well into the 1960s—and, in some cases, beyond—the best way for Black athletes to find opportunity both academically and athletically was by attending HBCUs, especially in the South, where Jim Crow severely limited and often completely forbade any university integration. Up until the end of September 1962, not a single Black student attended school with a single white student in the state of Mississippi in graduate or professional schools, universities, colleges, or junior colleges. Trade schools, high schools, middle schools, primary schools, and preschools in the Magnolia State were also wholly segregated. And the same could be said for Alabama. Most other Deep South states weren't much better, and the border South represented only marginal improvement. Thus, HBCUs drew the best and brightest in the classroom, in the theater, in the orchestra pit, in the art studios, and on the fields, courts, tracks, and other facilities. They created doctors and lawyers, teachers and business owners, professors and artists. They also emphasized skilled trades, agricultural, mechanical, and technical education. In very real ways these institutions split the difference between Booker T. Washington's call for Black self-sufficiency (and accommodation to the realities of Jim Crow) and W. E. B. Du Bois's call for a "Talented Tenth" of educated elites to lead the way toward integration and true equality. Indeed, Washington was the driving force behind one of the premier HBCUs—his Tuskegee Institute in Alabama, which emphasized cultivating skilled labor and the trades—while other Black institutions, such as Howard University in Washington, DC, fostered an elite through a wide-ranging liberal arts and professional curriculum.

Grambling, Southern, Florida A&M, Jackson State, Prairie View A&M, Howard, Tuskegee, and other HBCUs provided outlets for athletes to star in football, basketball, baseball, track and field, and other sports while also providing opportunities that created a Black professional and leadership class. Starting with the creation of the Central Intercollegiate Athletic Association (CIAA) and the Southern Intercollegiate Athletic Conference (SIAC), in 1912 and 1913, respectively, four HBCU conferences emerged, two of which would become Division I schools in the Football Championship Subdivision (FCS). Two, including the CIAA and SIAC, would play at the level that later became NCAA Division II. There are also more than thirty HBCUs operating in today's Division III and nearly two dozen in the National Association of Intercollegiate Athletics (NAIA), an organization originally created to support small colleges and universities in athletics. There are more than one hundred schools categorized as HBCUs in the United States, the vast majority with origins in the last quarter of the nineteenth and first quarter of the twentieth century. In some ways, the high-water mark of Jim Crow also marked the apogee of HBCUs. This is, of course, no coincidence. The CIAA initially claimed to be the governing body for all HBCU sports, a status that lasted, at least tentatively, until they joined the NCAA in 1921.[1] The two other HBCU conferences soon followed.

These institutions, embodying so many elements of Black pride, became the epicenter of Black communities, real and imagined. They cultivated community, and within this community they cultivated "sporting congregations," a concept that evokes community but also religiosity. Today, institutions refer to athletic departments, and especially football and basketball, as representing the "front porch" of schools—the most visible manifestation of a university. Schools utilize their sports mascots and school colors well beyond the playing fields. At the highest levels, their teams play on television and exercise the talking heads on ESPN, but even small colleges tend to dominate their communities, their sports teams providing a public face to their institutions. For HBCUs, sports teams embodied the front porch and more—they became points of pride and identification, providing a gathering place and a rallying point. The "success, popularity, and distinctiveness" of Black college teams "increased the cultural power within the community."[2] The fact that these institutions existed because of segregation, but also became responses to racism, cultivated an inordinate sense of pride, dignity, and both tacit and explicit resistance. These institutions, in the words of historian Derrick E. White, undermine "the notion that segregated institutions were inferior."[3]

Increasingly by—and especially after—World War II, schools that had historically been overwhelmingly white took note of the pool of Black athletes and academics and carved out an advantage by recruiting Black athletes early and often. UCLA, with its explosion of Black talent in the late 1930s and early 1940s—Jackie Robinson and his cohort at the forefront—was an early example. By the 1960s, Michigan State University became one of the first predominantly white institutions to invest heavily in Black athletes. The Spartans became a national football power in the mid-1960s by recruiting and playing dominant stars like giant Bubba Smith, who, at 6-foot-7 and 285 pounds, towered over the era's much smaller competition. Michigan State did not just challenge the era's prevailing standards, it shattered them by starting Black players and having a largely Black lineup. In the November 1966 "Game of the Century," Michigan State had twenty Black players, including eleven starters, a quarterback, and two team captains. Notre Dame, meanwhile, had one Black player—future Pro Football Hall of Fame defensive lineman (and later Minnesota Supreme Court Justice) Alan Page. In the words of one journalist and historian, "Michigan State was the future. Notre Dame was the past."[4]

The game ended in a 10–10 tie, with Notre Dame choosing to play conservatively to preserve the draw, much to the chagrin of many observers. Part of the reason they could do so was because Notre Dame was a blueblood that would get the benefit of the doubt from pollsters, whereas, as an upstart, Michigan State likely would not.[5] And that is precisely what happened; despite the tie at Spartan Stadium, Notre Dame edged out Michigan State in both the Associated Press (AP) and United Press International (UPI) polls that year. There is no evidence that race played a role in these considerations, as Notre Dame has often been the recipient of undeserved special pleading in college football, but Michigan State certainly had become a football power precisely because of an approach to Black players that the bluebloods had still eschewed.

Often these opportunities were not unfettered. In far too many cases, when there were regional clashes between Northern and Southern universities on the gridiron or the basketball court, the Northern school, especially if it was visiting one of Dixie's citadels, was expected to keep its Black players on the bench—or, preferably, at home. Too often, this led to acquiescence; occasionally, it led to resistance. Although William "Big Bill" Bell was an All-Big Ten and All-American honorable mention as a Black star at predominantly white Ohio State in 1931, the Buckeyes caved to Vanderbilt's request that they exclude Bell when the two teams met that season.[6] Even more shocking—the game was played in Columbus. While no one protested OSU's decision to yield to the gentleman's agreement—at their own facility, on their own campus—in 1940 seven students mounted a protest campaign against New York University when the school chose to accede to the University of Missouri's request that they leave star running back Len Bates at home. The university's leadership suspended the "Bates 7." Naturally, Bates, who would later serve in World War II and then spend his career as a guidance counselor in the New York City public school system, was disgusted both that he was left at home and that the seven students faced such draconian punishment.[7]

Nor did Black players find a panacea at predominantly white Northern universities, where they often confronted racism, sometimes even as fans cheered for them to help their teams. As historian Donald Spivey writes, "With the team facing a tough third or fourth down and in desperate need of a yard or more for a vital first down, you might well hear some diehard fans yelling 'Give the n——the ball!' Paul Robeson heard it at Rutgers University, Wilmeth Sidat-Singh heard it at Syracuse, as did Ozzie Simmons of Iowa, Brud Holland of Cornell, Willis Ward of Michigan, Bernie Jefferson of Northwestern, Lou Montgomery of Boston College, Kenny Washington of UCLA, and Leonard Bates of New York University."[8] And like Bates, several of these players saw their teams betray them under the auspices of the gentleman's agreement. Their use as players did not save them from the indignities of racism.

Nor did it protect them from violence on the field. Ozzie Simmons of the University of Iowa suffered severe injuries in a 1934 game against the University of Minnesota, and Johnny Bright of Drake University was maliciously targeted and suffered brutal injuries against Oklahoma A&M (now Oklahoma State) in 1951. In some cases that violence turned fatal, as with Jack Trice of Iowa State University, who died after injuries he suffered in a game against the Golden Gophers in 1923. It is possible that bad luck or their skill as players made them targets as much as their race, but in none of these situations was race entirely incidental.[9]

There are numerous paradoxes attached to HBCUs, including the indignities that came with integration. These schools were products of enforced, often violent segregation, beginning as projects responding to white supremacy. But they also became significant cultural, economic, and symbolic institutions on their own. Black Americans did not clamor to be with white people. What most wanted was simply for the best opportunities to be available to them and to not be second-class citizens in their own countries. During an era of segregation, HBCUs thus became institutions that provided these opportunities. But given state funding and majoritarian sentiments about predominantly white institutions—especially flagship institutions in the South and Midwest—those institutions gained a prestige and a place in the imagination even of Black Americans proud of their HBCUs.

Yet Black institutions offered something else as well, for what most African Americans wanted was, in the words of Derrick E. White, "political integration and cultural autonomy."[10] There was surely tension between these two desires, but they also serve as a reminder that while Black Americans resented the forced restrictions that virtually eliminated them from the civic sphere, they also had intense pride in Black accomplishment so often manifested in Black institutions, at the forefront of which were HBCUs, community schools, the church, and Black-owned businesses. And in an era when HBCU football teams were among the most visible manifestations of those institutions, the success of those teams proved to mobilize entire communities and to instill pride, albeit a pride that also raised an uncomfortable question: What if . . . ? What if we could play against the traditional predominantly white powers? Even more pointedly, what if we could play *with* them? In other words, would it be better to be able to play against (and beat) Southeastern Conference (SEC) powers like the Alabama Crimson Tide, Louisiana State Tigers, or University of Mississippi Rebels—or would it be even better to be able to represent them? That the latter proved to be what happened does not change the fact that there could have been another path forward.

Things were more complicated because segregation seemed to be working for a wide range of the segregated institutions in the South well into the 1960s. From 1945 to 1970, at least thirty-one all-white teams from the South or border regions won national championship recognition from at least one of the bodies that granted that honor when voters, not games on the field, decided the national champion. To narrow the criteria slightly, during those same years one of these segregated teams topped the AP poll (which began declaring the final top twenty teams in the country in 1938) nine times and topped the UPI poll (which commenced in 1950) ten times.[11]

In a world where segregation was not only not punished but rewarded in national polls, white supremacy on the gridiron seemed to validate white supremacy. That these institutions refused to play the HBCU powerhouses of the era created a bubble that was virtually impenetrable and seemed entirely self-perpetuating. Since the national media ignored programs like Florida A&M, Grambling, Prairie View A&M, Southern, Tennessee State, and Howard, it was as if those schools and their talented teams did not exist when it came time to give out mythical national championships in an era before a playoff system existed.

And for all its revolutionary tenor, the 1960s at times saw the reinforcement of this whitewashing of the top of college football. During that decade, the all-white teams at the University of Mississippi (1960 and 1962), the University of Alabama (1961, 1964, 1965, and 1966), Louisiana State University (1962), the University of Texas (1963, 1968, 1969), the University of Arkansas (1964), the University of Tennessee (1967), and the University of Georgia (1968) were recognized as national champions by at least one organization. Perhaps ironically, in the future these Southern power programs would be among the teams with the highest percentages of Black players.

Five case studies that effectively bracket the era help show the slow nature of change in college sports in the 1960s.

"NEVER, NO NEVER!": WHITE SUPREMACY AND FOOTBALL AT OLE MISS (AND TEXAS, AND ARKANSAS)

Ole Miss—the University of Mississippi—was a football juggernaut in the late 1950s and 1960s, an era that saw a run of SEC dominance similar to what it has had in the twenty-first century. From 1959 through 1962, the Rebels finished second, second, fifth, and third in the AP poll and second, third, fifth, and third in the UPI poll. Three organizations awarded Mississippi the championship for 1959, seven granted them that honor in 1960, and four did so after the 1962 season. Thus, the Rebels never were consensus national champions, but they were regulars in the national title discussion for several years, even as the state cemented its reputation as the most violently intransigent when it came to Black challenges to the white power structure.

The nadir of this massive resistance came during the 1962 football season, one that Ole Miss proudly counts as a national championship campaign. In fact, football was central to the events that resulted in deadly riots on the university's Oxford campus in the waning hours of September when James Meredith, a twenty-eight-year-old U.S. Air Force veteran, tried to become the first Black student to attend the school. Negotiations for Meredith to attend Ole Miss had been going on for months. Court battles had gone back and forth, and the state's preferred tactic of delay seemed to be bearing fruit until the Kennedy administration reluctantly but decisively intervened.

"I love Mississippi! I love her people—our customs! I love and I respect our heritage!"[12] exclaimed Mississippi governor Ross Barnett, who had become a hero to white Mississippi and indeed across the white South in the previous days, weeks, and months because of his vocal stand against Meredith's presence at Ole Miss. His fists clenched and his voice full of emotion, he was barely able to get those fifteen words out before the frothing crowd of more than forty thousand white football fans swallowed them in hysteria on the night of September 29, 1962. Mississippians from across the state and region were gathered at Jackson's War Memorial Stadium to see their beloved Ole Miss Rebels football team take on the visiting Kentucky Wildcats. They waved their Confederate flags as the band wore their Confederate Grays—literal replicas of the Confederacy's Civil War uniforms. They whooped and hollered and shouted the school's "Hoddy Toddy" cheer and sang the "Never! No, Never!" song, decrying integration and echoing Barnett's campaign promises. They cheered the playing of "Dixie," letting out blood-curdling rebel yells, and generally allowed their delirium to carry them to that dangerous level of conformity that only a mob high on a heady mix of championship football and massive white resistance could achieve in the South in the 1960s.

Barnett's speech before what Ole Miss historian James Silver called the "reasonless, incoherent, delirious" masses made confrontation with a violent climax not only inevitable but, in the twisted logic of the rabid segregationist lexicon, also patriotic.[13] White supremacy and therefore the exclusion of Meredith—but really, any and all Black Americans—in this context became bound up with Americanism. In the words of journalist Michael Dorman of New York's *Newsday*: "The crowd was in Barnett's palm. He had the opportunity here to strike a forceful blow, for either law and order or lawlessness. But he did neither. He had whipped the crowd into a frenzy. Now he let that frenzy fizzle. He uttered not one word of advice on how to cope with the crisis."[14]

But by doing neither, Barnett did not find a path between two extremes. Instead, the implication of his consistent brinksmanship throughout the integration crisis was that lawlessness was an acceptable alternative. Football became the backdrop for a value system that would see the beautiful Ole Miss campus, and especially the Grove, the picturesque epicenter of football Saturday tailgating, engulfed in flames. Two would be dead after the riots. Meredith would ultimately matriculate at Ole Miss, graduating in the summer of 1963 after a lonely year.

Ole Miss football would continue to be a force for a little while longer, though by the 1970s and for several decades following, the events of 1962 would haunt the team on the recruiting trail. Even other once ardently segregationist opponents would use the 1962 crisis as a wedge against Ole Miss to draw Black recruits who might have ended up in Oxford.

But in 1962 and for several years beyond, segregation was no impediment to national football glory. Indeed, the decade would end with a game, widely regarded as the de facto national championship, between two fierce, undefeated SEC rivals—both still lily white.

On December 6, 1969, the host Arkansas Razorbacks and the visiting Texas Longhorns stood astride the college football world as Southern universities had for a decade, and as with those other Southern powers, neither team had a Black player, though both universities had, however reluctantly, enrolled Black students. In 1948, Arkansas had become the first Southern university since Reconstruction to admit a Black student without a court order or other threat of litigation. Texas, the target of considerable litigation (which it lost), had desegregated its graduate programs in 1950 and enrolled its first Black undergraduate in 1956.

Devoted football fan and U.S. president Richard M. Nixon was in attendance that day in Fayetteville. A national television audience watched as the two titans fought for regional and national football supremacy. Visiting Texas entered the game ranked #1 in the country. The host Razorbacks were #2. And in this "Game of the Century," a game that seems to take place every few years in college football, Texas emerged with a 15–14 victory after coming back from a 14–0 deficit, completing a two-point conversion in the first half and a daring deep pass call in the fourth quarter that allowed the team to seal the victory despite its six turnovers on the day. Texas claimed the national championship in what author Terry Frei has called "Dixie's Last Stand"—the last clash with national import between all-white teams.[15]

BAM AND THE BEAR OF 'BAMA

Another decade-ending event, this one connected to the desegregation of college football, has become shrouded in myth and legend, serving to buttress the reputation of one of the sport's legendary figures by revealing him to be a force for change who flew in the face of the conventions of his era and his region while creating a feel-good redemption narrative.

Paul "Bear" Bryant was indeed a legend. He won 323 games as head coach of the University of Maryland, the University of Kentucky, Texas A&M University, and, most famously, for a quarter-century at the helm of the Alabama Crimson Tide, which he led to six national titles. He also oversaw segregated programs for the vast majority of his head-coaching career and for the entirety of his time as a college assistant coach. His teams at Maryland, Kentucky, and Texas A&M were all white, as were all his Alabama teams until the 1970s. The myth that emerged around Bryant involved the integration of Alabama, where he played in the 1930s, but at no point prior to the 1970s did he challenge white supremacy on—or, for that matter, off—the gridiron.

The myth runs as follows: Bryant recognized that integration was coming and that Alabama needed to accede, and so he scheduled the

University of Southern California, which had a number of Black star players, to play Alabama at Birmingham's Legion Field in September 1970. After USC, and especially their star running back Sam Cunningham, ran rampant against the Crimson Tide, which suffered a 42–21 mauling at the hands of the Trojans, Bryant brought Cunningham into the vanquished locker room for his players to behold. The result explains, as the subtitle of one book has it, "how one game changed the South."[16] Allegedly, Cunningham's dominance was the final proof that Alabama needed to integrate to continue to compete.

The problem is that this story is riddled with inaccuracies.[17] To be sure, USC came to Tuscaloosa and hammered 'Bama, racking up 559 yards of offense, with Cunningham responsible for 135 of those yards and two touchdowns. But it is absurd to maintain that this was a major strategy by Bryant or that this game "changed the South." By 1970, desegregation was still happening at a glacial pace across the Old Confederacy, but many schools across the region already had Black players, Black lettermen, Black starters, Black stars. Jerry Levias, who had been recruited by head coach Hayden Fry to Southern Methodist University, starred for the Mustangs beginning in 1966. And Cunningham was not the first Black player to score a touchdown in Alabama or against an Alabama SEC power. In 1969, Tennessee—which had two Black stars— routed Alabama, 41–14, in Birmingham's Legion Field. Kentucky fielded the first Black player in the SEC when Nate Northington became the first Black scholarship athlete in the history of the SEC in 1967. In 1969, Kentucky continued to break the mold when Wilbur Hackett became the first Black SEC football captain. Six SEC schools had fielded Black players before the 1970 Alabama–USC game. And rumors aside, Cunningham never accompanied Bryant to the Alabama locker room. Bryant may have known what needed to happen, but to imply that he was some sort of pioneer in 1970, a quarter of a century into a head-coaching career in which he had never coached a Black player, does a disservice to those who really were pioneers and who really did take risks. Further, it gives credit not to the Black trailblazers but to good old boy white coaches.

FROM THE GRIDIRON TO THE HARDWOOD: HOOPS AND HOPES

Jake Gaither did not move to Tallahassee and Florida A&M University to be the HBCU's head football coach, even though he became a legend in that capacity. His initial duties at Florida A&M were to serve as athletic director, to be an assistant football coach under Big Bill Bell, and to be the head coach of the college's basketball team, a position he had held at his previous postings. Basketball played a similar role in the winter that football did in the fall at many HBCUs—a source of visible pride and accomplishment, another example of sporting congregations. The National Collegiate Basketball Association—comprised of HBCUs—hosted a national postseason tournament.

When the NCAA staged its first end-of-season basketball championship tournament in 1939, it was an all-white affair. It also was a second-tier event to the National Invitation Tournament (NIT) held in New York, which was fully integrated. In 1940, the NCAA tournament broke the color line, but not with a Black player; rather, Rice University's Mexican American player Placido Gomez represented the Owls in the eight-team tournament that was otherwise lily-white. Interestingly, the second act of integration of the NCAAs came when Utah, which had lost in the first round of the NIT, replaced Arkansas in the NCAA tournament in 1944 and Wat Misaka, a Japanese American player, appeared for the Utes. The NCAA tournament would not field its first Black players until well after World War II ended: In 1947, starting center Joe Galibar and backup forward Sonny Jameson appeared for City College of New York.[18]

As happened in football, predominantly white basketball teams sometimes were willing to accommodate segregation rather than fight it. The NAIA, an organizing body for mostly small colleges, hosted its own postseason tournament, including in its rules an explicit parenthetical clause dictating "Colored players not eligible."[19] When Indiana State was invited to participate, their young coach, John Wooden, cravenly brought the team without its only Black player, Clarence Walker. The NAIA changed its policy the next year, and then only as the result of pressure from both the U.S. Olympic Basketball Committee and schools that chose to boycott the event rather than accommodate the segregationist policy, as Wooden, the future Wizard of Westwood who would go on to lead a dynasty at UCLA, had been willing to do.[20] At other times, teams limited their Black players, adhering to an informal coaching rule about how many Black players to play where: "Two blacks at home. Three on the road. And four when behind."[21]

In 1950, CCNY won a rare double, taking the more prestigious NIT and the growing-in-stature NCAA tournament with two Black starters, Ed Warner and Floyd Lane. Bill Russell and his future Celtics teammate and fellow Hall of Fame inductee K. C. Jones (who also coached the Celtics to two titles in the 1980s) carried the University of San Francisco to back-to-back titles in 1955 and 1956, at a time when the NCAA tournament winner was increasingly coming to be seen as the legitimate national champion. In 1959, future Hall of Famer Oscar Robinson took the University of Cincinnati to the national title game but lost to the University of California. Cal's Golden Bears would be the last all-white team to win an NCAA basketball title.

The NAIA continued to try to split the difference, dividing the country into thirty-two districts, each of which provided one team to the tournament. One slot was allotted to a "Black" district, and thus to an HBCU. From 1957 to 1959, Tennessee State, under coach John McLendon, a coaching giant on a par with Gaither and Grambling's Eddie Robinson, earned that slot—and each time they won the title.

WILL THEY WANT TO DANCE? MISSISSIPPI STATE TESTS THE UNWRITTEN LAW

As in football, while change on the college basketball courts of the South and across the country took place in the postwar years, the 1960s saw an acceleration of that change. And, as in football, protagonists in Mississippi and Texas would prove to be decisive.

In 1963, Loyola of Chicago, with five Black starters, was one of the teams favored to win the NCAA tournament. Their second-round opponent was to be Mississippi State, a team with a history of success on the basketball court and one of the top programs in the SEC. And, of course, they were all white. Indeed, in the wake of the 1962 Ole Miss integration crisis, many Mississippi State boosters took joy in the fact that while their rivals in Oxford had succumbed to integration, their Bulldogs continued to embody white supremacy in the Magnolia State.

Mississippi and many Deep South states had an "unwritten law" that they simply would refuse to participate in postseason events against teams with Black players. The two most relevant examples were postseason college bowl games in football and postseason tournaments in basketball. In fact, one of the main impetuses for the unwritten law came when Mississippi State played a Denver University team with Black players in a Christmas basketball tournament in 1956. When university president Ben Hilbun learned that the team's next opponent, the host University of Evansville, also had a Black player, he ordered the team to return home.

And yet many within the MSU basketball program, numerous students on campus, and even some fans chafed against restrictions that forbade them from playing teams with Black players. The agreement had caused them to turn down NCAA tournament automatic bids after they won the SEC crown in 1959, 1961, and 1962. As the 1963 NCAA tournament approached, voices emerged encouraging MSU to ignore the old unwritten rule and compete in the NCAA tournament no matter who they might face.

No voice was clearer than Mississippi State's coach, James H. "Babe" McCarthy, who used the platform of his statewide radio show to try to appeal to Mississippians to support his team's competing in the tournament: "It makes me sick to think that these players, who just clinched no worse than a tie for their third straight Southeastern Conference championship, will have to put away their uniforms and not compete in the NCAA tournament. . . . This is all I can say but I think everyone knows how I feel."[22] MSU's players agreed, especially the team's seniors, who had seen so much success come to an unceremonious end after the completion of their SEC season.

Unlike in past years, Bulldogs alumni and fans and Mississippi State students were vocal in their support of the team's traveling for tournament play no matter the opposition. President Dean W. Colvard gave a wishy-washy response, committing himself to no path forward and frustrating the students. Faculty, too, overwhelmingly supported defying the status quo, with numerous faculty bodies—including entire schools and departments as well as the faculty athletics committee—supporting the team's going to the tournament.

The feeling was not universal, of course, as segregation still was the most powerful political force in the state. The state's largest newspapers, the *Jackson Daily News* and the city's *Clarion-Ledger*, certainly fanned the flames of resistance, maintaining an ardently white supremacist stand, as they would throughout the civil rights era.[23] The Mississippi State legislature and Governor Barnett, who had become a hero in the white South for his defiance in the face of the Meredith challenge, seemed to have learned from the Ole Miss fiasco and left the decision where it belonged—at the level of university leadership. This would be only one of many consequential decisions Colvard would make, and he would become one of the most important presidents in MSU's history, providing leadership during some of the university's most vital years of growth and change. In the end, he allowed the team—casually known as the "Maroons" because of the predominant school color—to compete in the NCAA tournament.

But that was not the end of the controversy. A number of Mississippi state legislators saw an opportunity and jumped on it during an election year. They accused Colvard of "capitulating" and hinted at threatening Mississippi State's funding appropriation. Senator Billy Mitts, who was once a Mississippi State cheerleader, called on the state's college board to "refuse permission for any institution under its jurisdiction to engage in any athletic contest with integrated teams." A surprisingly lively debate emerged in what University of Mississippi history professor James Silver had called the "Closed Society" of Mississippi. Segregationists rallied but got a surprising amount of pushback, on and off campus. Ole Miss football coach John Vaught, who had led his team somewhat quietly through a campus crisis a few months earlier, declared that the Mississippi State players "deserved to go, and I'm glad they're getting the opportunity." Mississippi would maintain a segregationist consensus for years to come, but there were breaches emerging in what had once been impenetrable defenses.

Barnett remained relatively quiet on the issue, largely because the Southern Association of Colleges and Schools (SACS) had put all the state's colleges and universities on "watch" as a result of the intervention of Barnett and others in the lead-up to the Ole Miss crisis. Barnett made clear during the Mississippi State debate that he was "a strong believer in and an advocate of segregation in every phase of activity in all our schools."[24] There was no doubt that he opposed integrated sports. As he explained in 1960, "If there were half a dozen Negroes" on a team at a Mississippi university, "where are they going to eat?" And perhaps more to the point, in a Mississippi, and indeed a South, obsessed with "miscegenation, . . . [a]re they going to want to go to the dance later and want to dance with our girls?"[25] But in 1963, he entrusted the final decision to the political appointees who made up the Board of Trustees of Institutions of Higher Learning. He and most other segregationist politicians, including Senator Billy Mitts, expected the college board to rule in a way that would protect segregation. However, past boards had seen these kinds of decisions as internal administrative matters, and any unwritten rules had always been enforced not by the decree of trustees but rather by the power of the purse of the state legislature.[26]

In something of an upset, and only after heated debate, the board voted to allow Mississippi State to travel by an 8–3 vote, fought off a motion to fire Colvard, then voted 9–2 to support the beleaguered Mississippi State president. Nevertheless, Mitts and former state senator B. W. Lawson obtained a temporary injunction to prevent the team from flying out.

Thus began a series of what one player called "cloak and dagger stuff."[27] The series of machinations and maneuvers had become necessary as Hinds County and local sheriffs tried to serve the injunction, and Mississippi State officials as well as the team engaged in evasive moves. Several university officials left town and checked into hotels under aliases in cities outside of Mississippi. Meanwhile, the team engaged in its own chicanery, sending the freshman team to the Starkville airport while the varsity players waited for a call in the athletic dormitory. Weather delays further caused confusion, but eventually the team flew out, later than expected but unserved. An associate justice of the Mississippi Supreme

Court stayed the injunction, arguing that it had been "issued without authority of law and improvidently issued without notice."[28]

Loyola defeated Tennessee Tech in the opening round of the Mideast regional, setting up the clash against Mississippi State, whose SEC title had granted them a first-round bye. Coach McCarthy was suitably fulsome in his praise of his opponents, calling them "the best basketball team we've ever played since I've been at Mississippi State." Leland Mitchell, an All-SEC shooting guard, was one of several MSU players who simply did not see the big deal: "I don't see anything morally wrong with playing against Negroes, Indians, Russians, or any other race or nationality. Most of us boys have already competed against them in high school or in hometown sandlot games. In my opinion it's just like playing against anyone else."[29] Reflecting years later on his experiences in 1963, Mitchell recalled, "We wanted to play. We had just won the SEC tournament for the third year in a row and we hadn't been allowed to play in the NCAA tournament the last two years. For us the biggest thing was getting to play in the tournament because it was something we felt we deserved." In retrospect he recognized that "it was much more than a basketball game. We were making history. We were ambassadors for the South, though none of us realized it at the time."[30]

MSU jumped out to a quick 7–0 lead. From that point on it was all Loyola, who used tenacious defense and rebounding and generally superior athletic ability to win by 10, 61–51, with Loyola's four Black starters scoring 59 of the team's 61 points. Leland led his team with 14 points and 11 rebounds, but he fouled out with more than six minutes remaining in the game. Mississippi State's disappointed team members were gracious about Loyola and its players. Leland later remembered that despite the racial implications of the game, especially for his team, "there wasn't one incident, and not because we weren't trying or trying to be nice."[31] McCarthy dismissed any racial explanation for the outcome, peevishly responding to a question, "The color didn't make any difference. I don't even want to talk about that because it wasn't important," and maintaining that his team would happily play a team with Black players again in the future, barring the state passing a law forbidding it. A few weeks later the college board repealed the unwritten law.[32] Leland later admitted that despite the absurdity of the situation that got them to the tournament, the team "didn't know the significance of what we did. It didn't hit us until later."[33]

BASKETBALL TAKES A TURN: TEXAS WESTERN DEFEATS KENTUCKY

The 1966 NCAA men's college basketball tournament championship game is widely seen as the single most important contest in the history of college basketball. "What a piece of history!" exclaims Nolan Richardson, a legendary national title–winning coach for the University of Arkansas and a former player at Texas Western, the winner of that game. "If basketball ever took a turn, that was it."[34]

That year Texas Western (which in 1967 would become the University of Texas at El Paso) played traditional juggernaut Kentucky and its legendary coach Adolph Rupp in the national finals at the University of Maryland's Cole Field House in College Park. Perhaps indicative of the status of the college game at the time—even its championship—tip-off was scheduled for 10 p.m., the game did not appear on a major network, and in some of the cities where it was aired it appeared only on tape delay.

Rupp had led Kentucky to NCAA championships in 1948, 1949, 1951, and 1958, and almost everyone had them penciled in for the Wildcats' fifth championship when they faced the upstart Miners from El Paso, who came into the game ranked third in the country and with a 27–1 record, but whom few gave any chance to win. The game also ended up being a symbol of an era of transition as Western Texas, with five Black starters, upset Kentucky and its unrepentantly all-white squad, 72–65. Though not necessarily a crusader, Western Texas coach Don Haskins—like Branch Rickey and Bill Veeck and so many white allies before him—also was well aware of the moment and what it meant. First and foremost, Haskins, hired in 1961, wanted to win, and he did not allow prejudice to limit the ways in which he might do so.

Heading into the game, sportswriters who had never seen the Miners play but knew they were overwhelmingly Black conjured up images of a particular style of basketball and ran with that in their columns—asserting a run-and-gun style, dribbling acrobatics a la the Harlem Globetrotters, and generally letting their imaginations run wild. Perry

Wallace, who would become the first Black basketball player in the SEC when he joined Vanderbilt's team the year after the Texas Western triumph, explained the mindset years later: "There was a certain style of play whites expected from blacks. 'N——ball' they used to call it. Whites then thought that if you put five blacks on the court at the same time, they would somehow revert to their native impulses." One *Baltimore Sun* columnist claimed, "The running, gunning Texas quintet can do more things with a basketball than a monkey on a 50-foot jungle wire." This unfortunate choice of words was all the worse because, as journalist Frank Fitzpatrick wrote years later, "In fact the opposite was true. Texas Western walked the ball up court, ran a rigidly patterned offense, and emphasized defense—allowing just 62 points a game."[35] As historian Charles H. Martin argues, "Unlike the wide-open, up-tempo style that many of the Miners had learned on urban playgrounds, Haskins insisted on the patterned, highly-structured offense made famous by his mentor at Oklahoma State, Henry Iba, coupled with tenacious defense."[36] Kentucky was the run-and-gun team, running the ball up court and relying on speed and quickness.

In the wake of the Miners' victory, a new series of myths emerged. Western won with defense and rebounding, but the narrative soon emerged that Haskins had filled his roster with Northern ringers whose eligibility was dubious and who won through thuggish tactics. In his 1976 book *Sports in America*, James Michener (who had written a book condemning campus protests and defending the shootings at Kent State in 1970) excoriated Texas Western and utterly misrepresented the game, which he called "one of the most wretched stories in the history of American sports." Texas Western's players were "loose-jointed ragamuffins" who were "hopelessly outclassed" by Rupp's "tall and beautifully coached" team, which was "impressive in its pregame drills." He described the El Paso school as having "conscripted a bunch of black players from New York City high schools."[37]

The reality of the two teams was quite different. Texas Western had seven Black players (and four whites and a Hispanic player, often overlooked). Four of those Black players graduated from Western Texas. The three who did not missed out by a semester or so and went on to successful careers. Meanwhile, four of Kentucky's five starters, including future NBA player and coach of the 1980s Lakers dynasty Pat Riley, never graduated. As for Texas Western's unconscionable recruiting of out-of-state players? Kentucky had ten players on the roster who were not from the Bluegrass State, while the Miners had nine non-Texans on their roster. Although nominally concerned that Texas Western's Black players were being ill served, Michener succumbed to wide-ranging generalities and reductionist stereotypes (admittedly bolstered by a series of articles in *Sports Illustrated* from 1968) that did not hold up to even rudimentary scrutiny.[38] Meanwhile, for years after the game Rupp obsessed about the loss, frequently implying that the Miners must have used ineligible players, an unsubstantiated accusation that long infuriated Haskins.[39] Although the 1966 championship game result has been depicted as one of the greatest upsets in all of sports, one has to question this narrative in one sense—Texas Western was the number-three team in the country and had lost just one game all year. In terms of status, Kentucky was obviously well ahead of Texas Western—a blueblood facing off against a no-name—and the racial dynamic gives the game a historical resonance that elevates the sense of upset. But it needs to be said that Texas Western was an outstanding team that won on talent, work ethic, guile, and brains. The historic nature of the game should not allow history to diminish the team as merely plucky—and thus lucky—underdogs, though underdogs they were.

Rupp did not play a Black player until December 1970, by most accounts under duress from University of Kentucky officials and some politicians. Rupp's longtime assistant Harry Lancaster later recalled that after Rupp met with university president John W. Oswald, the old coach lamented, "Harry, that son of a bitch is ordering me to get some n——s in here. What am I going to do?"[40] He held out for a few seasons after that, but eventually succumbed to the inevitable. Haskins, meanwhile, received some pressure from his university's president, Joseph Ray, to start at least one white player.

Texas Western made history, and they did so in the face of racism. Excluding Black players from college basketball today is nearly unfathomable, but until Texas Western, it was common. Texas Western was one of several universities—three in Texas, also including the University of Houston and North Texas State—that utilized Black players as a way to break into the ranks of elite sports. As Martin has shown, these types of programs were driven by a combination of "opportunism, self-interest, pragmatism, ambition, and occasionally even a touch of idealism" in their efforts to recruit Black athletes.[41] This allowed them to challenge segregation, even if that was not their primary purpose. Texas Western, with its win over Kentucky, "provides the most successful story of an ambitious nonelite school that sought to gain regional and national prominence through athletic success."[42]

* * *

In the 1960s, college sports were in a period of transition, as was most of American society on matters of race. By the second half of the decade, however, prominent athletes across the professional and amateur ranks would grow more vocal and more aggressive, and would be far less willing to accept crumbs from the table of a sporting world still controlled overwhelmingly by whites even as Black athletes were taking their rightful place in the games.

CHAPTER 6

Oh Say Can You See?

Rebellion, Anger, and Contested Americanisms

POWER TO THE PEOPLE!
By the late 1960s, Black and Brown athletes were no longer content with simply having a seat at the table. A generation and more of these athletes and their white allies fought to have access, to get the opportunity to compete, to play, to excel. But as the 1960s progressed, athletes knew they wanted more—that they deserved more. At the same time, large numbers of Black Americans were no longer content merely to call for integration. They wanted power. On top of all of this, the debate over the Vietnam War was coming to a crescendo. All these trends would play out in the athletic arena as well, whether in the form of Muhammad Ali's refusal to be inducted into the military or an unorthodox performance of the national anthem at the World Series. And with each of these events, the response was swift, furious, and at times unhinged.

THE ALI SUMMIT, THE VIETNAM WAR, AND "RADICAL" POLITICS
In June 1967, Jim Brown, having retired from the NFL and traded playbooks for movie scripts, was in London filming *The Dirty Dozen* when he received a phone call from Jabir Herbert Muhammad, Muhammad Ali's manager and a son of Elijah Muhammad, the leader of the Nation of Islam. Muhammad needed Brown to talk to his friend Ali, who had refused induction into the U.S. Army in Houston weeks earlier on the

grounds of conscientious objection to the conflict in Vietnam. In Ali's words, "I ain't got no quarrel with them Viet Cong."[1] Herbert Muhammad admitted to Brown that many of the people surrounding the champ "wouldn't mind him going into the service, but they couldn't tell him that."[2]

The world heavyweight champion faced an uncertain future that included the possibility of jail time, never mind losing his title belt, but he insisted that his newfound religious beliefs—he was also recently named a minister in the Nation of Islam—were sincere. Three years earlier Ali had failed the qualifying test to serve in the military because of poor writing and spelling skills, but the Army recalibrated the tests in 1966, suddenly pushing Ali's scores above the acceptable limit and reclassifying him as 1A, eligible to serve and be drafted. Ali was naturally confused by this change but did not make any reference to being a conscientious objector at that time. This brought out the cynics and the superpatriots, who claimed that by refusing to step forward on three occasions when called to do so at the U.S. Army induction center in Houston on April 28, Ali had engaged in a carefully orchestrated moment of anti-Americanism. He had refused induction because, as he had been informed by his attorneys, he had to "exhaust his administrative remedies" to be able to have the opportunity to have his case heard before a civil court. Ali continued to reiterate his religious beliefs and to take all the criticism coming his way. After enduring a grueling few days, including the events in Houston, he kept quiet at the behest of Elijah Mohammad. He did, however, call his mom in Louisville. "Mama, I'm all right," the champ said, "curled up" on a bed in the Hotel America. "I did what I had to do. I sure am looking forward to coming home to eat some of your cooking."[3]

Humanizing moments aside, Herbert Muhammad wanted to confirm the depths of this sincerity that had infuriated a nation, which immediately attacked the patriotism of Ali—most would have still defiantly called him Cassius Clay—and many of his detractors would have combined this nationalistic fervor with a racist edge. "He was already considered a loud-mouthed Negro while he was Cassius Clay," according to sociologist and sports activist Harry Edwards. "When he joined the Nation of Islam, that exacerbated it even more."[4] But many millions of people, including Black Americans and fellow athletes—indeed, fellow activist athletes—also questioned Ali's decision. It was this state of doubt that Elijah Muhammad hoped Brown could help clarify. The result would be "the simple, dangerous assertion of" Ali's "human rights."[5] It also would reveal how, in the words of Brown biographer Dave Zirin, "The line between those trying to get their share of the system and those trying to overthrow it was never a clear one in those days of social tumult."[6]

Brown, the son of a domestic worker and an absent father in deeply segregated Georgia, later reflected, "I came up with the concept of having Ali meet with the top black athletes. We had a desire to find out the truth about his protest."[7] Brown, like Jackie Robinson and Jim Thorpe before him, was a transcendent athlete who seemed to succeed in every sport he ever attempted. He was obviously a football superstar. There are many who argue that he is the greatest player ever to carry a lacrosse stick. He played basketball at Syracuse and was drafted by the NBA's Syracuse Nationals despite the fact that he had quit playing after his junior year. Casey Stengel sent him a letter gauging his interest in trying to play for the Yankees, even though Brown insists "I wasn't that good" at baseball. In his last day as a varsity athlete at Syracuse, on a day when he also had a lacrosse game, he won the discus, shot put, and javelin at a track and field meet, despite only having fiddled around with the javelin a handful of times. His prowess in the throwing events helped Syracuse win the meet before he ran off to play his lacrosse match. He once won six events in a meet—in addition to his throwing prowess, he could high jump 6 feet, 3 inches and run the 100-yard dash in 10 seconds flat—so he got the notion that he might be able to compete in the national decathlon championship. He did so with ten days of practice under his belt, placing fifth.

Brown and Ali were legitimate friends, not just famous jocks who traveled in the same rarefied air. In his memoir, Brown devotes an entire chapter to Ali. The first words in that chapter are a series of words describing "one of the nicest human beings you would ever like to meet": "Brave, Outrageous, Indomitable, Incandescent."[8] The night the man then known as Cassius Clay beat Sonny Liston for the heavyweight champion in one of boxing's great upsets, Brown was there. The two spent two hours in Clay's hotel while Malcolm X, another Clay adviser and friend, cooled his heels.⁹ Clay wanted Brown to know that he had joined the Nation of Islam and was a devout follower of Elijah Muhammad, and that the NOI's leader had bestowed him with the name Muhammad Ali. The two would wander urban neighborhoods in the mid-1960s dropping in on barbershops, stopping people on the street, and in general communing with the people, their people, Black people.

So Brown used his connections to pull together a constellation of Black sporting superstars who also took political questions seriously. Brown convinced Bill Russell and young basketball prodigy Lew Alcindor, who had just finished his sophomore year at UCLA and would in 1971 change his name to Kareem Abdul-Jabbar after his own conversion to Islam, to join him in Brown's old Cleveland stomping ground. Russell was perhaps especially important for Brown to corral, for by the mid-1960s, Russell and Brown had established themselves as "the two most transformative sports figures of the era," according to Russell biographer Adam Goudsouzian—a mantle that Ali would soon claim.¹⁰

Brown enlisted a former Browns teammate, John Wooten, to help him pull together other NFL players with activist inclinations, drawn mostly from Brown's former Cleveland teammates, but also from other teams. These included former Browns defensive back Walter Beach; former Browns and then Green Bay and future Hall of Fame defensive end Willie Davis; Sid Williams, another of the Browns; former Chiefs running back Curtis McClinton; Bobby Mitchell, the future Hall of Famer who had been the first Black player with the Washington Redskins; and Jim Shorter of the Redskins. The only nonathlete in the group was thirty-nine-year-old lawyer Carl Stokes, who a few months later would win the mayoral election in Cleveland, then America's ninth largest city, becoming the first Black person to be elected mayor of a major American city. In 1967 Stokes was in the midst of what would be one of the most understated careers in American history; as his obituary, read into the Congressional Record, proclaimed, "He was a leader, a visionary, a role model, and above all, a pioneer."¹¹

Brown drew up "a guest list with open minds." He later said, "People don't realize that the United States government was what we were fighting. And that's a very powerful force and they did want Ali" to acquiesce and go into the Army "to make an example out of him and that was one of the reasons that I called the meeting because he was basically alone and this great force was going to try and bring him down and I conjured up this idea of bringing top athletes who were like-minded. Certain athletes," he added, "did not get invited."[12]

Most of the athletes Wooten contacted chose to head to Cleveland, which came as no surprise to him. "After I called all of the guys and explained what we were meeting about, they didn't ask who's going to pay for this or that, they just asked where and what time," Wooten said.[13] "I guess everybody paid their way to fly there and nobody refused," Brown later mused. "Let me put it to you this way: to me, there was no one at that table but soldiers."[14]

Alcindor was among those who didn't waffle as to whether to go to Ohio. "Muhammad Ali was one of my heroes," he later said. "He was in trouble and he was someone I wanted to help because he made me feel good about being an African American. I had the opportunity to see him do his thing [as an athlete and someone with a social conscience], and when he needed help, it just felt right to lend some support."[15]

"The principal for this meeting, of course, was Ali," McClinton later said. "Our assembling there was about Ali defining himself, because that definition was a part of us." But if Ali provided the spark, Brown fanned the flame: "The principal of leadership for us was Jim Brown. Jim's championship leadership filtered to all of us."[16] But Russell's presence was vital, too. According to a girlfriend of the beleaguered heavyweight champion, Ali "worship[ed] Jim Brown and Bill Russell."[17]

The meeting took place when Cleveland was facing the same racial tensions cities throughout the country were experiencing in the last years of the 1960s. Just a year before the Ali Summit, the city's predominantly Black Hough neighborhood had erupted in riots after a white bar owner refused to serve a Black patron who requested a glass of water. Five nights of violence and rioting followed.[18] Nonetheless, Cleveland had also become something of a "hotbed for black power, energy, and Black Nationalism" and an "epicenter of black political and social progress." Stokes's election would both be a result of and fuel this phenomenon, making the city an appealing landing point for Black migrants seeking jobs and perhaps to get away from the Jim Crow South. "Black people were coming to Cleveland from all over the country to see what we were doing here politically and economically, because no other city was doing it like we were," according to Arnold Pinkney, a longtime entrepreneur and political activist and a former Black Economic Union (BEU) treasurer. And, of course, the Browns were especially beloved in Black Cleveland because of their history with Black players, such as Marion Motley, Bill Willis, and the otherworldly Brown.[19]

On the sunny Sunday afternoon of June 4, the group gathered at the offices of the Negro Industrial Economic Union (NIEU) at 105–15 Euclid Avenue in Cleveland's lower University Circle neighborhood, in many ways the heart of Black Cleveland. Their goal was to ascertain just how serious Ali was about his claims of conscientious objector status to the Vietnam War. The NIEU housed the BEU, an organization Brown had founded in 1966 after his retirement from football "to promote economic empowerment and independence among black Americans, believing that would lead to political influence and eventual civil rights."[20] The BEU provided economic development in communities across the country, not just in Cleveland, and had received more than a million dollars from the Ford Foundation. The BEU motto, splashed across the top of the first issue of its newsletter, was "PRODUCE, ACHIEVE, PROSPER."[21] According to Brown, the gathering that day "represents the philosophy that we were establishing in the BEU and beyond. It represents so many things, because, man, I'm proud of it. I'm proud of the people that came."[22]

But on the day of what came to be known as the Ali Summit, "every cultural force convulsing the nation came together—race, religion, politics, young vs. old, peace vs. war."[23] And, as Harry Edwards put it, "The anti-war movement really hit the headlines when Ali refused induction and made his statement about not having any quarrel with the Viet Cong. And then to refuse to comply with the draft, that lined up all of those people who were on one side or the other of the Vietnam War."[24] Hundreds gathered outside of the meeting site "to get a sense of what could be happening and why those stars were congregating."[25]

To any outsiders paying attention, the meeting may have seemed like a group of radical Black athletes providing a rubber stamp to Ali's antiwar stance. It was anything but. Indeed, many of Ali's advisers hoped his peers "would persuade the boxer to take a government deal, which promised a quick, comfortable deployment if he would drop his protest."[26] And many believed that Brown and the others would "talk some sense into him." After all, these men all "spoke the same language, the language of the elite black athlete." They all had "not only survived, they had prospered on the playgrounds of professional sport" and thus "they would be able to tell him how lucky he was to be where he was. Take the deal. Go ahead. That would be the message."[27]

It turned out that the assembled stars, far from arriving in Cleveland with a preconceived notion of what they wanted, went to listen. They certainly "were not going to give Ali blind support."[28] And yet while many went in skeptical, possibly even hostile to a position that could be—and was—painted as anti-American, far from convincing Ali to temper his stand, they emerged convinced of Ali's commitment to his cause.

Brown had called the group together with Wooten's help, but the two largely remained silent during the meeting, watching and listening "as the rest of the group took turns interrogating Ali."[29] "I wanted the meeting to be as intense and honest as it should've been, and it was because the people in that room had thoughts and opinions, and they came to Cleveland with that purpose in mind," Brown said.[30] "I felt with Ali taking the position he was taking, and with him losing the crown, and with the government coming at him with everything they had, that we as a body of prominent athletes could . . . stand behind Ali and give him the necessary support."[31]

Ali's presence itself proved to be a difference maker. In the words of Ali biographer Jonathan Eig, "Usually, Ali could count on his size and physical grace to make an impression when he entered" a space, his physicality leading the way for his "gregarious personality." But his size was not going to impress NFL and NBA players. After all, "almost everyone in the room was big, strong, and confident." But Ali's personality really did win over the men, "overpowering" them "with his energy and steady stream of lightning-fast speech." He "cracked jokes"; he wandered the room "like a preacher working the aisles of his church, establishing eye contact, calling the men by their first names, making each person in the room feel as if he were addressing them individually." He remained poised in the face of tough questions and "never got defensive. He spoke passionately and confidently and with good humor, clearly enjoying the debate."[32] Brown noted that Ali "was funny as hell," and while the intent of the assembled athletes was "moderation and balance" he "was such a dazzling speaker, he damn near converted a few to the Nation of Islam! Guys were nodding their heads, going Hmmmm."[33]

"The questions flew fast and furious," and Ali's answers "would determine whether Brown and the other athletes would throw their support" to Ali or whether the Louisville Lip would float on his own. "F. Lee Bailey would have been proud in the way we questioned" Ali, Wooten later said. "Those guys shot questions at the champ, and he took them and fought back. It was intense, because we were all getting ready to face the United States public relations machine—the media, and put our lives and careers on the line. What if this fails? What if he goes to jail? The champ stood strong." Mitchell found himself one of several of the men who began as skeptics but found themselves nodding along with Ali's words: "During those hours, he said he was sincere and his religion was important to him. He convinced all of us, even someone like me, who was suspicious. We weren't easy on him. We wanted Ali to understand what he was getting himself into. He convinced us that he was." In the end, "our presence there was more to" provide "the freedom for Ali to go left or right," McClinton later said. But "after about 15 minutes of being there, I'm saying to myself, 'No way is this guy going to change his mind,'" according to Davis. "We didn't have a right to tell Ali what to do," Williams noted. "All we could do is show our support for him in whatever he was going to do. That decision was up to him and he made it."[34] Russell later recalled just how firm Ali was in his commitment: "He said 'I know I'm right. And if you want to talk me out of it, that's not going to happen.'"[35]

Ali remained steadfast, making it clear that he would not fight in Vietnam, even if given a ceremonial position far from the front. His words were wide-ranging, covering his religious beliefs, the Nation of

Islam, Elijah Muhammad, and a range of Black political and civil rights issues. In the end, Ali proclaimed, "Well, I know what I must do. My fate is in the hands of Allah, and Allah will take care of me. If I walk out of this room today and get killed today it will be Allah's doing and I will accept it. I'm not worried. In my first teachings I was told we all would be tested by Allah. This may be my test."[36] The fight promoter, Bob Arum, later reflected on Ali's taking on a room that might have been intimidating for even the most accomplished athlete: "Here he was in a room with these great athletes who were all college educated, but he was able to convince all of them that the path he was taking was the correct one. And people at that point and time didn't realize how smart Ali was."[37]

Alcindor, then twenty years old and still dominating the hardwood at UCLA, despite his age, was clearly committed to the cause. He asked whether his fellow college athletes should join in antiwar and other protests. "Kareem was the youngest, and he was up there standing tall," Brown later said, using the name Alcindor would adopt four years later.[38] "I was just happy to be invited," Abdul-Jabbar said years later. "I was told they wanted me there because the youth of America, black youth, needed someone who more or less represented their point of view." He didn't display nerves. "I didn't feel any butterflies but I probably should have."[39]

Beach, by then working in local Cleveland politics and referred to as "Dr. Beach" by former teammates both admiring of his intellect and, in the way of athletes, mocking the garrulous former defensive back, "wanted to know how Ali's protest fit philosophically into the broader civil rights struggle." Yet others were concerned that Ali's stand, however courageous, might "worsen the dehumanizing treatment that already came as a cost of their black skin."[40]

Adding to the initial skepticism of several of the group was the fact that many were deeply critical of the Nation of Islam. But beyond that, nearly half were veterans of the U.S. Armed Forces and worried that Ali's antiwar stand stood as an insult to the military, and thus to their own service. Brown had graduated from Syracuse as not only one of the greatest athletes on the planet, but also, having been a member of the Army ROTC, as a second lieutenant. Wooten, Mitchell, Beach, and Shorter had all been in the armed forces. Stokes had served in World War II.

"Truthfully, I didn't feel extremely comfortable with the actions Ali was taking at the time," McClinton, who had done his service in the Army Signal Corps, would recall many years later. "But I acknowledged him as a citizen. He had a right to speak his mind, and we wanted to support that."[41] Davis would later be even more blunt: "My first reaction was that it was unpatriotic." He had intended to make it clear that Ali "owed it to his country to serve in the military."[42] "I came there ready to talk him into going into the service," Mitchell recalled. "I actually felt that way. He whipped my behind pretty quick, because he can talk. But when it was all over, I felt pretty good walking out of there saying 'We back him.'"[43]

McClinton believed that some of the skeptical arguments made Ali pause, at least momentarily. While acknowledging Ali's religious devotion, they tried to appeal to his sense of patriotism. McClinton said he told Ali, "Hey, man, all you'd do is get a uniform and you'd be boxing at all the bases around the country. . . . [Y]our presence on military bases gives that motivation to military men" and would be a way to "recognize them and give them respect." McClinton believed that this argument created "a very dynamic conflict within" Ali, because "the whole issue of his transition to Islam, all of that had to be laid out and baked like a good cake. He knew all the ingredients. But what was he really?" McClinton thus saw Ali's joking and laughing during the meeting as "a way of dealing with it to move forward."[44]

One of the ironies of the event and the way it played out is that for all of the skepticism of the Nation of Islam among the participants of the meeting and society at large, the NOI did not want Ali to oppose the war. Ali's visible presence in the ring raised the NOI's profile but also provided riches in the form of donations from Ali and his allies. Ali's stand focused greater attention to the Nation of Islam at a time when such attention meant increased surveillance. And many within the NOI simply cared about Ali and the consequences he might face, including assassination. Indeed, Ali's manager, Herbert Muhammad, also represented Elijah Muhammad, and his call to Brown in London had gotten the ball rolling that led to the Ali Summit. For very different reasons and with very different motivations, had the Nation of Islam gotten its way

Ali would have acquiesced as his white conservative critics thought he should.

Brown later admitted to the *Plain Dealer*, "Herbert [Muhammad] wanting Ali to go into the service was a shocker. I thought the Nation of Islam would never look at it this way." He had assumed that Ali would get "special consideration so he could continue his career," but "couldn't talk to Ali about that, so he reached out to me and I had the dilemma of finding out a way to give Ali the opportunity to express his views without any influence." He "never really told Ali about my conversation with Herbert. I never told anyone, really."[45]

There were many people with a financial interest in finding a way for Ali to fight. Among these was Jim Brown. Brown was a partner at the time with boxing promoter Bob Arum's Main Bout, Inc., which staged Ali's fights. Before Ali had even been convicted, boxing officials were planning a tournament to find Ali's replacement as heavyweight champion, but it soon became clear that all of the possible contenders were pretenders—none was remotely worthy of stepping into the ring with Ali. This reality led some in boxing to envision a scenario whereby Ali could be persuaded to accept a "symbolic role" in the military. Joe Louis had performed boxing exhibitions for soldiers during World War II. Might Ali do the same, thus avoiding prison and allowing him to return to the professional heavyweight ranks within a year or two?[46]

A group of influential Louisvillians, early sponsors of Ali's career, tried to intervene, hoping to convince him that the substantial money he stood to lose should make him reconsider—but to no avail. Meanwhile, at the time Arum was a part-time fight promoter and a full-time lawyer in New York. It was in his interest "to negotiate a scenario with the Army in which Ali could fight exhibitions, do his service in the ring, and continue to make money."[47] So he went to one of the senior partners at his firm, Arthur Krim, an influential entertainment lawyer and adviser to President Lyndon Johnson, who, presumably with the president's blessing, "proposed a deal": that Ali "doesn't have to go in, he doesn't have to wear a uniform, he just does exhibitions at Army bases." He may even have been able to continue to fight professionally. It was this proposal, which Arum brought to Brown, that had kicked off the idea of the Ali Summit.[48]

Thus, in the mind of Eig, "the meeting was about money first, principle second."[49] This cynical take ignores that whatever Brown's motives were, Ali's motives matter, too, as do the motives of the other athletes, such as Russell and Alcindor, for whom money played zero role in their decision to fly to Cleveland. For Arum and Main Bout, surely money was a central motivator. After all, as Eig rightly argues, "Main Bout depended on closed-circuit TV revenues to thrive, and it seemed unlikely that millions of customers were going to line up outside movie theaters to watch Jerry Quarry versus Thad Spencer" when Ali was undoubtedly "the company's greatest asset, but he was worthless to them if he wasn't fighting." Arum never denied his interest. As he later said about his role in helping initiate the meeting in Cleveland, "I wasn't setting it up for the athletes to rally around Ali. Who the fuck cared at that point?"[50] Seemingly feeding Eig's argument about the various self-interests involved, the NIEU was going to "handle the closed-circuit shows of Ali's fights" in each of the cities where the organization had a presence. Ali would thus "be a prime producer of revenue." But this really does not seem to have been central to Brown's thinking at the time. The more important consideration was simply that Ali was a friend, and "the business situation came out of friendship, not the other way around," so "the only thing he wanted Ali to do was whatever Ali wanted to do."[51]

Brown had long advocated for "green capitalism" and Black economic empowerment, embracing the idea of leveraging capitalism to accomplish political goals. But in this case, "Ali's principled opposition to the war" trumped the abstractions of economic leverage. Brown, who undoubtedly had an economic interest in the champ continuing to fight, nonetheless pursued the greater good once he realized Ali's commitment, even as Arum referred to Ali as "a dead piece of merchandise."[52]

The Ali Summit lasted for more than three hours. The press was gathered. Given the number of superstars on location, it would have been nearly impossible to keep it quiet even if they had wanted to. According to Cleveland sports photographer Tony Tomsic, "The meeting was supposed to be a secret, but word got out a little bit. I remember I called

Sports Illustrated. I told them about Ali, Brown, Russell, Alcindor. They said, 'Come on. If that was going on, we would have heard about it.'"[53]

At a table set up for a press conference, Russell, Ali, Brown, and Alcindor sat from left to right, with the others standing behind them. Nearly all of them wore "solemn suits and stern expressions."[54] Whatever the gathered press and other observers expected from Ali or the group, Ali made it clear that there would be no big breaking news story. "There's nothing new to say," he declared by way of introduction.[55] Brown said the group supported Ali and his rights as a conscientious objector and were impressed by his sincerity. After the long meeting, Brown told the assembled media and crowd, "We decided that the champ is sincere in his religious beliefs."[56]

This event marked a moment of transformation in a time of flux. The war in Vietnam was becoming a flashpoint in American society—though the war was increasingly unpopular, outright opposition to it was still seen by most Americans as largely the domain of radicals. Ali had already lost the goodwill of millions of Americans because of his declaration that he was a member of the Nation of Islam, a decision exacerbated by the change from what he called his "slave name," Cassius Clay, to Muhammad Ali, the name personally bestowed on him by Elijah Muhammad. The Nation of Islam scared mainstream white people, and with the emergence of Black Power at roughly the same time, Ali had become hopelessly associated with Black radicalism. The Ali Summit marked a vital moment in the confluence of civil rights with antiwar activism and radical politics more generally.

Russell had entered the summit as skeptical as any of the attendees as to Ali's goals and seriousness. He leveled his own "blunt assessment of the politics at stake, pondering with pointed inquiries as to what Ali's ultimate goals were."[57] "I envy Muhammad Ali," Russell told *Sports Illustrated* soon after the summit. "He has something I have never been able to attain and something very few people possess. He has absolute and sincere faith. I'm not worried about Muhammad Ali. He is better equipped than anyone I know to withstand the trials in store for him. What I'm worried about is the rest of us."[58] In Cleveland but also at other times in Ali's life, Russell said, "I saw a man accepting personal responsibilities, someone who conducted himself in a way that the people he came in contact with were better for the experience."[59]

The entire situation was treacherous for the athletes involved. "We didn't care about perceived threats," Wooten later recalled. And there does not appear to be substantial fallout for any of the athletes—those perceived as dangerous and radical were already in that camp, and outspoken Black athletes already knew that in some circles they would never be accepted. "We weren't concerned," Wooten continued, "because we weren't going to waver. We were unified. We all had a real relationship with each other and we knew we were doing something for the betterment of all."[60] Brown admires his colleagues: "The fact that they were at that table meant that whatever they felt, whatever nerves they had, they controlled it. They said 'Fuck the nerves.' . . . All the individuals were there because they wanted to be. That's the sort of thing that can get you blackballed forever."[61]

Russell reflected on Ali's case in a *Sports Illustrated* article he wrote with Tex Maule, which appeared just a couple of weeks after the summit: "The hypocritical and sometimes fanatical criticism of Ali is, it seems to me, a symptom of the deeper sickness of our times. I feel sorry for the court that tries him: it must be sensitive to public opinion and it cannot operate in a vacuum. If Ali is acquitted some people will say they were afraid not to acquit him. If he is convicted the judge will have to give him the maximum sentence. That is because of the emotional climate of the country today."[62]

The government pursued its case against Ali. Two weeks after the Ali Summit and one day after the publication date of Russell's thoughtful *Sports Illustrated* article, Ali was convicted of draft evasion, sentenced to five years in prison, and fined $10,000. Boxing officials stripped him of his heavyweight title and exiled him from the sport. He appealed, allowing him to stay out of prison. The Supreme Court would overturn the decision in 1971, arguing that Ali's induction notice was "invalid because it was grounded upon an erroneous denial of his claim to be classified as a conscientious objector."[63] Nonetheless, Ali lost more than four years of his prime as a fighter.

"It was a different time back in 1967," Hall of Famer Willie Davis remembered decades later. "There was more strife amongst the African American community. The world was different then." In 2014, William Rhoden wrote in the *New York Times*, "The moment itself would be remembered as the first—and last—time that so many African American athletes at that level came together to support a controversial cause." For Abdul-Jabbar, "The Ali Summit was just one moment in a chain of events. Each of those moments is like someone in an old-fashioned fire brigade, passing along a bucket of water to throw on the fire. The hope is that each generation galvanizes the next to stand up and be counted when the circumstances call for it. To paraphrase Bob Dylan, the battle outside is still raging." Or, as Brown put it, "What you realize when you are born where I was born is that the no. 1 issue in American life is racism." Being Black "is a burden you carry."[64] Meanwhile, "the time dictated the passion in all of us."[65] "What I would rather have people concerned about are juries in the South that make a mockery out of our court system or a murderer acquitted in the South and writing a magazine article about how he did it. Such injustices are far more important to the future of our country than the draft status of Muhammad Ali—or if you prefer, Cassius Clay." Brown thus linked the story of Emmett Till, whose killers sold their story to *Look* magazine, to that of Ali, reminding people that there was a continuum but also that in some ways Ali's case was a distraction.[66]

In December 2016, just months after Ali's death, *Sports Illustrated* honored Brown, Russell, and Abdul-Jabbar with the Muhammad Ali Legacy Award. By then the former champion, once so hated, had been recognized as "The Greatest" not only in the ring but beyond it as well, largely as the result of his push for human dignity. "Together," the magazine said, "they set the standard for the black athlete, showing that the fight for equality is not one that can wait until your money has been made, but a battle to be waged even at the peak of your athletic career."[67] They embodied, in other words, what Howard Bryant has identified as "The Heritage"—that is, the burden and responsibility but also the right of Black athletes to defend and build on what came before them. By the late 1960s, the mere right to play was no longer enough. The Black

athlete looked beyond that, even if in so doing, in fighting for fundamental rights as Americans, their critics weaponized their own ideals of
"Americanism" against them.

"When I look through all my adult life," Willie Davis later recalled,
"there's always been a period where something happens that causes the
country to struggle, be it racial or whatever. I look back and see the Ali
Summit as one of those events. I'm very proud that I participated." "We
knew who we were," said McClinton of the Summit participants. "We
knew what we had woven into our country, and we stood at the highest
level of citizenship as men. You name the value, we took the brush and
painted it. You raised the bar, we reached it. You defined excellence, we
supersede it. As a matter of fact, we defined it."[68]

As Dave Zirin points out, "Coaches and team executives"—and we
can add some journalists and fans to this list—"tend to be conservative
creatures who believe that any engagement with the outside world by
'their players' qualifies as a distraction from what happens inside the lines
and will lead to the short-circuiting of their well-tuned machines. This
trope"—and its twin, "stick to sports"—"is used to whip players into line
and coerce them to just 'shut up and play.'" In Zirin's telling, the photograph of the Ali Summit participants "reveals this directive to be the
mendacious and self-serving tripe that it is."[69]

"Ali, before he came back" after the end of his banishment and the
Supreme Court's decision, "was a true warrior," Brown noted admiringly.
"It was unbelievable, the courage he had. He wasn't just a championship
athlete. He was a champion who fought for his people. He was above
sports; he was part of history. The man used his athletic ability as a platform to project himself right up there with world leaders, taking chances
that absolutely no one else took." In the end, "from the standpoint of his
ability to perform and his ability to be involved with the world, Ali was
the most important sports figure in history."[70] Ali "always stood for what
is right. He was born with that. . . . He looked around to see how black
people were treated, and he couldn't tolerate it." Brown repeatedly reiter-
ated that Ali was a "warrior" in interviews over the years. And this status
transcended boxing. Ali had a love for people, Brown argued: "Not just
for black people, but for all good people—which does not get reported,"

and this love made Ali special. "Powerful people have a love for all people—that's how they have the strength to be warriors. The strongest warriors are strong on the inside, not from their physical strength. You don't become a warrior because of your occupation. You become a warrior in your soul. Ali didn't let his occupation curtail his soul."[71]

JOSÉ FELICIANO'S ANTHEM, JOSÉ FELICIANO'S AMERICA

When the Puerto Rican guitarist and singer José Feliciano got up to sing the national anthem before Game 5 of the 1968 World Series, pitting the host Detroit Tigers against the St. Louis Cardinals, on the afternoon of Monday, October 7, he was a relatively little-known singer-songwriter. Just minutes later, he would be infamous after a rendition of "The Star-Spangled Banner" that led to the sort of false outrage Americans are the best in the world at mustering. But in the midst of the debate over the Vietnam War that had found Ali at its epicenter, many Americans were prepared to engage in the hypernationalistic patriotism that had flared during the two world wars and was always percolating beneath the surface during the Cold War. The line between mock outrage and real outrage is a fine one, and the former can fuel the latter. This is precisely what happened in 1968, as the rocket's red glare of American patriotism's ugly side burst in the air and, according to one historian, "*The Star-Spangled Banner* changed forever."[72]

Just moments before the first pitch, Feliciano, a lifelong baseball fan, took his assigned place in the rich green center field of Tiger Stadium. He had flown the red-eye to get in and chatted with and sang a bit to Tigers stars Al Kaline and Denny McLain in the clubhouse before heading out to the emerald outfield. Feliciano, a blind twenty-three-year-old, was wearing his sunglasses and a maroon suit. He was accompanied by his faithful guide dog, Trudy. Though his sunglasses were to protect his eyes, the dark shades, combined with his long, dark hair, "hinted at sinister possibilities," in the words of historian David Zang.[73]

Born in Puerto Rico and raised in the Bronx, Feliciano was a fan of the New York Yankees. A self-taught singer and guitarist, he was recognized as a virtuoso at the latter. He had been part of the booming folk scene, performing at one point on the same bills as Bob Dylan in

Greenwich Village's legendary scene, but he also was comfortable in traditional musical environments, having played Las Vegas with Frank Sinatra. He embraced rock as well, reaching number three on the *Billboard* charts with a cover of the Doors' "Light My Fire." His first album would garner him six Grammy nominations and three wins, including for Best Vocal Performance. But, in the words of one *New York Times* writer decades later, "Taking liberties with Jim Morrison," the lead singer of the Doors, "is one thing. Taking liberties with Francis Scott Key proved more contentious."[74]

The Tigers' management had asked Ernie Harwell, the team's radio voice, to find national anthem performers for each of the games the team would host in the World Series. Harwell, who would go on to a decades-long career—more than four of those in the Tigers' radio booth, where he became a legend—had invited Feliciano to do the anthem. He had "unwittingly risked his young career" in backing Feliciano. Harwell was a songwriter and "was attuned to popular music trends," and Feliciano was on Harwell's radar as a result of his "laid-back, soul version" of the Doors song that had become a hit. But Harwell had also heard that Feliciano was working on his own interpretation of "The Star Spangled Banner": "I had heard from people in music whose opinions I respect that he had an interesting version of the anthem," Harwell explained when controversy erupted.[75]

Singer Margaret Whiting had done a "straight ballad" version of the anthem before Game 3, the first in Detroit, with virtually no notice taken.[76] Perhaps ironically, soul superstar Marvin Gaye performed before Game 4, and while he did not rouse controversy, Harwell had been more concerned about his performance than about Feliciano's. Team management "worried about Marvin because of his Motown connection," Harwell later remembered, and so they told him to "ask him to sing it a little more traditional."[77] "Yeah, I'll sing it straight," Gaye promised, and he largely did.[78] He was accompanied by a brass band that "prevented him from going too far afield," but as the song progressed Gaye slowed things down, "extending the drama and pathos of the song and giving special emphasis to its concluding celebration of freedom," according to musicologist and culture scholar Mark Clague, though there appear to have been no complaints.[79] Despite the approach to Gaye to ensure a relatively straitlaced performance, Feliciano says Harwell never asked him to do the same. "He didn't have a chance to talk to me, which I'm glad of," Feliciano would later tell an interviewer. "Because if I'm told not to do something, I'll do it anyway."[80]

Feliciano did not have an orthodox national anthem planned, and though he never thought he was doing anything wrong, that didn't mean that he wasn't running a risk. There was a microphone stand in front of him that would deliver his rendition to the stadium, filled to capacity, and an NBC microphone taped to that mic stand that would deliver the performance to an estimated 55 million viewers and into posterity. "I had about ten seconds of should I or shouldn't I," Feliciano later recalled.[81]

It was just Feliciano and his guitar, though there was some miscommunication on this point. The stadium announcer introduced Feliciano but also the house band, Merle Alvey's Detroit Tigers Dixieland Band, as accompanying Feliciano, who had not been told about the band and obviously did not see them when he got on stage. When someone in the band asked what key he would use, he replied that he would just accompany himself on guitar. There was no way the band would be able to accompany him. Feliciano's version was in 4/4 time rather than the traditional 3/4.[82] The stadium announcer asked the fans to join in singing the anthem, but if the band would be flummoxed by Feliciano's rendition, the fans would be hopelessly lost. The performance that followed, which stuck to Francis Scott Key's words but tinkered with melody and rhythm, sparked outrage, which would seem utterly unfathomable today given the wide array of anthem performances that even the most hidebound critics have enjoyed, except for the fact that sparking outrage over national anthems has become something of a stock-in-trade in the United States. Alvey's band "stood dumbfounded behind Feliciano as he sang."[83] Most of the members of the band, visible for only a few seconds on television, held their horns at their sides; "one mouthed the words, another laughed, and the rest tried to look straight ahead as Feliciano strummed his way to history."[84]

After the third line of the song, "what so proudly we hailed," NBC camera operators refused to focus on Feliciano and his unorthodox presentation. They "cut to a shot of the flag, the color guard, the teams, and the stadium—anything to avoid showing the singer delivering arguably the most important performance of the national anthem since its very first airing in Baltimore."[85]

"His National Anthem was one for the ages," according to Zang. "Each note of the performance—hauntingly beautiful and gentle in retrospect—seemed wildly unorthodox at the time. It was nuanced in a way" that the era's traditional "prideful, bombastic versions . . . were not."[86] While some descriptions of his rendition have called it "bluesy and 'languid,'" "infused with a Latin-jazz feel," a "sweet soul, gospel-tinged interpretation," as having "a folk flair" that was "overlain by a plaintive, pleading lyric line injected with several soaring, blues-inspired passages," it was almost immediately clear that the consensus might not be so kind.[87] At the very end, Feliciano threw in a couple of "yeah, yeahs," which one historian calls "an innocent flourish to a flawless performance" but which may well have been the final salt in the wound of those inclined to rub salt on their self-inflicted wounds.[88] The Tiger Stadium crowd responded with "stunned murmuring blended with cascading boos and puzzled applause to produce a sound like distant, rumbling thunder."[89] Though on the whole, at the time—as opposed to what would follow almost immediately—"fans seemed more stunned than angry."[90]

Feliciano hoped to spend a few innings enjoying his favorite sport. He went to the press box, and at one point broadcaster Tony Kubek asked him, "Do you realize what you've done?" Feliciano was clueless, and while Kubek offered support, a storm indeed had descended.[91] Feliciano's sunglasses and long hair did not help, nor, almost certainly, did his ethnicity or his blindness.

Meanwhile, calling the performance "wildly unorthodox" is one way to put it. Critics were not so gentle.

Mickey Lolich, who pitched the Tigers to a crucial win that day, nonetheless brought the controversy into the clubhouse, claiming that because of the anthem's length (it was less than two minutes long) Lolich was "so upset that I couldn't straighten myself out in the first inning," an excuse that seems awfully sensitive for a professional athlete to make in the biggest stage of his sport.[92] The fact that he gave up three runs in the first inning, including a two-run home run to Orlando Cepeda, before settling down was probably actually not José Feliciano's fault. To be fair, years later Lolich clarified and expanded on his experience. "As you know," he remembered, "Jose sang his version of the National Anthem, which by today's standards would be fantastic. But in those days it was a little bit different. And, it was sort of a long version. And, when he got done, I basically, almost had to start re-warming up again. And I hadn't even gotten around to throwing a breaking ball. And when I went out to pitch the first inning, I hadn't even thrown a curve ball yet."[93]

Again, Feliciano's anthem version was less than two minutes long. Marvin Gaye's version of the anthem in Game 4 had also lasted just less than two minutes; in fact, it was about twelve seconds longer than Feliciano's rendition.

Other players reacted to the performance. Tigers pitcher John Hiller later recalled, "That came out of nowhere. We weren't expecting anything different. We said, 'Oh my God Ernie—what did you do?'" Another Tigers pitcher, John Warden, was standing near Hiller on the third base line and remembers thinking, "Holy cow, what's that? What's he doing? And everybody's looking around at each other. And you can hear the fans are sort of—you hear that background rumble."[94]

Tiger Stadium received two thousand complaints in the first hour after the performance and claimed that the negative-to-positive ratio was 100-to-1. Military veterans in Phoenix allegedly threw their shoes at the television set. A television channel in San Diego received two hundred calls in five minutes, most of them critical. Ernie Harwell, perhaps slightly defensive since he had used his influence to invite Feliciano, claimed that his mail was split evenly between praise and condemnation of the performance but nonetheless admitted that "editorials lambasted it" while "civic groups passed angry resolutions." One critic from the public attacked Harwell, claiming, "Anyone who'd let that long-haired hippie ruin our 'Star-Spangled Banner' has got to be a communist."[95] Indeed, Harwell later claimed he received a lot of letters levying this accusation.[96] Conservatives even criticized the fact that Feliciano sat and that he wore sunglasses, apparently unaware of (or insensitive to) his blindness.

In an era when newspapers dominated, the Feliciano story was front-page news across the country—in St. Louis and Detroit, of course, but literally from coast to coast. The front page of the Detroit *Free Press* the next day captured the tone that would follow: "Storm Rages over Series Anthem."[97] According to a range of journalists across the country, the performance was "bizarre," a "star-spangled goof," and akin to "a tiger tootling on a tin can." One observer wondered if Feliciano "forgot the tune," while another wagged, "I thought the dog was singing instead of the guy."[98] The *Free Press* published the critiques of the city's citizenry. One complainant called it "just a desecration to hear it sung that way." Another asked, "Are there no groups about who are prepared and willing to sing this difficult song the way it is meant to be sung?" Another lamented, "I got sick. No wonder our country is losing its dignity." The generation gap doesn't explain every critique, as one wrote, "I must be old by today's standards, 26, because I didn't appreciate the way José Feliciano interpreted our national anthem."[99] Joe Oyler, whose brother Ray played for the Tigers, agreed with this assessment, if a bit more bluntly: "I'm young enough to understand it, but I think it stinks."[100]

It is hard to say which complaint was most histrionic, but one contender wrote, "No matter how wrong our country might seem to some people, it did not deserve the horrible rock-and-roll rendition given the anthem . . . and it makes one ashamed. . . . [O]ur only hope is that no other country is receiving the games."[101] The performance also brought out the hypocrisy that so often accompanies anthem-connected critiques: One fan at the ballpark proclaimed, "I didn't stand up, that wasn't the national anthem he was singing."[102]

Even Zang, who would later write a very sympathetic account of Feliciano's experience in 1968, acknowledges, "I should point out that I heard the anthem on live television. Even as an eighteen-year-old, I thought the performance was shocking. My current assessment of the rendition as gentle and beautiful is by no means shared by many older colleagues for whom I have played it in recent years. Some have left the room in mid song."[103]

Given that the year was 1968 and that rock 'n' roll seemed to create the ultimate cultural divide, many thought Feliciano's rendition "smacked of rock 'n' roll." Thus, "Feliciano's decision to bring the two together at the high mass of American sports rituals was akin to appointing Yippie leader Jerry Rubin as commissioner of baseball."[104] Certainly some people appreciated Feliciano's rendition. They were in the minority. One wrote "his clear emotion-packed voice gave a truly contemporary flair to a song old yet relevant." Aware of the controversy brewing over the performance, another wrote, "If we aren't willing to accept a different rendition occasionally, with common sense and tolerance . . . we are not fostering goodwill."[105] Fourteen-year old Susan Omillion loved it: "I was in class. On the way home, I heard that something had happened at the ballpark. People were talking on the streets, on the porches along the way. When I got home, during the news, they showed a clip of this guy playing the guitar and singing the anthem as no one had ever heard. And it was like, 'Wow, this is cool.' There is so much negativity that I thought was unnecessary, unfair. I don't know, a 14-year old, what do they do? Back in those days, if you're me, you start a fan club."[106] And she did.

The record company RCA Victor understood that many people liked the performance, as young listeners "flooded radio stations with requests to hear Feliciano's *Banner* again." Bootleg versions of the song appeared on New York streets the day after his performance. The label responded by rush-releasing a 45 single-sided version of the stadium recording and sent copies to radio DJs. They then produced a commercial single, which was announced in *Billboard's* "Spotlight Singles" on October 23. The B-side was Feliciano's cover of the Beatles' "And I Love Her," which one historian has described as possibly being "a clever answer to questioning critics who doubted Feliciano's true feelings about his native land" but which also revealed both the artist's connection to pop currents as well as a certain level of savvy marketing. The record immediately charted on *Billboard's* top 100, reaching as high as number fifty.[107]

Tony Kubek, the color analyst for NBC's broadcast of the game, who had played for the New York Yankees for nine years in the 1950s and into the mid-1960s and had heard his share of World Series anthems, said of Feliciano, "I think he did one heckuva job. I feel the youth of America has to be served and this is the type of music they want."[108] Bill Freehan, the Tigers' catcher and one of the team's key players, said during the controversy, "I met José Feliciano five minutes before he came out to sing. He is a baseball fan and he was proud and nervous about being asked. I can't condemn the rendition because I know how much he wanted to be accepted. . . . I know one thing: He made Marvin Gaye . . . sound like a square."[109] Tim McCarver, a former Cardinals great who was a catcher on that 1968 team and would go on to a long career in broadcasting baseball on television, spoke about the performance decades later: "The social unrest and the political situation was the backdrop for the series that season," and while Feliciano's version of the anthem "was longer than most versions . . . it didn't bother me at all. It bothered some people. . . . But back then even our sideburns bothered people."[110]

Two days after the performance, one newspaper defended Feliciano in an editorial titled "Why All the Furor?" While maintaining a preference for "a standard rendition" of the anthem, it also argued that Feliciano "brought a special kind of meaning to the song" and "gave expression to the feelings of another America too rarely felt in our national and patriotic institutions. Feliciano was saying that nothing is static, that nothing lies beyond examination or change, that this too is America."[111] The *New York Times* editorialized, "Hearing our national anthem sung to an unfamiliar tune should not make that anthem any less meaningful." The piece not only defended Feliciano and his rendition, but also explicitly criticized his detractors and defended freedom of expression. Another *Times* critic in the same issue said, "Thank God for people like José Feliciano" and seemed mystified and even angry at the criticism the performance had faced.[112]

Harwell earned his reputation for being a decent man with great integrity as he defended Feliciano in 1968, and he would continue to do so to anyone who would listen for the remainder of his life. (Harwell passed away in 2010 at the age of ninety-two, having retired from the Tigers booth in 2002.) "I feel a fellow has a right to sing any way he can sing it," he said even as the controversy roiled.[113]

In a bizarre way it might be nice to realize that Americans have always had a stupid reactionary streak that merges politics with popular culture. But at the same time, when the enduring idiocy takes on a patina of the threat of violence, as it has in recent years, one wishes we had been able to stamp it out with reason earlier. Of course, malign idiocy's immunity to reason is what makes it so virulent.

Feliciano, meanwhile, suffered a great deal from the backlash to his performance. He defended his rendition in the wake of the game and as the controversy raged. "I was afraid people would misconstrue it and say I'm making fun of" the anthem, Feliciano later said, though he did admit that his attempt to update the anthem was intentional. "America is young now, and I thought maybe the anthem could be revived."[114] "I sang it that way to express love for my country. I am very happy that I did it that way. It's the way I feel." The World Series performance was the first public version of the rendition, though he "had worked on the arrangement for sometime by myself awaiting the opportunity." He left the stadium after a few innings because he had another commitment, but he did not leave the controversy behind. Many radio stations chose to stop playing his music. He tried to defend himself, nearly pleading, "I owe everything to this country. I wanted to contribute something to express my gratitude for what it has done for me. . . . I'm for everything it stands for."[115]

But this was not enough for the self-proclaimed patriots who had also decided that they were the gatekeepers of the patriotism of others, a tendency that carries forward to the present day and the controversies over anthem protests in sports. At one point, according to Harwell, who according to some accounts almost lost his job over the performance, "The American Legion wanted to pass a resolution that everybody had to sing it on note," an example of the absurdity that stemmed from Feliciano's heartfelt if possibly naive rendition of a song that simply isn't all that wonderful musically and that has never been easy to sing.[116]

To be fair, Feliciano's Grammy wins for his 1968 album came in 1969, just a few months after the World Series imbroglio, but if anything, this shows the gulf between the music world and the sporting one—and at the time, the sports world represented more mainstream standards. At the same time, Feliciano was not so easily dissuaded from his own strong beliefs—from that point on he opened each of his shows in the United States with his version of the anthem. He was also emboldened after the furor began to settle down, and his rendition became a minor hit. He began to assert that his version of the song may have "reinvigorated" patriotism for young people. "The song had practically passed into oblivion. Now it's back in every home as it should be," he claimed.[117]

Feliciano was one of the first people to start to "step across the gulf between sports and rock 'n' roll." Before long, musicians across genres began bringing their own flair to the national anthem, another door Feliciano had opened, even as many tried to slam it shut on him. Many of these renditions "clarified through the lens of hindsight just how respectful and melodic Feliciano's rendition had been."[118] As Mark Clague argues, "Feliciano's rendition indeed marked a historic turning point. It shattered the anthem's musical orthodoxy, opening new opportunities for pop stylists to offer sincere, personal arrangements of Key's song." Musically, he tested the song's structure with his 4/4 meter, the first public performance to do so, and he broke several musical barriers in terms of his use of "rhythmic displacement and tuneful ornamentation" that resulted in a "soulful feel."[119] Historian Marc Ferris maintains that Feliciano's "version remains one of the most heartfelt and original interpretations ever recorded" and that he "turned the song into a vehicle for individual expression."[120] In Feliciano's own interpretation, "I opened the doors for anyone who wants to do the Anthem . . . in their own way. I was the first one and usually pioneers get the stones and everybody else gets the accolades. So I'm happy to get the stones."[121]

Fortunately, Feliciano's time in the wilderness was brief, which doesn't mean it was not difficult or painful. He continued to be popular in the Latin American community, and he won six more Grammy Awards, sold more than 1.9 million albums, got a star on the Hollywood Walk of Fame in 1987, and won myriad other honors, awards, and accolades, though disc jockeys and programming directors at some radio stations blackballed him. But a couple of years later, in 1970, his bouncy "Feliz Navidad" became a holiday hit and is now a Christmas season staple.

Just as the Ali Summit foreshadowed America's increasingly roiling conflict over Vietnam, Feliciano gave the world his version of the song at a time when "the political events surrounding Feliciano's anthem . . . distorted its reception." Horrifying the first wave of observers and then enthralling younger listeners who clamored to hear it on the radio and bought the 45 single, "it hit the airwaves in a year when public opinion was shifting against the Vietnam War" and America—indeed the world—was caught up in one of the most chaotic years in history.[122]

In October 2003, Feliciano was invited to perform the national anthem before another Game 5, this time in Miami before the National League Championship Series between the Cubs and the host Marlins. A sold-out crowd gave him a warm reception and response to his performance, and tens of millions saw it on television. There were no outraged calls to television studios. There were no furious letters to the editor. There were no overwrought op-ed pieces. In the words of David Zang, it had taken thirty-five years, "but the healing hands of time had already finished their work."[123]

Feliciano was later asked to sing the anthem for Game 1 of the 2012 National League Championship Series. In all three instances where Feliciano sang the anthem, the team that hosted him went on to win the World Series. As Clague wryly notes, "Given the undercurrent of superstition in baseball, teams would be wise to invite Feliciano to perform whenever they reach the postseason. His anthem is a proven winner."[124]

Feliciano finally even returned to Detroit and played the song at the Tigers' home stadium. On May 5, 2010, the day after Ernie Harwell—by then long a Detroit legend—died, Feliciano was invited back to reprise "his individualistic version of the anthem" at Detroit's new Comerica Park.[125] He "received an enthusiastic ovation."[126] He was invited back yet again on May 25, 2013, in honor of the forty-fifth anniversary of the 1968 World Series.[127] Once again, he was met with an ovation.

In 2018, Feliciano was asked to sing his anthem at a ceremony for twenty people from seventeen countries who were taking the oath of citizenship. He played the same guitar he used in 1968.[128] After the ceremony he had a message for the new American citizens: "I welcome you all with open arms. And this is America. America will always be great because of the people who come to it and make their homes here. Thanks so much, and congratulations."[129] He then gifted the guitar, freighted with so much history, to the Smithsonian.

And Susan Omillion, the fourteen-year-old girl who started the fan club? She became José Feliciano's wife. She met him three years after his anthem performance and he was invited to dinner at the Omillion home.

He learned that her father was in the hospital, so he went for a visit, brought his guitar, and put on an impromptu performance. He and his fan club founder and president became friends. Eleven years later, they got married.

In September 2018, Feliciano was invited to sing the anthem again at a Tigers reunion to commemorate the fiftieth anniversary of the 1968 team. Before heading to Comerica Park, he met with fans at the Detroit Historical Museum. When he sang the anthem before the Tigers game—his fourth time playing the anthem in their home stadium—he was wearing a Tigers jersey with "Feliciano 68" on the back.[130] The Tigers were playing the Cardinals, their 1968 World Series opponent, in a regular season matchup. Yet again he received a standing ovation.[131]

Roberto Clemente and the Changing Face of Baseball

On September 15, 2022, Major League Baseball held its annual Roberto Clemente Day to honor the legendary Pittsburgh Pirates star. On that day, the Tampa Bay Rays became the first team in major league history to start nine Latin American players in the same game. They represented five countries: Colombia, Cuba, Mexico, Venezuela, and the Dominican Republic. The Rays routed the Toronto Blue Jays, 11–0. All nine of the players, as well as two Tampa base coaches, received special MLB dispensation to wear jerseys bearing the number 21, which Clemente wore for the entirety of his eighteen-year Hall of Fame career, and which evoked the wearing of #42 by all MLB players on Jackie Robinson Day every season. Yandy Diaz, who hit a three-run home run for Tampa Bay in the win, said he felt "very happy, especially on a day like today. I think the Latinos are really putting a stamp on the game of baseball."[132] It is perhaps especially appropriate that this confluence of circumstances took place on the day honoring Clemente, because on September 1, 1971, in the heat of a pennant race, the Pirates were the first team ever to start an all-minority lineup, with five Black players and four Latinos, including Clemente in his customary right field.

Clemente, decidedly not sticking to sports, died in a plane crash while delivering humanitarian aid from his home island of Puerto Rico to earthquake-devastated Nicaragua on December 31, 1972. The

6.5-magnitude earthquake, which hit on December 23, killed and injured thousands of people, uprooted families, and devastated more than 350 square blocks of property in and around Managua, leaving more than three hundred thousand people homeless. The rickety plane, overloaded with relief supplies, crashed into the Atlantic Ocean soon after takeoff from San Juan. Clemente's remains were never recovered. He left three young boys, aged six, five, and two years old. He died a legend, but more important, he died a hero. Yet in many ways he also "found his greatest fame only after his untimely death."[133]

The National Baseball Hall of Fame waived its rule that a player must be out of the game for five years before being eligible for election, and he was inducted into Cooperstown in 1973, becoming the first Latin American and Caribbean player to be enshrined in baseball's Valhalla. A five-tool player, Clemente was a fifteen-time All-Star, two-time World Series winner (his performance in the 1971 Fall Classic was one of the greatest in baseball history), the 1966 National League MVP, a four-time batting champion, and twelve-time Gold Glove winner with one of the greatest outfield arms in the history of baseball. He had gotten his three thousandth hit in his last at-bat of the 1972 season. Clemente was a no-doubt first-ballot Hall of Famer even absent the tragedy that made him a sentimental favorite.

Clemente was not the first star player with Latino roots. The flow of Latino players to the major leagues was a trickle before Minnie Miñoso's ascension to the majors with Cleveland in 1949 and his emergence as a regular and a star with the Chicago White Sox in 1951. Miñoso, a Cuban, began his career in the Negro Leagues, but his talent was undeniable and he would play in the major leagues until the mid-1960s, with brief (and gimmicky) cameos in 1976 and 1980 to make him a four- and then a five-decade player. Miñoso was not the first player of Latino descent—those debuts had predated even Jackie Robinson, albeit with light-skinned players who effectively passed as white—but he was the first star Black Latino player. Clemente, who began his career in the Dodgers organization, would be the first superstar. In fact, perhaps ironically, Branch Rickey had left the Dodgers for the Pirates organization and had seen Clemente toiling for his old organization. Rickey managed to snag Clemente in the Rule 5 Draft, which is intended to prevent teams from stockpiling minor leaguers who could otherwise be on major league rosters, after the 1954 season. Clemente made his debut for the Pirates in 1955.

The radical sports journalist Dave Zirin has identified the similarities between Robinson and Clemente, which are telling, even if Clemente was neither the first Latino nor even the first dark-skinned Latino player in the majors. Both were military veterans, and like Robinson, Clemente was "struck by the gap between the ideals he fought for and the reality on the ground." Both "played with a fire and flair that transcended statistics," though each certainly had great numbers. Both "possessed a fierce pride with no patience for bigotry or prejudice." Both "came to represent something far more important, vital, and political than just a ballplayer." And both had legacies that have "grown more powerful over time." Yet perhaps "the most chilling similarity to Robinson is the way iconography has robbed Clemente of politics, of his true self."[134]

Clemente had to deal with dual bigotries, both because of his skin color and because of his Puerto Rican heritage. But he also carried himself with steadfast dignity and refused to accede to second-class citizenship. Racism in the immediate post–Jackie Robinson era was still a near constant. Well into the 1960s, Clemente regularly faced segregation during spring training in Florida. In 1955, the Pirates established their spring training home in segregated Fort Myers, in Lee County on Florida's southwest Gulf Coast. And those segregation rules extended even to Major League Baseball teams and their Black players. So while his white Pirates teammates stayed in the Bradford Hotel in downtown Fort Myers, Clemente and other Black players stayed with families in the Black Dunbar Heights neighborhood on the east side of the railroad tracks. Dunbar Heights had a vibrant community, but the Black players were nonetheless forbidden from many of the upscale amenities their white teammates experienced—beaches and public pools were off limits, and almost every downtown business had restrictions for Black patrons. Black players were not allowed to participate in a team outing at the Fort Myers Country Club. Rickey, supposed ally of Black players, expressed his annoyance at the local rules but also expected players to acquiesce to them—to not cause trouble. And fans were segregated as well when they attended Pirates spring training games. These conditions prevailed into the 1960s, even after Clemente had established himself as a superstar.

In the wake of the murder of Dr. Martin Luther King Jr. in April 1968, baseball and its hapless commissioner, William Eckert, floundered, not having any idea how to react. Clemente had come to admire and to know King a little bit, and he was frustrated and angry that the major leagues planned to play on, allowing players to make their own decision whether to play while providing no actual leadership on the issue. "They come and ask the Negro players if we should play," Clemente later remembered. "I say, 'If you have to ask the Negro players, then we do not have a great country.'" Pittsburgh's players voted "overwhelmingly" not to play their season opener against Houston and requested that the next day's game—scheduled for the date of King's funeral—be canceled. Clemente and a white teammate, Dave Wickersham, issued a statement on behalf of the players: "We are doing this because we white and black players respect what Dr. King has done for mankind."[135]

Clemente knew early on that he was vulnerable when he was a young player, but he refused to be afraid to speak out: "They say Roberto, you better keep your mouth shut because they will ship you back," but "from the first day, I said to myself: 'I am the minority group. I am from the poor people. I represent the poor people. I represent the common people of America. So I am going to be treated as a human being, I don't want to be treated like a Puerto Rican, or a black, or nothing like that. I want to be treated like any person that comes for a job.'" It is telling that Clemente linked race and class in his analysis of the plight that Black and Hispanic players faced in professional baseball. "Every person who comes for a job, no matter what type of race or color he is, if he does the job he should be treated like whites."[136]

But he also was often mocked for his language skills, despite the fact that operating in his second language he had a leg up on virtually every sportswriter he encountered. Journalists also targeted him as lazy; for example, when he dealt with nagging injuries, management and journalists often accused him of lollygagging. When he spoke out, he was accused of being moody or temperamental. Reporters mocked his speech patterns. But he always carried himself with dignity and refused to be pigeonholed. According to Clemente biographer David Maraniss, "Clemente wanted to speak English and insisted on doing so." But "his fear of being misinterpreted could make him seem reserved and defensive, especially when writers lurked in the clubhouse." According to Clemente teammate Steve Blass, "I always had a theory that here was a very bright man who had taken verbal risks with English before and had been burned and didn't care for it to happen again. I think the writers relating what he said in" pidgin English "was actually secondary to the fact that he had concepts that he was trying to convey" and journalists "wouldn't understand because his English wouldn't convey it as well as his Spanish. And I think that frustrated him."[137]

Clemente's experience of racism, but also the dual struggle he faced as a Puerto Rican whose first language was Spanish, reflected the issues and demeaning stereotypes faced by Hispanic players. Mockery of language served to reduce the humanity of Latino players. In the late 1970s, Garrett Morris would play the role of Chico Escuela, a Latin American player with a very limited English vocabulary. Chico's catchphrase, "Basebol been berry berry good to me," served to capture the popular mindset about Latino players while simultaneously recognizing the increasing role they had in the modern game. Morris, who was SNL's first—and, during his time on the show almost always only—Black cast member, was outspoken on matters of race and hilariously pilloried white supremacy. He unquestionably played Escuela with a certain wink and nod, but it still can be jarring to see the depiction today.

Clemente paved the way for the future generations of Latino players who would come increasingly to dominate the sport: "Sparked by his encounters with Jim Crow," Clemente "took baseball and the United States media to task on their practices to marginalize Spanish-speaking players" and "more than any other player of his generation, Clemente took on the role of advocate for the Puerto Rican image in the United States."[138] Indeed, he often "defined himself as Puerto Rican, rather than by the color of his skin," because "while he was proud to be a black Puerto Rican" Clemente "never wanted to be categorized or limited by race."[139]

The 2022 World Series, pitting the Houston Astros against the Philadelphia Phillies, was the first since 1950 not to have a single Black U.S.-born player on either roster. This caused Dusty Baker, an African American who played in the 1970s and 1980s and finally won his first World Series as manager of the victorious 2022 Astros, to say, "That's terrible for the state of the game. Wow! Terrible! I'm ashamed of the game. Quote me. I'm ashamed of the game."[140] But there were plenty of players who would have been excluded from Organized Baseball prior to Jackie Robinson. Baseball absolutely struggles with a low percentage of African American players, but it has a large Latino player pool that would have fallen under Jim Crow. It is worth noting that some of the most beloved players of the past generation—including David Ortiz, Albert Pujols, and Pedro Martinez—would not have played in the major leagues prior to 1947, and two of them—Ortiz, better known as "Big Papi," and the incomparable Martinez—made much of their fame with the Red Sox, for whom they could never have played until at least 1959.

CHAPTER 7

Raised Fists, Black Shorts, and a Fallen Queen

Race, Politics, and Sex-pectations in Track and Field

RAISED FISTS, BOWED HEADS: THE 1968 OLYMPICS

Part of the reason Feliciano's story faded from public consciousness is that even before RCA Victor stamped copies of the vinyl 45 single of his anthem performance, another, much bigger furor emerged over a national anthem performance in Mexico City—or rather, over what happened during a national anthem performance in Mexico City.

The year 1968 was tumultuous, roiling, and chaotic, not just in the United States but worldwide, and Mexico City was not immune to the year's events. Ten days before the Olympics began, the government called up troops, who massacred students in Tlatelolco's *Plaza de las Tres Culturas* who were, tragically and ironically, protesting police violence.[1] Clearing out the protesters was part of the larger effort Olympic host cities often make to clean up the city for visitors, scrubbing away any sign of poverty, homelessness, and other signs that the host is a real city rather than a Potemkin Olympic Village.

The 1968 Olympics hosted the greatest track and field competition in history. In thirty-six events, fourteen world records were set, with another twelve Olympic records falling in the thin October air of Mexico City. Lee Evans won the 400 meters in 43.86, a time that cut the world record by more than three-tenths of a second. The silver medalist, Larry Jones, had set that original record two weeks earlier and broke his own mark in taking second in the fastest 400 ever run. Dick Fosbury, an American high jumper, not only set the Olympic record but transformed his event by jumping over the bar backward, a change in style that revolutionized the heights athletes could jump. The world record in the men's triple jump fell five times by three athletes, with the top five surpassing the mark that had been the world record coming into the competition. American Jim Hines became the first 100-meter sprinter to break the 10-second barrier. And the Games saw the first African Olympic gold medalists in the 1500 meters (Kip Keino of Kenya, in an Olympic record time) and the 3000-meter steeplechase (Amos Biwott, Keino's Kenyan countrymate), marking the beginning of African dominance in the middle- and long-distance events.

But the most spectacular performance of all was Bob Beamon's long jump. Beamon, who had been a part of the University of Texas at El Paso's outstanding track team (there was clearly something in the air at Texas Western/UTEP in the late 1960s), shattered the world record to such an unfathomable degree that the word "Beamonesque" entered the sporting lexicon. He jumped 29 feet, 2½ inches (8.90 meters)—22 inches (55 centimeters) beyond Ralph Boston's and Igor Ter-Ovanesyan's marks—setting a record that would last until 1991 and that still stands as the second-longest legal jump in history.

Beamon, who had been active in a new wave of seemingly more radical Black politics on college campuses, was one of a dozen athletes thrown off the UTEP track team for being part of a boycott of a meet against Brigham Young University, which had a wide range of racist and discriminatory practices against Black athletes and students born of the racist teachings of the Church of Jesus Christ of Latter-day Saints (LDS), with which BYU was inextricably affiliated. Sports Illustrated devoted one part of the magazine's groundbreaking 1968 series, "The Black Athlete: A Shameful Story" to the experiences of Black athletes at UTEP. While UTEP had done a great deal to bring in Black athletes, helping explain the advantage they had developed in their athletic program in the second half of the 1960s, the university community had done little to make Black students, a large percentage of whom were recruited athletes, feel welcome outside of the sporting arena. Jack Olsen, the author of the series, was blunt: "The University of Texas at El Paso is a bad place for a black man," though it was hard to tell "where the prejudice originates." In the words of basketball player Willie Cager, "We were suckered into coming here. I come from the toughest, blackest, poorest part of the Bronx. I won't be unhappy to go back."[2]

Ironically, Beamon and his teammates had been the targets of some scorn in February 1968 when they violated a boycott of the New York Athletic Club's (NYAC) big annual indoor track meet at Madison Square Garden.[3] The NYAC did not accept Black members yet was happy to allow Black athletes to compete at the meet. Many Black athletes and a wide range of track clubs, including college teams, boycotted the meet. Several of UTEP's Black athletes did not. Of the nine Black athletes who participated in the meet, five were from UTEP's team. Beamon, from the Jamaica neighborhood of Queens, reinforced Cager's assertions about traveling to the Madison Square Garden meet: He attended because it allowed him to get a free trip home and to escape oppressive El Paso. Beamon won the long jump at the meet.

Thus it may have come as a surprise when the Black UTEP track stars led the boycott of an Easter weekend track meet against Utah State and BYU in Provo. The athletes had a brief encounter with activist sociologist and former track star Harry Edwards after the NYAC meet, and he may have encouraged them to think more deeply about the prospect of protest going forward, though there are questions as to just how influential he was. Either way, the team chose to boycott the meet, leading to the suspensions. There had been tensions for a while—many of the athletes had not wanted to run in the Texas relays at Austin that took place after the assassination of Martin Luther King Jr. Then, in addition to the race issue, the BYU meet fell on an Easter holiday that was important to a number of the Black athletes who came from devout families. The race issue at BYU was important, but the protest did not take place in a vacuum.

UTEP's men's track team had a legitimate shot at winning the school's second NCAA championship that year, but the diminished squad they sent, minus the suspended athletes, still finished a respectable ninth. It is also worth noting that a number of athletic programs, teams, and athletes mobilized against competing against BYU in the late 1960s and early 1970s. BYU and the LDS's blatantly racist policies had allowed for "the strategic use of BYU as a platform on which to articulate expressions of anger, grievance, and redress" that in turn "dramatized—publicly and forcefully—the concerns of America's blacks."[4]

Thus, while Beamon will forever be remembered for what he did in the long jump pit in Mexico City, he had been a part of the larger protests going on in 1968, and he had paid a price, as had myriad other college athletes—and as would more in the years to come. But all of this was just prologue for the events in Mexico City, culminating in the awards ceremony for the men's 200-meter dash.

In that event, held on October 16, 1968, Tommie Smith broke his own world record of 20.0 seconds with a time of 19.83. Smith, a onetime world record holder in the 400, was followed by Australia's Peter Norman in silver medal position, with Smith's teammate, training partner, rival, and sometime friend John Carlos winning bronze. Ho-hum—another Mexico City track and field event with a spectacular performance.

Yet the enduring image from the athletics competition in the 1968 Games and from the 200-meter dash was one of raised fists, bowed heads, black socks, and an almost imperceptibly small pin. The repercussions of a protest during the national anthem after another record-setting performance were immense, fueling outrage, more ugly American hyperpatriotism, and a shamefully severe backlash against three athletes whose courage would only be recognized years—even decades—later.

The story is so often told that it warrants only a quick summary here. Black Olympians (and some white allies) had debated how to use their platform to confront racism in American society. The time was especially ripe in light of the campaign to exclude apartheid South Africa from the Olympics, a campaign that had been successful and, more importantly, was explicitly tied to questions of white supremacy. With the help of Edwards, the athletes developed the Olympic Project for Human Rights (OPHR).[5] While many athletes talked about boycotting the 1968

Olympics, the decision was to go in solidarity, with relatively few plans beyond that.

There was an incident even before the Olympic team departed for Mexico City from Denver. A white member of the Harvard crew team, coxswain Paul Hoffman, was wearing an OPHR pin as he prepared to board for Mexico City. The very white, very privileged Harvard crew teams had been vocal in their support of Black athletes and the OPHR, and several of them were part of the 1968 U.S. crew team that would represent the country at the Games. An irate U.S. Olympic Committee (USOC) official, Robert Paul, approached Hoffman, pointing to the OPHR pin on Hoffman's lapel and claiming that it violated uniform rules. Hoffman calmly pointed to sprinter Wyomia Tyus and told Paul, "See that woman over there? If you get her to take her button off, I'll take mine off." Paul relented, perhaps indicating that he knew better than to tangle with the quiet but steadfast Tyus, or perhaps indicating that Paul and officials like him, as Hoffman believed, "had this problem" talking to Black athletes.[6] But the incident also revealed the USOC's "heightened sensitivity to any appearance of subversion or protest" even before the athletes arrived in Mexico City.[7]

During the national anthem ceremony, Smith and Carlos shed their spikes, wearing only black socks (to embody poverty in the Black community), bowed their heads, and raised their fists in a Black Power salute. They wore their OPHR pins. Norman wore one of the pins in solidarity.

The outrage was immediate. Officials expelled Smith and Carlos from the Olympics, and their track and field careers were over. Young journalist Brent Musberger, in an excoriating piece in the *Chicago American*, referred to the two men as "dark-skinned Stormtroopers," a galling comparison with Nazi Germany for which Musberger was never really held to account even as his career trajectory shot upward.[8] In a tumultuous era of athlete activism, Smith and Carlos had engaged in the most visible examples—and they paid a price. Perhaps tellingly, Norman found himself the subject of heated criticism back in Australia as well.

WYOMIA TYUS AND THE ART OF SUBTLE PROTEST

Smith and Carlos were the central players in the Mexico City drama. They were not, however, alone. One of the most impressive, and certainly overlooked, performances in the 1968 Olympics was the sprinting of Tyus, the "Swiftie from Tennessee State." One of the legendary "Tiger-belles" from Tennessee State University's track and field program, Tyus won two gold medals with world record times, her sixth and seventh world records in her career, in the 100-meter dash and the 4x100-meter relay. In winning the 100 she repeated her gold from the 1964 Tokyo Olympics, making her the first person—man or woman—to repeat in track's signature event on its grandest stage. Tyus, always modest, has said, "I don't focus on my records. Time never broke a tape."⁹

The Tigerbelles were arguably the most dominant track program—maybe the most dominant athletic team, full stop—in history, college or pro. Coach Ed Temple's women's team transformed the sport in an era when the NCAA barely recognized woman athletes, not even bothering to host a women's championship until 1982. Temple was the U.S. women's Olympic head track coach in 1960 and 1964 and the Pan-American track coach in 1959 and 1975, remarkable recognition for a coach toiling away in a women's track program at an HBCU in the 1950s and 1960s. He coached fifteen Tigerbelles who won Olympic gold medals, eight silver medalists, five bronze medalists, and produced seventeen other Olympians for both the U.S. and national teams. Nearly all of these athletes earned degrees, in many cases graduate and professional degrees. And he did all of this—developing a program unlike any in the history of the sport, maybe any sport—as an unpaid volunteer. Temple's day job was teaching sociology at TSU. And the school's track facility was laughable—"an oval ribbon of dirt, unmarked and unsurfaced," located near a pigpen maintained by agricultural students.¹⁰

Temple made the Tigerbelles a success, but he was not without his flaws. He was exceptionally strict in ways that revealed a paternalism that often slid into sexism and even misogyny. He tried to dictate and restrict his athletes' dating lives, at least in part because Black women's sexuality had been turned into the hypersexualized stereotype of the jezebel and he wanted to protect them from that. But even more, he pushed hyperfeminine expectations onto his charges, demanding "that they perform traditional, heterosexual, white-defined femininity." In words that were once probably considered harmless and clever but induce cringes today, he would often say, "I want foxes, not oxes." The Tigerbelles were expected to fix their hair and makeup immediately after meets and to dress up to travel, to be "ladylike." Temple's rationale was at least somewhat understandable in an era when colleges were expected to take responsibility for students in loco parentis: "Every single one of these girls had never really been away from home. I was responsible for them. I felt responsible for them. I had promised their parents I would look after them and that's just what I did."[11] And as time passed he softened somewhat; as the 1950s and 1960s progressed, his athletes pushed the limits of his rules and, while he never formally relaxed them, many were recognized in the breach.[12] Nonetheless, operating with no scholarships, Temple had not only created a dynasty unlikely ever to be matched again, his "Tigerbelles opened the door for women, not only in track and field, but in all sports."[13]

Part of the problem woman athletes faced is that whatever Temple's excesses, they *were*—Black and white—sexualized. When Wilma Rudolph struck multiple golds in the Rome Olympics, she earned the evergreen quadrennial title "darling" of the Olympics. "This queen of the 1960 Olympics is a slender beauty whose eyes carry a perpetual twinkle, as if she were amused, and a little puzzled, at what is going on around her," the writer practically hyperventilated. It got worse: "Miss Rudolph is five feet, 11 inches and weighs 132 pounds. Vital statistics: 34-24-36." And of course she "has the legs of a showgirl."[14]

Proof of the way the larger sporting world viewed woman athletes came when *Sports Illustrated* featured "Flamin' Mamie's Bouffant Belles" of the Texas Track Club from Abilene in a 1964 cover story—the first time women's track and field had gotten the honor of the *SI* cover. Flamin' Mamie was Margaret Ellison, who cultivated her buxom Southern belles and who argued, "I'm trying to change the stereotyped image of the track girl."[15] Yet the emphasis was on their fashion, their bouffant hairdos, and their looks. As Gilbert Rogin wrote, "The Texas Track Club is celebrated on two counts—its athletic achievement and the uncommon beauty of its girls, who compete in dazzling uniforms, elaborate makeup and majestic hairdos." He argued that "the Texas Track Club has done more to promote women's track in the U.S. than if its members had, say, won the national AAU championships," an absurd assertion that got the chronology and facts entirely wrong—how many Americans had heard of Flamin' Mamie's team prior to the *Sports Illustrated* cover story?[16] The magazine had created the buzz when it could have just as easily put any of a number of accomplished athletes—not least Wilma Rudolph or Wyomia Tyus—on the cover and in a feature. Rogin, a serious track fan and journalist, had encountered the team at a meet and eventually went to Texas to meet them and accompany them on a road trip, which led to the *SI* story. He consciously chose to write "primarily about the athletes' beauty regimen rather than their running" because, by his own damning admission, "it was all just a stunt. It wasn't a track story."[17]

Leering letters to *Sports Illustrated* confirmed that the cover story "worked" if lecherous sexism was the goal: "Let the Russian amazons have the Olympics. Dames like 'Flamin' Mamie's Bouffant Belles' can just stand in the starting blocks and they'll get my vote for first every time. Wow!" Eddie Smith, a fellow Texan and the writer of this letter, may as well have been a cartoon wolf drawn by Tex Avery. Eddie Steinberg of Brookline, Massachusetts, was no subtler: "As a patriotic American in an Olympic-year, I would like to volunteer my service as team trainer."[18] In the wake of the article, the women participated in a meet at the University of Oregon in Eugene, in some ways the epicenter of American track and field. As soon as word spread that the Flamin' Mamies were there, "clusters of male spectators arrived out of nowhere. Binoculars were visible peering out of windows from the men's dormitory across the street."[19]

This coverage and the attention that followed galled many in the women's track community, including Tyus. And why wouldn't it? The Texas Track Club, despite the drooling fawning of journalists and the practically tumescent responses of readers, experienced a fraction of the success of Tennessee State's women's team. None of the Texas Bouffant Belles made an Olympic team. But they brought a look to the table. And they were white. As Tyus's memoir coauthor says about the 1964 *Sports Illustrated* cover story, it was "a breathtaking testament to the interlocking powers of racism and sexism" because "the article effortlessly erases the accomplishments of Black female athletes while simultaneously mocking the aspirations of white female athletes."[20]

Tyus had personal reasons, too, for resenting Ellison. Tyus had made the U.S. national team that Ellison had inexplicably been chosen to coach. The majority of the team did not take Flamin' Mamie at all seriously as a coach. "We were not at all happy about the choice of Ellison as coach," Tyus later wrote, "but there was nothing we could do. It's not like it is now, when everybody has their individual coach and that coach goes too. Back then you were stuck with the coach they chose. You still did your own workout, and the team coach would only put in her two cents here and there, but you were supposed to listen to her like she knew something." Ellison did not know much. "Naturally we knew not to do anything Mamie told us to do. We had seen her before at meets with her skintight outfits and her bouffant hair. She would come out to the track—heels *this* high—and you knew she couldn't coach. She couldn't tell us anything besides how to put on eye shadow, tease our hair, and wear skimpy clothing."[21]

The *Sports Illustrated* article did not exactly undercut the argument that Ellison was not much of a coach. She almost breathlessly asserted that one of her athletes, a sprinter, "can jog five miles without stopping"—a basic foundational accomplishment that the typical high school athlete can complete, never mind a track and field athlete aspiring toward the ranks of the elite.[22] Later Ellison commented on the workouts one of her athletes was expected to perform as a sprinter at Odessa Junior College, where she was on a partial track scholarship at a school with one male track athlete—the two made up the entire track program; the workout she listed would have been a perfectly reasonable workout for a college track athlete. Yet Ellison's "dour observation" was that her college coach "was killing her."[23]

And as if all this folderol wasn't complex enough, on top of it all, woman athletes had become "pawns in the propaganda posturings of the United States and Soviet Union in the Cold War."[24] After only five years of coaching, Flamin' Mamie had been chosen to coach the U.S. team facing the Soviet Union (and other countries) in Moscow, a regular

Cold War faceoff. Indeed, it is highly likely that without the Cold War context, woman Olympians—and especially the numbers they added to the medal count against the Soviets, East Germans, and the rest of the Eastern Bloc—would have gotten even less attention. Making things more complicated still was the fact that "the contrast with the Soviet women's track program served to highlight both the physical differences of the two superpowers' athletes and the apparent disadvantage American women faced against the Soviets." The fact was that "American track women continued to gain popularity in part because the 'big-boned muscular' athletes of the Soviet Union served as a convenient 'other' for American society to transfer lingering concerns over the masculinizing effects of sport on women's bodies."[25] They had become instruments, but that instrumentalization also gave them an opportunity—albeit one fraught with sexism and caught up in the complexities of the Cold War.

If Black men had to deal with indignities and violence just to compete in sports, Black women had to endure the double bind of race and sex (and often a third element, class) in order to compete. This double—or triple—bind, what some refer to today as intersectionality, was especially acute because HBCUs themselves often perpetuated it, treating women's sports as an afterthought, a second-tier activity. Women of all races had to deal with sexist attitudes and paternalism in order to partake in sports. And sometimes the "Flamin' Mamies" got the attention that should have gone to the "Swiftie from Tennessee State"—or literally any among hundreds of other athletes.

For women, then, there was a ceiling. And for Black women that ceiling was especially low. Professional sports leagues were limited. The one that flourished, the All-American Girls Professional Baseball League (AAGPBL) during World War II, was often seen as a novelty and a placeholder for when men came back and Organized Baseball could return to its fullness. Yet the AAGPBL was a competitive league whose players took the game seriously and whose fans came to recognize the quality, even if the mores of the era did not allow for their imaginations to conceive of professional sporting opportunities for American women. And the AAGPBL was segregated, which led to the interesting eventuality that a few Black women played baseball with their male counterparts in the Negro Leagues, albeit in small numbers and only fleetingly.

Meanwhile, even as the OPHR picked up steam, women had been effectively excluded. They were expected to provide support in the form of being seen but not heard. As historian Amy Bass has written, in a struggle like the OPHR in the 1960s, "the assumed 'right on' priority becomes that of placing the black male on equal footing with his white counterpart before dealing with the inequities faced by women—white and black."[26] Even the women's training situation before the Olympics was second-class—while the men's team prepared for the Games in South Lake Tahoe, the women were consigned to an essentially media-free environment in Los Alamos, New Mexico, which had the benefit of high altitude like Mexico City but otherwise reinforced the sense of second-class citizenship that exclusion from the OPHR had done. Tyus was especially "appalled" at how these various exclusions showed that the men took the women for granted, treating them as if they "had no minds of their own."[27] Years later, Tommie Smith would lament, "They should have been involved."[28] Harry Edwards calls "the lack of due attention paid to the status, circumstances, outcomes and contributions of Black women—either as athletes or in the struggles for change more generally" a "glaring omission."[29]

The women were clearly not as visible as Smith and Carlos, and the medalists' very public shaming, their being sent home, their careers almost instantly ending, quite clearly had the chilling effect Avery Brundage and the other Olympic solons had hoped for. But that is not to say that women were not involved in ways that were subtle but still risky. Tyus, who should rightfully have been one of the shining stars of the Games, made her own discrete protest. "As part of my contribution to the protest for human rights," she recounted in her memoir, "I had worn black running shorts for the relay," and in fact she wore them for her triumphant individual 100-meter competition as well, "rather than the regular white running shorts that were issued to us—although I'm not sure anyone noticed."[30] Given how much of the Smith and Carlos protest had been symbolic—the black socks without shoes on the podium, the raised fists, the OPHR button—Tyus's hidden-in-plain-sight symbolic gesture fit in perfectly.

At the post-relay meeting before the press, the woman athletes were asked about Smith and Carlos—a form of erasure of their own accomplishments, to be sure, but also likely inevitable given the context. "What is there to think?" Tyus said. "They made a statement. We all know that we're fighting for human rights. That's what they stood for on the victory stand—human rights for everyone, everywhere. And to support that and to support them, I'm dedicating my medal to them. I believe in what they did."[31] After Smith and Carlos were thrown out of the Olympics, Tyus was quoted as saying that she thought it was "awful," maintaining that the two athletes "did not hurt anybody."[32] Reflecting back, she later wrote, "I don't remember planning it in advance. I was in support of what the whole movement was about, so I was ready to say something. It was not about what they did in that one moment" but rather "it was about human rights," from what happened to the student protesters in Tlatelolco before the Games to "what was happening to people all around the world. That's what the whole human rights project has always been about: we are all in this together."[33] Given how the women had been kept at a distance and even shunned by the men, this gesture was even more gracious than it seemed. The women would have had every right to let the men dangle in the wind. Instead, they backed Smith and Carlos.

Tyus was mindful of the Cold War context, global movements for liberation, and America's own hypocrisies on matters of civil and human rights, and her Olympic triumphs allowed her to speak out even if in so doing she was barely heard. Because while her comments were thoughtful and far-reaching, "none of that got printed, of course, only the fact that I had dedicated my medal—that we all, the whole relay team, had dedicated our medals. That was ok with me—as long as the press understood why we did it."[34] But the press had not really earned that benefit of the doubt, and while ignoring some of Tyus's comments might have protected her, that is surely not why they didn't fully quote her. Almost certainly her gender explains the silence. A double gold medalist, the first repeat 100 gold medalist in history, Tyus was still treated as an adjunct to the men's events—and to the men's protests. As Bass has put it, Tyus and her teammates were put in a position that "was limited to one of support rather than advocacy."[35]

And so the question becomes, did her protest and comments cost Tyus? The answer is in the absence. Women's sports were an afterthought in 1968, and Tyus's accomplishments were barely recognized. Only Beamon's epochal leap was clearly more impressive, but otherwise her back-to-back 100-meter victories deserved to be recognized alongside Evans's or Hines's or, outside the social context, Smith's victories. All broke world records—but so did Tyus, who also accomplished what no one in the history of the sport had ever done. In the sport's feature event, she ran the best result in history. She tied the world record in 1964 and broke it in 1968. That got erased.

Tyus certainly believed her gender was the key factor in that erasure. When asked why her protest and subsequent support for Smith and Carlos drew no attention, she stated, "Because I was a woman. Who cared?"[36]

Tyus could not be sure of the consequences of her actions. "It's a difficult thing to measure," she correctly pointed out. Her response was largely ignored. Was this because she was a woman? Was it because in the wake of the Smith-Carlos protest everything was going to be sucked up in the wake? Tyus argued that "no one ever really looked at all that I had done: back-to-back gold medals in the 100 and three gold medals total and breaking all kinds of records." As she savvily noted, "But if it was that, it wasn't only that. It was also because I'm not only Black but a woman." She is clear that other than broadcaster Howard Cosell, who praised her accomplishments, no one else "was trying to notice me or give me a flag even when I had done something that no one else in the world had ever done"—and this had happened even before Smith and Carlos had run their race.[37]

"At the time," Tyus wrote, "they were not about to bathe a Black woman in glory. It would give us too much power, wouldn't it? Because it would have been a moment, if you think about it: 'She won back-to-back gold medals; nobody in the world has ever done that. Let's paint the US all over her—let's drape her in a flag!' You would think. But no. I would never see them hanging a flag on me. Because one thing the Olympics is not about is giving power to the powerless."[38] This is a profoundly important assertion supported by most serious scholarship on the Olympics: The Games are much more about validating than questioning the powerful.[39]

Tyus was used to being in the shadows. She had followed Wilma Rudolph—a multiple-time world record holder and gold medalist in the 1960 Rome Games in the 100, 200, and 4x100—at Tennessee State and the Olympics, after all: "If the other person in the room is someone like Wilma Rudolph, there's nothing wrong with them getting the attention. And of course it's not just Wilma; if I go into a room and someone is talking to me, and then Serena Williams walks in, no one's going to be talking to me anymore, and my little story is no longer going to be on the page. I'm not offended by that. It's just the rules of the sports game."[40]

But while Tyus was willing to take a backseat when it came to publicity, she always felt that the second-class status of women in the movement was a real problem. When asked "if the movement would have been better at achieving its goals if it had included women . . . [o]f course I'm going to say yes. We should have been included in the organizing, should have been consulted. It would have made a difference. But we weren't." She reflected, "Partly it was a sign of the times, where we were as people, not just Black people but the world: women were expected to follow, to do what the men said. In '68 they weren't thinking about what women in general were saying or doing. No one was. Women's words and women's lives were not considered worthy of attention." And that issue transcended race. "That was not a Black thing; it was an all-race, worldwide sexist thing. Men know better, men are stronger. That's what most people thought. But I didn't grow up that way. My parents taught me that I'm as good or better than anybody, male or female."[41] Indeed, she grew up as a "tomboy" whose father had an "optimistic vision for both gender and racial equality," and when the Tyus children were young they "joined the young neighboring white boys" in a whole range of sports and games.[42]

That's why not bringing women into the OPHR and the organizing that went on before the Games "was a problem." Tyus "felt that bringing us into the organizing would have been consistent with the whole idea of the movement, or at least what the movement came to be: a movement about everybody everywhere who was struggling for human rights." That inclusion is why she had gotten involved to begin with. And "considering that it was all about inclusion, it would have made sense for women to be brought in, front and center." Inclusion did not happen automatically.[43]

Temple had always been concerned that Tyus's otherworldly performance was "overshadowed" by everything surrounding Smith and Carlos, and while it is not the kind of thing Tyus generally is concerned with, she wrote, "I know he was right" because "when anyone wants to talk to me about what I've done, and they ask what Olympic team it was, and I say '68, they say, 'Oh, you were with *them! *Those guys, those guys, those guys!' And I say, 'No, I won my medal first, so they were with *me.*' I like teasing people. Because that's the first thing they bring up."[44]

And while infelicitous in their approach, those people are not entirely wrong. Tommie Smith and John Carlos (and, for that matter, Peter Norman) took a heroic, very public, and very consequential stand. They suffered greatly. They faced massive public criticism and lost their track and field careers. They were forced out of the Olympic Village. And they spent years in the wilderness—even if today they are generally seen as heroes, especially by the kinds of misfits who write history and journalists who glom on to that history. But Tyus's experience is valid too. Ironically, had she not been ignored in 1968, she might have been demonized. In a weird way, sexism and paternalism shielded her. But her story is important because that sexism and paternalism is important and serves as a reminder that even within progressive and even radical movements there were retrograde beliefs with regard to sex and gender. Tyus was a hero herself who did not get the credit, but also the blame, that she deserved. In those Olympics, she "earned her place in the pantheon of sports heroes," Billie Jean King—herself a member in good standing of that pantheon—has said.[45] Her place is secure, but her fame really ought to be far greater, not only for her athletic accomplishments but also for the role she played in the struggle for human rights.

As Elizabeth Terzakis, the coauthor of Tyus's memoir, writes, "By throwing her support behind" Smith and Carlos, "Tyus played a significant—if under-recognized—part in bringing the movement for human rights into the arena of international athletic competition."[46] In just a few years, however, increasing numbers of woman athletes would speak out and demand to be heard. Women in sports, as in society, were growing newly discontented, even radicalized, fighting for the rights that Black male athletes did before them but without the scope and scale of HBCU athletics to give them a forum and a platform.

As it had been for Black men, change was slow to come. But a few words would make a difference. Thirty-seven words, to be precise.

OF PIXIES AND PRINCESSES: *DECKER V. BUDD*

Mary Decker was to middle-distance and distance running what Babe Didrikson, Jim Brown, Jim Thorpe, and Jackie Robinson were to sports more broadly—she really could do it all. Over the course of a career that stretched from the beginning of the 1970s through to the cusp of the twenty-first century, Decker at one point or the other held the American record in every event from the 800 through the 10,000 meters. She also accumulated a pile of world records, including an unfathomable six in 1982, from the mile through the 10,000, and most believe that had she made even a modest effort at the marathon she would have broken that American and maybe even world record too. As it was, with no real event-specific training, she ran her only marathon at the age of twelve, running a time that showed immense promise in the earliest days of the women's marathon as an official event. In her career she set thirty-six U.S. records and seventeen official and unofficial world records. She is "the greatest distance runner, male or female, in American history," who had a "powerful yet graceful stride" that always "made it look easy," with an "unparalleled combination of speed and endurance."[47] She also had just about perfect running form. Because she rose to great heights so quickly, she came to be known as "Little Mary Decker." She went from angering boys by being faster than them on the playground to joining a track club and competing in the long jump, 100-meter dash, and 400 meters to running in elite middle-distance and distance events in a span of just a few years. Throughout her career she cultivated an uncanny ability as a frontrunner—set a blistering pace; destroy the competition's legs, lungs, and confidence; and finish strong (and in first).

She broke through in 1973 in a USA-USSR dual meet in Minsk. These meets were hallmarks of Cold War sport—both proxy conflicts to determine superiority and efforts at sporting diplomacy—and the Soviets frankly dominated them, using an advantage in the women's competition in particular to pull away. At Minsk the Soviets once again dominated, but the breakthrough star was Decker, who defeated 1972 Olympic 800 silver medalist Nijolė Sabaitė in that event. Decker "emerged as an overnight sensation" after her surprising win, and "the American public celebrated the surprising victory of its newly discovered 86-pound phenom." Journalists from the United States "contrasted her youth, slight stature, and pigtails against the power, muscle, and strength of the Soviet athletes." As historian Lindsay Parks Pieper points out, "Significantly, the teenage runner routed the more muscular Soviets while upholding Western gender norms."[48] Decker thus "embodied and espoused nationalistic femininity. Her athletic successes, girlish appearance, and vocal condemnation of Eastern European runners seemed to prove that women could excel in track and field without succumbing to masculinization." This combination of the politics of gender and the politics of Americanism reached its pinnacle in late Cold War–era athletes like Decker, who could "repulse the Red Menace" and look like the all-American girl in doing so.[49]

This narrative would continue to develop as Decker's career exploded, and at least part of the narrative was how Decker looked, even if she fell short of some of the performances of Soviet runners: "The U.S. public appreciated that Decker stayed petite and attractive while the Eastern European runners seemed to increase in bulk and power." As renowned *Los Angeles Times* sports columnist Jim Murray pontificated—in ways that would not have been unfamiliar to readers of the coverage of Babe Didrikson—"women's international track and field stars are beginning to look like someone you might call 'Bubba.'" While "90 percent of the adult female world wants to look like Bo Derek," one of the era's "It Girls," Eastern European and Soviet athletes seemed to be "working more toward looking like Bo Schembechler," the football coach at the University of Michigan. "In a world of perfect '10s'"—a reference to one of Derek's movies—the Soviet Bloc athletes were "minus-3s." Decker, though, was atypical, in a good way.[50] Once again, women could prove instrumental in fueling American sporting nationalism, as long as they looked the right way.

And Decker played into this narrative, willingly disparaging her competitors. She referred to one of her competitors, Tatyana Kazankina, a triple gold medalist from the Montreal Games who had set a world record in the 1500 that Decker had not yet been able to match, as "Ted" for what she called "obvious reasons." But she did not stop there: "When I first ran against her as a young girl in Moscow years ago, I used to beat her in the 800. The girl I ran against now looks like her brother." And Kazankina was not an outlier in facing Decker's gendered scorn. "All I know" about the East German women, she said, "is they have hair growing in places where normal women don't. And the runners I've seen look different than I do."[51] Because she "both epitomized and embraced feminine forms during the heightening of the Cold War," she also won fans—men, perhaps, in particular. "We are fools for Mary Theresa Decker. Hopelessly smitten," gushed Rick Reilly in the *New York Times* in the buildup to the Los Angeles Games. "She is what we like. She wins. She smiles. She is a girl we can carry in our wallet."[52]

Known for her punishing workouts—and thus the injury issues that plagued her—Decker's career as "America's sweetheart" also carries with it a patina of disappointment, as she never had success at the Olympics, the quadrennial event where track and field is front and center for a week or so and where legends, reputations, and fame beyond the track and field world are all made. She was too young to qualify for the 1972 Munich Games, injuries kept her from competing in Montreal in 1976, and in 1980, the United States boycotted the Moscow Games. Decker was peaking at the 1980 U.S. Olympic Trials, crushing the opposition by two seconds in the 1500 and looking like she was "ready to take on the world in the Moscow Olympics." Speaking on behalf of a number of competitors, she later said, "We athletes talked about it all the time. I don't remember anyone who thought it was a good idea or that it would have any influence on the Soviets. I was still young, at just 22, and I felt that I would have other Olympic chances."[53] She also admitted, "I was bitter about it and I'm sure the other 600 athletes on the Olympic team were too."[54]

In 1983, she had made history at the world championships by winning the unprecedented 1500–3000 double, a ruthless and unforgiving schedule that she nonetheless won, leading pundits to call the feat the "Double Decker" (and sometimes the "Decker Double"). "Helsinki was going to be a pure track championship," she later recalled. "In some ways it was better than the Olympics. There were no politics, no boycotts. Everyone would be there. Everyone wanted to perform their best."[55] For all her accomplishments, Decker went into both of her Helsinki races as an underdog to the mighty Soviet and East German running machine, which held eight of the top ten slots in the 1500 heading into the meet. Decker was ninth. The rankings in the 3000 were similar. "No one thought I could beat the Russians because they were so tough and had great speed at the end. I decided not to play games with them. I just wanted to take it out hard at the start, and run hard all the way."[56] Her plan worked. Both races were hard fought—the 3000 became so physical that Decker thought her Soviet Bloc rivals were borderline cheating—but she won tight but clear victories at the end. Decker had become not just a known, record-setting commodity in American track circles, she had become a star; no longer "Little Mary Decker," she had risen to royalty, becoming "Queen Mary."[57] Her feats in 1983 and the season she had more generally were enough to earn her the honor of being *Sports Illustrated*'s "Sportsperson of the Year" for 1983, beating out all other athletes—women and men.[58]

But the world championships, important though they are to track and field fans (who tend to see them as every bit as important of a competition as the Olympics), were to be a prelude to Los Angeles and the events at the LA Coliseum, the grand old stadium that would host the track and field events and the eyes of the world, at least on the open side of the Iron Curtain. And that would take place in Decker's California backyard. She was in constant demand, though, which would get in the way of the monastic training she preferred. And then her preparation approaching the Olympics would be curtailed by her old injury bugaboo.

The Olympics still succumb to gendered narratives. It seems like every Olympics—Winter and Summer—sees the emergence of the "pixie" or "darling" or "queen" or "princess" of the Games; when she wins gold medals, as is her fate, she becomes a "Golden Girl." The anointing of this title involves a complicated calculus that combines traditional conceptions of beauty with athletic success and at least the simulacrum of a vivacious personality. Usually, the titles also go to a young athlete—often, though not always, to gymnasts in the Summer Games or figure skaters in the Winter Games, but also sometimes to an athlete who stands out to male sportswriters for her sexual allure. Usually (though again, not always) this athlete is American. She has a compelling story that can be told in the kind of gauzy feature that is the hallmark of Olympic coverage, where people become experts for a few days of watching sports they will not even think of for another four years and where a compelling enough backstory creates instant fans. Then, of course, for much of the history of the modern Olympics, politics have been a factor—the geopolitics of the Cold War being the most obvious historical example. Add all of these together and women often found themselves serving instrumental roles in Olympic competition, especially as their participation became more acceptable—or at least resistance to that participation futile—and as their golds, silvers, and bronzes added to that ever-important medal count against the Soviets, East Germans, Chinese, or whomever the geopolitical foes du jour might be.

The 1984 Los Angeles Olympics saw such a perfect storm, and if Decker was not *the* chosen Olympic princess—that honor went to bubbly and dominant gymnast Mary Lou Retton, for whom the pixie role seems to have been invented—she certainly took the weight of the track competition on her shoulders. Meanwhile, although the Soviets—and as a consequence nearly the entirety of the Eastern Bloc—boycotted the 1984 Games, watering down the competition significantly, Americans made up for it by throwing the most brazenly jingoistic Olympics in recent history, matched only by the 1936 Games hosted by Adolf Hitler and the Nazis in Berlin. Ubiquitous chants of "USA! USA! USA!" seemed to cross from Olympic patriotism to what Frank Deford called "Large Boor Freestyle Jingoism." He watched the spectacle unfolding around him and wondered, "God only knows what the 2.5 billion people around the globe who are watching the Games will think of a vain America, so bountiful and strong, with every advantage, including the home court, reveling in the role of Goliath, gracelessly trumpeting its own good fortune while rudely dismissing its guests."[59]

But Decker's feature race—the 3000 meters, a race that even in track circles is rarely a marquee event—carried with it a multiplicity of meanings. Not only was it a chance for another American gold medal, another American podium appearance, another pumped up playing of the national anthem, but Decker even had a geopolitical foil in the form of Zola Budd, a South African who had been fast-tracked to British citizenship, and thus eligibility to compete for Great Britain at the Olympics. She did so with the help of the London tabloid the *Daily Mail*, which had supported her shockingly fast visa process—what usually took years for a normal applicant took just a couple of weeks for Budd. When her visa was granted, the front page of the *Daily Mail* screamed "Wonder Girl Zola."[60]

South Africa had been excluded from Olympic competition for a generation, meaning that Budd should have been ineligible, especially as a white South African beneficiary of apartheid. The fast-tracking of her British visa certainly felt like a very privileged form of special pleading for a white South African. Most Americans could not have come close to articulating South African apartheid policy, never mind that America's approach to South Africa in the Reagan years was a policy known as "Constructive Engagement" that amounted to coddling and acquiescing to South Africa's racist regime. Nor did it matter that Decker was as apolitical as they came. Budd was a pixie of her own, and Americans love a morality play where they can ascribe to themselves virtue, even if on matters racial the history of the United States is abysmal and even if coddling South Africa had become something of its own national sport. In the "hype-driven" LA Games, the Decker-Budd clash created considerable "frenzy."[61]

Furthermore, though Decker was conventionally attractive and suitably feminine and had become a favorite of the armchair fans who adopt track loyalties every four years, she was rather ill-suited to the role of pixie or princess or anything along those lines. Hypercompetitive, laser-focused, and sometimes irascible, Decker wasn't inclined toward the demure. She was far more likely to jab a competitor with a well-placed elbow than she was to give a princess wave, and why not? Distance and especially middle-distance running—and the 3000 really is the latter—can be shockingly physical. Decker was small, but she was a fierce competitor who did not much care about making friends with the competition. But she also did not have much interest in cultivating media-created rivalries. Zola Budd was a promising young runner, "waif-like" and "with a penchant for running dazzling times barefoot."[62] But she had nothing comparable to Decker's résumé or experience, and while casual fans had picked up on the Decker-Budd rivalry talk, serious track and field fans knew that the field was deep and that anointing Decker and Budd the gold and silver, in one order or the other, was premature at best, even if Decker was the favorite.

Throughout the postwar period, the role of apartheid South Africa served as perhaps the key international question that revealed the impossibility of keeping the Olympics clean from politics.[63] Even prior to the rise of the National Party and its apartheid policies in 1948, South Africa was a deeply segregated country by law and custom. But the implementation of apartheid created the most rigidly racially stratified nation on earth, exacerbated by the fact that whites represented a small minority of South Africa's population and showed a willingness to engage in the most brutal means to maintain white supremacy. Once South Africa was finally removed from the Olympics (an intermittent process that took the entirety of the 1960s to fully take hold), it still haunted the putatively apolitical Games like a specter. Controversial rugby tours involving South Africa's national rugby team kept South Africa in the Olympic conversation. The clash between Decker and Budd (which also became a deeply gendered conflict whereby two world-class athletes and tough competitors played the infantilized, feminized roles of "princess" and "pixie") at the 1984 LA Games became a proxy battle between claimed Western superiority and the evils of apartheid, despite the fact that Americans had few claims to superiority on the racial issue, in sport or beyond.[64] Meanwhile, in the interregnum between the 1983 World Championships in Helsinki and the Olympics, Nike started running ads featuring Decker—the first time the footwear company, known first and foremost for its connection to running and track, had featured a real athlete. Decker was, in this sense, Michael Jordan before Michael Jordan was.

The race created an enduring image, and it was not of Decker triumphantly winning the 3000, vanquishing Budd, and earning another podium and national anthem for the United States. The image is of Decker sprawled out on the infield after tangling legs with Budd. Her coach, Dick Brown, had suggested a change of tactics for the 3000 finals: Take it easy for a few laps, get a feel for the pace, and win in the final laps. "That turned out to be the biggest mistake of my life, to let someone else lead," Decker said later. "I always ran my own race at my own pace. But we thought maybe with the Olympic pressure, we should play it a little safe." So while she took the lead initially, she let the pack catch up with her—including Budd, who took the lead, taking with her a pack of athletes including Decker, Budd's Great Britain teammate Wendy Sly, and Romania's Maricaca Puică. There was a lot of contact, much of it between Decker, who for all her elite background did not have much experience running in packs because of her frontrunning nature, and the unquestionably talented but inexperienced Budd. At the 1,720-meter mark of the race, "something more serious happened," according to track and field historian Amby Burfoot. "To this day no one is quite sure what. Legs tangled, and Mary pitched almost headfirst onto the grass infield of the track. She tried to bounce back up and rejoin the race, but encountered such searing hip pain that she couldn't get to her feet."[65] In the words of legendary TV sports broadcaster Al Michaels, Decker going down "was stunning."[66]

Budd maintained a lead in the ongoing race for another lap, with boos cascading down on her from the partisan (one chronicler uses the adjective "boorish")[67] crowd. She ended up finishing seventh. Puică, the Romanian, won the race, taking the gold medal. Sly won silver, and Canada's Lynn Williams held on for bronze. Puică took a victory lap, and the inflamed crowd shifted their emotions long enough to give her loud applause. Romanians, having defied the Eastern Bloc boycott, had become popular at the Games, and Puică certainly benefited from these Cold War proxy sentiments.

Meanwhile, "the race was over," as one chronicler of the controversy writes, "but the controversy it stirred became a boiling pot of outrage, sympathy, and finger-pointing."[68] After her own competition was done, and "struggling with her own disappointment," Budd tried to speak to Decker: words of consolation, an apology, something. Decker waved her off: "Don't bother." This sealed Decker's reputation for bad sportsmanship in some circles, though in context it is hard to imagine a serious expectation that Decker would respond with hugs. She later wrote an apology letter to Budd and received a warm response in return. "I believe I handled the situation with dignity," she later said. "I didn't call her a name or anything. I just said 'don't bother apologizing. It won't help.' It's too bad neither of us had the race we wanted. At least she stayed on her feet."[69] The "much-adored" Decker found many Americans turning on her in light of her "refusal to move beyond the 'brutal kilometer.'"[70]

In a number of postrace events, Decker broke down in tears, earning her, unfairly, the moniker of "crybaby." Decker's response to this perfectly captured the gender double bind competitive women faced: "If you're strong and confident, you're considered bitchy. If you cry because you fell over and your whole dreams since you were twelve go down the toilet, you're a crybaby."[71]

South African–born Cornelia Bürki, who had moved to Switzerland to become a legendary distance runner in that country (and avoided the sort of criticism Budd faced) had passed Budd at the end of the race for sixth and witnessed the exchange between Budd, whom she had befriended, and Decker. Bürki later remembered confronting Decker, blaming her for the accident on the track and receiving a blistering response. "All people remember is what they saw and heard on television. Everyone saw" Richard Slaney "carrying her off the track, and heard her blaming Zola" in the days and months that followed. "No one cared about the little girl who just wanted to be a runner."[72] Meanwhile Budd faced harassment, including death threats, upon her return to London.

In the immediate wake of the race, the outcome was seen almost as a tragedy for the American. The *Los Angeles Times* ran a pair of stories, one on Decker ("MARY," with the subhead, "The Queen of Track Suddenly Becomes Frightened Child") and a corresponding one on Budd

("ZOLA," subheaded "Post-Race Rebuke by Decker, Her Idol, Bewilders Youngster"). The article on Decker, by Alan Greenberg, certainly plays up the gendered angles on the fallen American: "Mary Decker, America's sweetheart, broke her date with destiny and a lot of hearts, including her own, Friday night." But "at the bitter end her throne was not the Olympic medal stand but a portable medical rescue unit. Her beautiful smile never blazed across world television" and instead she was carried off the infield by "hulking British discus thrower Richard Slaney," her fiancé. But even this somehow confirmed her royal standing. "As befits a queen, Decker's feet never touched the ground once she left the track. But this was no conquering hero, this was a crying, distraught womanchild of 26 being carried off in her lover's arms, brown eyes liquid with tears as she peeked over his shoulder, curled up like a frightened child." Then Greenberg shifted from metaphors of royalty to those of melodrama: "And so concludes another gut-wrenching episode in the scintillating but star-crossed career" of Decker. "But this was no scripted soap opera. These tears, these traumas are real."[73]

Betty Cuniberti, writing Budd's side of the story, emphasized the emotional price Budd paid due to the response of the crowd and her "bewildered" response to Decker's postrace shunning. It is a sympathetic profile of a very young athlete who may have made a mistake in the race but who faced serious consequences beyond the scope of any sins she might have committed. In the wake of the crowd's booing, she was "very upset emotionally," and she was deeply upset by what had happened in the race against a hero whose picture she kept on her desk back in South Africa. "All she said was, 'How's Mary?'" according to Dick Whitehead, manager of the Great Britain track team. But of course, gender was never far from the fore in depictions of Budd, either. The race "was to be Budd's coming-out ball. But instead it was more like a gangland rumble." Between the physicality of the race and the outsized report from the crowd, the message was clear: "Welcome to the Big Girls' race, Zola."[74] It was, stunningly, Budd's first true international race, and she learned hard lessons as a result. Sports journalist Rick Reilly summed up Budd's complicity, or at least any possible intent: "The very last person Zola Budd wanted to hurt was Mary Decker. Mary Decker was her hero."[75]

Though Decker qualified for the 1988 Seoul Games, she was past her peak and underperformed, finishing well out of the medals. She tried a comeback for the Atlanta Games in 1996, but by then the sport had passed her by, and she got embroiled in a doping scandal in her efforts to regain past glories.

"I just seemed to have an Olympic jinx," Decker mused years later. "But I feel good about all the other contributions I made. I didn't have women to emulate when I started. People who saw me out running in the early 1970s reacted like I had three heads or something. Today's high school and college girls have a lot of opportunities. A lot of us who came before them made these a reality."[76]

Zola Budd returned to South Africa, where she would continue to be beloved. In the Black community the "combi" taxis, one of the most popular forms of transport, are known as "Zola Budds" because of how they zip perilously but surely through the streets and on the highways, and some people began to refer to the big, bulky, cumbersome buses that often get into accidents as Mary Deckers.

Budd and Decker (running under her married name, Mary Decker Slaney) would face off five more times. Decker Slaney would win them all. On July 20, 1985, with considerable media focus, the two faced off at the Peugeot Talbot Games in a much-hyped 3000-meter rematch. Decker Slaney won handily (in a time more than three seconds faster than Puică's winning time in LA) with Budd finishing in fourth, nearly 13 seconds behind. *Time* magazine, still lamenting the Olympics, labeled the race "The Way It Might Have Been."[77] *Newsweek*, too, played up the redemption angle, seeing the race as an opportunity for Decker Slaney to "rise from the agonizing fall," while Budd had become "an image of the kid pushed too far too soon." But in the end, "Slaney's smile transcended the statistical paraphernalia. She had greeted Budd before the race and consoled her when it ended. And she had beaten her. Her image and her stature were intact at last, and it was with a sigh of relief that Mary Decker Slaney could tell the world, 'I'm just so happy that it's finished.'"[78]

A month later, at the Weltklasse Zurich one mile race, Decker Slaney was even more impressive, winning in a world record time of 4:16.71—with Puică finishing second, in 4:16.71, and Budd third, with

4:17.57—in a blisteringly fast race. Just nine days later in Brussels, at the Ivo Van Damme Memorial, the three finished in the same order in the 1500, with all three under 4 minutes and with 2.72 seconds separating Decker Slaney from Budd in third. Another week later they met for the last time on Europe's lucrative track and field circuit. Same three performers, same places, in a rematch of the 3000, with all three running significantly faster than Puica's Olympic gold medal time. "I had the best year performance-wise ever in 1985," Decker later reflected, and these races certainly contributed to that.[79]

The two met one last time, in 1992. Zola Pieterse had married, and her career, while respectable, had not really taken off after the promise of 1985. She still holds national records in both Great Britain and South Africa, but one imagines what that race in America's Olympics, those cascading boos, the response from her girlhood hero—when she was still that hero-worshipping girl—might have done to her. On October 16, 1992, at the Sydney mile, Mary Decker Slaney, who other than in that Olympics had been the princess, the queen, the goddess of track and field, faced off one last time with Zola Pieterse. They finished one and two, but the race was anticlimactic, as Zola's hero won by nearly ten seconds.[80]

* * *

The ability of women to compete in sport was no longer seriously in question by the 1980s. This was largely the result of the excellence of athletes like Wyomia Tyus and Mary Decker. And by that time the idea of exclusion of Black athletes would have been seen as absurd by even the most committed racists. But there were still barriers in sport, especially for those who spoke out on political and social issues, and if those speaking out were minorities, women, or both, the consequences could be stark. Much had changed in the twentieth century. But as we fast-forward to the twenty-first century we will see that the ability to speak still did not grant athletes the status of complete citizens. Athletes who deviated from the expectation to be seen and rarely heard would find that they were very much bound and very much not protected.

CHAPTER 8

Gaps between Ideals and Reality

Exclusion and Modern Sport

TITLE IX

There are thirty-seven words to Title IX of the Education Amendments of 1972: "No person in the United States shall, on the basis of sex, be excluded from participation in, be denied the benefits of, or be subjected to discrimination under any education program or activity receiving Federal financial assistance."[1]

Title IX's advocates modeled it after the Civil Rights Act of 1964 and saw it as a vital component of the legislative agenda of new wave feminism, though Title IX was only a small part of the Education Acts of 1972. The irony is that the inclusion of women in the Civil Rights Act had been intended as a poison pill to kill the landmark legislation. Representative Howard Smith, the powerful chairman of the Rules Committee and a committed segregationist, proposed adding women to Title VII of the legislation, which addressed equal employment opportunity. Although Smith actually supported expansion of women's rights—indeed, he had embraced an Equal Rights Amendment for decades by 1964—he figured the proposal would kill the bill's chance of passing. Instead, women benefited from the Civil Rights Act as a result of Smith's miscalculation. The proposed amendment, which was intended, in Smith's words, "to prevent discrimination against another minority group, the women," engendered a couple hours of mocking debate.[2] This led people to believe Smith's amendment had been a joke. Smith's inclusion of women may have been cynical, but it was not intended as a joke.

By 1972, women's rights were no longer a topic for mockery or strategic chicanery. Yet even after passage, the implications of Title IX for athletics were not immediately clear. Indeed, neither was the definition of "discrimination."

In some ways Title IX has been enormously effective. Although Title IX is wide-reaching and was never intended to be solely or primarily about sport, in terms of its public reputation, its implementation, and its implications, sports are indeed arguably the most visible area in which Title IX has had an impact—and its impact is demonstrable. This is true despite the fact that the words "sport/sports," "athletics," "extracurricular," or "NCAA" appear nowhere in the language. In the words of Laura Mogulescu, curator of the Center for Women's History at the New York Historical Society, which in 2022 ran an exhibition called "Title IX: Activism On and Off the Field": "In the 50 years since its passage, Title IX has played a hand in ushering women into higher levels of education and professional careers, opening doors to new areas of employment from corporate offices to athletic arenas, and remaking school curricula and classroom materials to discard outdated gender stereotypes."[3]

To understand why Title IX has been so important, though, a brief look at the place of women in sports prior to 1972 is warranted.

We need to be clear and celebratory about what Title IX has done but also clear about what it has not done. First, while Title IX has proven to be an enormous boon for women's sports, not all women's sports successes are the result of Title IX. Second, and more perniciously, Title IX has often been blamed at the university level for the elimination of men's college sports programs.

On the first issue, many women's sports exist outside of the traditional high school–to-college pipeline. Tennis is one of the most visible of women's sports where many of the most successful players have not been part of the school and especially the college system. The stars of the 1970s and 1980s—Billie Jean King, Chris Evert, Martina Navratilova, and others did not rise through the NCAA ranks. King's famous "Battle of the Sexes," in which she defeated former male professional Bobby

Riggs in 1973 in the Houston Astrodome (before which Riggs played the role of male chauvinist pig to perfection), certainly coincided with the political movements that fueled Title IX, but it took place completely outside of any framework to which Title IX applied. If anything, King validated Title IX; Title IX did not validate King.

Certainly, some women have utilized the NCAA in sports like tennis to move into the pro ranks. And just as the vast majority of athletes in all sports do not turn professional after college, so too has college provided opportunity for tens of thousands of tennis players who were never destined for the professional tour. But King, for example, has lamented that there were no scholarship opportunities available to her in the early 1960s when she paid her way to Los Angeles State College (now California State, Los Angeles) where she was, naturally, a dominant player who played practice matches against—and sometimes beat—the college's men's players.[4] King certainly would have benefited from Title IX, but the point here is that not all sporting successes at the elite levels fit within the NCAA framework, even before 1972. Pioneers like King fought for a generation for women's right to compete in sports, and that work needs to be recognized. In the end, Title IX should be seen as a consequence of these fights, not a cause of them.

On the second issue we need to be even more clear: There is nothing in Title IX that requires the closure of men's athletic teams. These are decisions universities have undertaken rather than provide or expand women's opportunities, but nothing in the law requires that any programs be closed. Indeed, Title IX does not even demand equal expenditures per se. Instead, the standard is the "Three Part Test," and an institution is in compliance if it meets *any one* of the parts of the test:

1. The number of male and female athletes is substantially proportionate to their respective enrollments; or

2. The institution has a history and continuing practice of expanding participation opportunities responsive to the developing interests and abilities of the underrepresented sex; or

3. The institution is fully and effectively accommodating the interests and abilities of the underrepresented sex.

It is quite clear that there are myriad ways, then, for an institution to demonstrate an effort at adherence to Title IX in college sports. Institutions that choose instead to kill men's programs have been given other options and decided not to take them. It is facile and cheap to blame women's sports and Title IX for a university's decision to, say, cut its men's wrestling program or to eliminate men's track and field.

THE TITLE IX GENERATION

Billie Jean King has called Title IX "the third most important piece of U.S. legislation in the twentieth century after the Nineteenth Amendment, which assured women's right to vote, and the Civil Rights Act of 1964."[5] King should know. She emerged as a star before Title IX, lamented not having benefited from it when she was college aged, and worked hard to support it after it was passed, starting the Women's Sports Foundation "in part to protect Title IX."[6] The legacies of Title IX are myriad, multitentacled, and far-reaching.

When I was competing in college track in the early 1990s, we hired a new assistant track coach. Because our men's and women's teams trained together and competed mostly at the same meets, our coaches were hired to coach events, not assigned to the men's or women's teams. The new sprint events coach had competed for Princeton's women's track and field team. But she was not an NCAA athlete. Instead, she competed for an organization I had never before heard of: the Association for Intercollegiate Athletics for Women (AIAW). Founded in 1971 and committed to holistic sporting development, but also to ensuring that women could compete for collegiate championships, the AIAW saw the need to organize women's collegiate athletics in a world where women's sport was an afterthought—if it was thought of at all. In the wake of the passage of Title IX it became clear that women's sports were ready to explode, but how that would happen was unclear—and the NCAA appeared to be in no hurry to facilitate that growth. As the 1970s progressed, the NCAA began to realize the importance of women's sports—or at least its own vulnerability in that arena—and worked to compete to draw women's athletics programs into the NCAA. By 1982, the NCAA effectively won that war, and the AIAW formally disbanded in 1983. The AIAW had envisioned a collegial world of women's college sports that developed the whole athlete, worrying less about elite competition than about access and opportunity. But when it folded, "the male model of athletics won out: intense and exclusionary competition, economic stratification, and less emphasis on academics."[7]

By the 1980s and early 1990s, women's basketball had surpassed track and field as the most visible manifestation of women's sporting excellence in the mainstream consciousness. Much of this stems from the dominant program that former star player–turned–coach Pat Summitt created at the University of Tennessee and the rise of the University of Connecticut women's program under coach Geno Auriemma. A ferocious rivalry developed between the two programs, with meetings between the Volunteers and Huskies becoming as hard-fought, tense, and competitive as any rivalry in sports. That Summitt had been a star women's player who rose to fame as a coach and Auriemma was a man coaching women's sport just added spice to a rivalry where occasional antipathy emerged within a framework of unquestioned mutual respect.

Summitt, who passed away in 2016 and received plaudits from across and beyond the world of sports, traced a straight line between the development of the AIAW, Title IX, and the move to the NCAA and the successes in which she played such a central part: "What these developments did was to make winning *available* to women. Previously, competition was a hobby—not a very socially acceptable one. But now that there were trophies, gold medals, and prestige on the table, women's sports surged. . . . I felt the effects immediately and personally."[8]

Those developments have also served the Women's National Basketball Association (WNBA), the most successful professional women's sports league in history, which celebrated its twenty-fifth anniversary season in 2021. The depth of talent, the quality of play, and the media attention have all improved and expanded in that quarter century, though the league still fights for recognition, pay, and respect. And tellingly, the WNBA, a league of women—of Black women, of gay and bisexual women, of moms and daughters—has been well ahead of the curve on its political commitments. Virtually always outpacing men on questions of racial justice, women's rights, and protecting the rights of the LGBTQ community, the WNBA has been the first in line, the most vocal, and the most courageous. In the words of journalist Kate Fagan, writing in an issue of *Sports Illustrated* largely dedicated to honoring the WNBA's twenty-fifth anniversary, "For nearly a quarter century the WNBA has been rowing against the headwinds of racism, sexism, and anti-LGBTQ sentiment."[9] WNBA players and teams have advocated for maternity rights in the workplace (both in and beyond the WNBA) and have supported same-sex marriage, gun control, and criminal justice reform. They have protested police shootings of unarmed victims and have generally called for police reform. They knelt early and often and longer than most athletes in most sports. Despite being paid a fraction of what their male counterparts are paid—and thus having a fraction of the job and lifetime financial security—these players have stood or knelt for what they believed in, and in so doing have elevated the profile of the league in many ways, even as it has inevitably generated criticism, hostility, and hatred. These actions and the play on the court have also gained them prominent fans, including the late Kobe Bryant, LeBron James, and the Obamas, among many others. Of course, WNBA players are so relatively underpaid that many go abroad to play in lucrative short-term professional leagues in China, Russia, and elsewhere. When Brittney Griner was arrested in Russia in 2022 on trumped-up charges (allegedly having a vape pen with traces of drugs in it) and sentenced to a decade in prison in Russia, she was there because, despite being an otherworldy talent in the WNBA, she was playing in a Russian league to supplement her relatively meager earnings.

Basketball is more popular than soccer by a long way in the United States, but women's soccer has reached unprecedented levels of popularity because of the successes of the dominant, charismatic, engaging (and politically engaged) United States Women's National Team (USWNT). Of the eight FIFA Women's World Cups that have been held since the inaugural event in 1991, the United States has won four times, in 1991, 1999, and back-to-back world championships in 2015 and 2019. The

1999 team, with Mia Hamm as the most visible of a slew of stars, is perhaps the most famous, and their performance finished with a spellbinding penalty shootout to defeat China in a tournament that the United States hosted. The most famous image of that tournament is an ecstatic Brandi Chastain stripping off her jersey and dropping to her knees in her black sports bra: an elite athlete celebrating a career-defining win, even though too many people just wanted to talk about the sports bra, a piece of sporting apparel women had been training in without something on top for well over a decade at that point.

Megan Rapinoe has been the brightest star in a constellation of stars that led the USWNT to the back-to-back wins in 2015 and 2019 and is looking to three-peat in 2023. And unlike the relatively apolitical 1999 team, many of the recent team members are deeply engaged with a range of causes, with Rapinoe, whose partner is WNBA legend Sue Bird, making them one of the great sporting super-couples, in the lead. In 2019, when the soccer magazine *Eight by Eight* interviewed Rapinoe and included a series of videos for their website, she was asked if she was excited about a visit to the White House and President Donald Trump if the team won. She replied, "I'm not going to the fucking White House!" This, of course, set off a firestorm between Rapinoe and the USWNT and Trump, who went off on the sort of tweetstorm for which he became known in the years during and surrounding his presidency. Nonetheless, most of Rapinoe's teammates supported and agreed with her.[10] The firestorm provided the backdrop for the knockout rounds of the tournament and effectively saw a president of the United States seeming to root against an American national team, with the ensuing element of spite elevating the team's already rarefied air of performance. They won, again. And they did not visit the White House. *Sports Illustrated* named Rapinoe its "Sportsperson of the Year" for 2019,[11] and *GQ* identified Rapinoe as its "Superhero of the Year" in the 2019 end-of-year issue. The magazine proclaimed, "In one summer, Megan Rapinoe went toe to toe with the president, achieved World Cup glory, and became a symbol of America at its most righteous."[12]

One of the ironies of the successes of the USWNT is that they emerged from a state of underdevelopment remarkable even by the standards of how women's sports have often been treated in the United States.[13] When the first national teams were put together in the 1980s, they were barely funded. They would gather to practice on high school fields, if they were lucky; their equipment and apparel were often hand-me-downs from the men's national team, which itself was barely a blip on the radar before the United States hosted the 1994 men's World Cup. But while the men have never really escaped beyond the middle range of the second tier of global men's soccer (and sometimes even that is a generous assessment), the women have been dominant. Thus, perhaps not surprisingly, the women have clamored for equal pay to their far less successful male compatriots. Yet when these discussions emerge, the commentary, especially from dismissive conservative male sports fans usually inclined toward deriding participation trophies, suddenly decide that in allocating resources to the women's team, the USWNT's successes matter less than how many fans attend which team's games. For these fans, it is all about winning—until it is not.

Because various iterations of women's professional soccer leagues do not have the backing of an institution like the NBA, which the WNBA enjoys, and because soccer tends to lose its luster after a given World Cup cycle passes, it has been challenging to develop a professional league in the United States, but the National Women's Soccer League (NWSL) has lasted for more than a decade and looks to be on firm footing.

Almost weekly, it seems, women are breaking barriers in sports beyond competing as athletes as well. Women are increasingly rising into front office administrative positions, in coaching in traditional male bastions, and in officiating. In 2021, the MLB Miami Marlins named Kimberley Ng general manager, making her the highest-ranking official in professional team sports in the United States. For years the San Antonio Spurs broke barriers with Becky Hammon, who climbed the Spurs' coaching ranks starting in 2014 and may have been set to become the first woman head coach in the NBA before she left the Spurs and took the head coaching job of the WNBA Las Vegas Aces in 2022. In baseball, the team that was the last to integrate became the first to hire a Black woman to serve in an on-field capacity at any level when the Red Sox hired Bianca Smith in January 2021 as a coach, albeit in their minor league organization. Nike, Oakley sunglasses, and Topps trading cards even signed her to sponsorship deals. Meanwhile, enforcing the laws on the fields and courts, in the NFL there were three women wearing the zebra stripes in the 2022 season (up from two in 2021), and in the NBA women make up approximately 10 percent of full-time referees, with those numbers growing every season. These are just samples; the trickle has not yet become a flood, but these advancements were almost unimaginable even around the turn of this century.

None of this is to imply that Title IX has been a magic bullet. There was a reason Billie Jean King continued to do work to secure the place of Title IX even after it had passed into law—legislation is, after all, only as good as its implementation and enforcement. And even as the USWNT was rising to elite status and before the WNBA took flight, a series of plaintiffs had to fight to ensure Title IX had teeth. Indeed, if the 1970s saw the victory of Title IX's passage, the 1990s saw courts ensure that victory bore fruit.

A quick sampling of some of the more significant cases gives a sense of the ways courts gave teeth to Title IX as it existed on paper. *Cannon v. University of Chicago* (1979) allowed private parties to bring suit to enforce Title IX without having to exhaust all administrative remedies—in other words, institutions could not simply drag their feet administratively to prevent a remedy.[14] In 1984, *Grove City College v. Bell* determined that Title IX applies only to schools receiving direct aid, but it could be applied to a private school that refused direct federal aid but had students who received significant aid.[15] *Franklin v. Gwinnett County Public Schools* (1992) allowed for monetary damages to be paid by institutions found in violation of Title IX, while that same year *Cohen et al. v. Brown University* affirmed the three-prong test.[16] Finally, in 1993, two other cases solidified the legal foundations of Title IX: *Gonyo v. Drake University* ruled that men cannot claim sex discrimination if an institution chooses to cut men's sports teams, and *Favia v. Indiana University of Pennsylvania* ruled that monetary and budgetary difficulties do not provide an excuse for not adhering to Title IX.[17] What is perhaps telling is that elite, theoretically progressive institutions like Brown University and the University of Chicago, self-professed conservative Christian schools like Grove City College, and state institutions alike had to be forced by the court to provide full access to athletics.

There is an irony of Title IX for HBCUs and women's colleges in that the dual impact of integration and Title IX meant that women who would otherwise have gone to underfunded but dominant Tennessee State found themselves able to go to the University of Tennessee at Knoxville or just about any university of their choosing. And there is a further Tennessee-related irony: Given the state's outsized role in gender and sports with the Tigerbelles and Pat Summitt's Volunteers, it is at least a little cruelly ironic that passage of the Equal Rights Amendment died when Tennessee failed to ratify. As Mogulescu argues, "Although society has changed in many ways, more work remains to ensure that all students have access to an education free of sex discrimination."[18]

In the summer of 2022, Serena Williams, one of the greatest athletes of this or any era, made an improbable run in the U.S. Open. The unlikelihood multiplied itself: She was nearly forty years old and was increasingly committed to her off-the-court life. She wanted to spend more time with her family, including the daughter she was eight weeks pregnant with when she won the 2017 U.S. Open. She wanted to commit more energy to her myriad business ventures. She wanted to live life beyond the tennis courts that have largely defined her when she followed her sister Venus into the professional ranks and the pair utterly redefined their sport. Lamenting the choices woman athletes have to make once they become mothers, Serena announced her pending retirement in *Vogue*: "I'm here to tell you that I'm evolving away from tennis, toward other things that are important to me."[19]

Women's tennis has been at the forefront of a comparable fight for equal pay that the U.S. women's soccer team has been waging for years. This is an argument that extends at least back to Billie Jean King's prime. In fact, one of the issues that inspired the 1973 "Battle of the Sexes" between King and Riggs was King's advocacy for equal pay for women playing in tournaments with a men's and women's draw. Riggs used that claim to equal remuneration as a foundation for the challenge. "I don't believe that women deserve the same prize money as the men, as Billie Jean King has been saying," Riggs announced at a news conference. He sent a telegram to King that read, "You insist that the top women players provide a brand of tennis comparable to the men. I challenge you to prove it on a tennis court."[20] Even after King obliterated Riggs in the nationally televised event, women's pay continued to lag behind that of men. The issue has reemerged in recent years, with men's tennis superstar Andy Murray having long advocated for pay equity.

"IF I WANT TO KISS MY BOYFRIEND, I'M GONNA KISS HIM": THE LGBTQ ATHLETE

Throughout most of the twentieth century, lesbian, gay, and bisexual athletes were invisible. This is not to say they did not exist—of course they did—but they had no choice but to remain in the closet. The danger for male team sport athletes was incalculable; for women it was not much better. In fact, sports—and especially team sports from Victorian Britain onward—were supposed to curb any urges young men might have, to suppress "unmanly" feelings, and to create homosocial bonds but crush homosexual urges. For women, there was always the question as to whether team sports might foster "unnatural" urges as well, or, as we have seen, whether sports would impact women's ability to reproduce. Sports were, then, somehow supposed to be asexual, even if everything about them, especially for men, seemed to be geared toward alpha male status, toward venerating the Big Man on Campus, toward creating larger-than-life heroes. After all, is any trope more enduring in Americana than the starting quarterback dating the head cheerleader?

Women broke this barrier long before men did. Fears that women would become lesbians as a result of sporting contact was a recurring subtext of those who looked askance at women's sports, and the homosocialization of women did occasionally result in athletes coupling—which, in turn, may well have drawn some women to sport. In the 1970s and 1980s, tennis once again led the way, and in matters of social change when tennis led the way, Billie Jean King was at the forefront. Though she had married relatively young, by the 1970s she was in a lesbian relationship even while maintaining her marriage. King was initially coy and then frank about being gay, becoming the first major professional athlete to come out in 1981. This paved the way for Martina Navratilova, the

Czech superstar who is one of the very few who can be mentioned in the same breath as Serena Williams, to come out first as bisexual, in 1981, and then later as gay.

Individual sports were one thing; team sports were another. The WNBA initially kept the very idea that the league might have lesbians in it at arm's length. But some teams realized that not only some of the league's athletes but also a large number of its fans were gay, and in the 1990s it was becoming increasingly socially acceptable to leave the closet.

So women led the way in individual and team sports, while gay (and straight) male athletes fended off rumors as slurs and played up their hetero status as soon as those rumors appeared. And gay panic could hurt athletes in myriad ways. Carl Lewis, for example, was certainly the male star of the 1984 Olympics, matching Jesse Owens's four gold medals in the 100, 200, long jump, and 4x100-meter relay. The end of his track career largely coincided with the end of the twentieth century, and many observers—UNESCO, the International Olympic Committee, and *Sports Illustrated* among them—named Lewis the athlete of the century. Yet, as historian David Goldblatt has written, Lewis "had global fame, an avid sense . . . of the commercial and extraordinary looks, and although he made a lot of money, it was not nearly as much as it should have been. Promised endorsements with Coke and Nike vaporized around the same time that the press was flooded with rumours and accusations that—Lord forbid—he might be gay."[21]

But the transition was slow for women as well. The 1999 USWNT very much embodied the straight female ideal, the team of girls next door with Mia Hamm at the forefront, whereas the World Cup–winning teams of 2015 and 2019, with Megan Rapinoe leading the way, represented a wider and more realistic range of depictions of women's sexuality. The WNBA was slow to embrace these realities even as the league developed a gay fan base. But before long some teams leaned into the diversity of their fans, and in the third decade of the twenty-first century the WNBA is undoubtedly the sporting league most accepting of gay athletes, coaches, administrators, referees, and fans.

The presence of openly gay men in professional team sports has in many ways long represented the final frontier for sporting accessibility.

After all, we know there have been gay athletes in American professional sports, but we will never know just how many; in most cases we will not know a fraction of the identities of athletes who kept a huge aspect of who they were hidden, and we will not know how they struggled—and how it might have impacted the kind of athletes they were. Sports, supposedly the ultimate meritocracy, kept gay athletes closeted, and as a result almost certainly kept dozens, hundreds, even thousands from continuing in sports past high school or college. Let's be clear: For the vast majority of the history of American college and professional sports, being an openly gay male was simply not a viable option—it would have resulted in mockery, harassment, and isolation at best, and almost certainly violence from teammates and opposition alike.

Glenn Burke invented the high five. This nearly universal gesture seems so elemental that it surely did not need inventing, and yet on October 2, 1977, when Dusty Baker hit his thirtieth home run of the season in the last game of the year, his Dodgers teammate Burke ran onto the field to congratulate Baker. As Baker finished his home run trot down the third baseline, Burke raised an open hand over his head and Baker responded as Burke had clearly indicated him to do—by slapping his upraised hand. The high five was born and spread like brushfire.

This ubiquitous dudebro gesture also found itself in another location. After he retired from baseball following the 1979 season—Burke played for the Dodgers and A's between 1976 and 1979—he continued to use the gesture in the Castro District, San Francisco's gay village and one of the first gay neighborhoods in the United States. Burke did not publicly come out as gay until a 1982 profile in *Inside Sports* magazine ("The Double Life of a Gay Dodger"), but by then the high five was not only the domain of jocks. It had also become "a symbol of gay pride."[22]

Burke was not out to his teammates, but some figured it out—or seemed to, anyway—because Burke never went out with the guys. "No one would say anything to me," he later said. He was popular in the clubhouse, and he "kept the locker room loose with his loud music, dancing, and impression of comedian Richard Pryor." He "got used to the 'f—' jokes. You heard them everywhere then." But, he said, "I knew who I was. I wasn't no sissy. I was a man. It just so happened that I lived in a different world." But there is certainly a reason why he and other athletes never came out. His Dodgers teammate Reggie Smith, looking back on baseball in the 1970s, says, "Homosexuality was taboo. I'm not going to sit here and say it was anything different. I'm sure it would have ruined his career. He would have not only been ostracized by his teammates, but management would have looked for ways to get him off the team, and the public would not have tolerated it."[23]

When he moved on to his hometown team, the Oakland A's, things became even more difficult, and it seemed like a noose was closing on him. A local newspaper reporter wrote about an unnamed A's player who regularly visited the Castro District. Fans started calling him a "f—" from the safety of the stands. A number of Oakland players were uncomfortable around him. Guys left the showers when he entered and tried to avoid rooming with him on the road. Once injuries began to take their toll, Burke knew his career was winding down: "I probably wouldn't have left" baseball "if there hadn't been the other problem, the gay thing. But put it all together, and it was too much." According to Jack McGowan, a former sports editor of the gay newspaper the *San Francisco Sentinel*, Burke "was absolutely a hero. It was not so much that he was masculine, but that he was superbly athletic, and we were proud because he showed the world that we could be gay and gifted athletes."[24]

Burke continued to be active in the Bay Area's burgeoning gay sports community and participated at a championship level in national and international competitions of gay athletes for several years. His later years were characterized by poverty and drug use, and he spent six months in prison in the early 1990s. He died of complications from AIDS in 1995 at the age of forty-two; his autobiography, *Out at Home*, came out two weeks later.[25] In 2013, Burke was posthumously part of the first class of inductees into the National Gay and Lesbian Sports Hall of Fame. In 2014, Major League Baseball honored Burke at the All-Star Game, and in 2021, the A's announced that their annual Pride Night celebration would thereafter be known as Glenn Burke Pride Night.

A small but growing number of former players have come out in recent years, as have some others in the game. Dale Scott, a longtime umpire in the majors, came out in 2014, three years before his retirement.

He followed in the footsteps of fellow umpire Dave Pallone, who was fired when his sexuality was revealed in 1988. Pallone sued and settled out of court with MLB.

The NBA, too, has had former players come out. In 2007, John Amaechi, whose five-year NBA career ended in 2005, publicly came out. He had played for two years for Utah, whose team owner also owned movie theaters and refused to allow *Brokeback Mountain* to be shown in any of them. He had also played with a deeply homophobic teammate, Tim Hardaway, who claimed that he "hated" gay people. Amaechi's coming out and the condemnation Hardaway received combined to cause him a real change of heart, and now Hardaway is a leading advocate for gay rights in El Paso. According to *Outsports*, which named Amaechi's coming out number fifteen in its hundred most important moments in LGBT sports history, "If it hadn't been for Amaechi telling his story, Hardaway likely would never have begun his journey of acceptance."[26] That said, in the wake of Amaechi's announcement only one person affiliated with the NBA—his former coach, Doc Rivers—and no one in an official capacity with the NBA itself, made contact with him. The league was, in Amaechi's words, "resoundingly silent."[27]

When Kobe Bryant called a referee a "fucking f—" in April 2014, Amaechi immediately challenged the Lakers' superstar. Bryant gave one of those "I'm sorry if you were offended" sorts of apologies and then fought the fine he received for his outburst. "When someone with the status of Kobe Bryant, arguably the best basketball player in a generation, hurls that antigay slur at a referee or anyone else—let's call it the F-word—he is telling boys, men and anyone watching that when you are frustrated, when you are as angry as can be, the best way to demean and denigrate a person, even one in a position of power, is to make it clear that you think he is not a real man, but something less," Amaechi wrote in the *New York Times* NBA blog, *Off the Dribble*. "Many people balk when L.G.B.T. people, even black ones, suggest that the power and vitriol behind another awful slur—the N-word—is no different from the word used by Kobe. I make no attempt at an analogy between the historical civil rights struggle for blacks in the United States with the current human rights struggle for L.G.B.T. people, but I can say that I am frequently called both, and the indignation, anger and at times res-ignation that course through my body are no greater or less for either. I know with both words the intent is to let me know that no matter how big, how accomplished, philanthropic or wise I may become, to them I am not even human."[28]

Like Hardaway, Bryant showed how players can be capable of change, becoming a legitimate ally to the gay community just as he became an ardent advocate for women's sports, including the WNBA. After Bryant's tragic death in a helicopter crash in January 2020, *Outsports* wrote, "His evolution represented a seismic shift in terms of LGBTQ acceptance in the testosterone-filled world of male professional sports."[29] There is no doubt that people like John Amaechi were central to that evolution.

Jason Collins's coming out was even more significant. Collins was still an active, albeit unsigned, NBA player when he announced that he was gay after the 2012–2013 season.[30] Collins, a Stanford graduate, had a long career in the NBA as a journeyman and role player, averaging 3.6 points and 3.5 rebounds per game over his career. For a while it looked like he would not be signed after his historic announcement, and the debate over the willingness or ability of teams in the NBA to sign openly gay players was ready to launch, complicated by the fact that Collins was unquestionably at the end of his career and would be a depth acquisition at most. He had made his sexuality public, thus making suspicions valid even if Collins was no lock to sign with a team. But in early 2014, the Brooklyn Nets signed Collins to a ten-day contract, which they extended, and Collins played in twenty-two games, starting one, and averaging 7.8 minutes, .9 rebounds, and 1.1 points per game in his time as a Net. Nonetheless, his time in Brooklyn—he had spent the first seven years of his career with the Nets when they were in New Jersey—made history in the NBA and in professional sports.

Collins was the first out active player in one of the "Big Four" pro-fessional men's sports leagues in North America. It should, however, be noted that Robbie Rogers, a soccer player who played in Europe and for the United States Men's National Team (USMNT) became the first out player in Major League Soccer in 2013, making him the true pioneer in North American men's professional team sports. Rogers and Collins had a conversation for *Out* magazine in 2017 about being openly gay athletes in professional sports. "I become a little sad when I think that when I retire, there really won't be any of us," Rogers lamented, referring specifically to male professional athletes. "Then who will be in the locker room, who will be in the sports arena changing the culture? The way to change things for more athletes to come out is for more athletes to come out. Which is sad, but that's the answer." Collins agreed: "Cheers to the next athlete coming out."[31]

Michael Sam broke the next barrier in men's team sports in 2014. The NFL represented what many assumed would be the last bastion to fall when it came to gay athletes. Sam, a defensive lineman, was a great college player for the University of Missouri, a consensus All-American, and the SEC defensive player of the year in 2013. He came out as gay after his college playing career, and the usual concerns about whether he would be drafted—and if not, if it was because he was gay—emerged. The NFL, perhaps more than any other sports league on earth, has created a narrative of aversion to "distractions," and the belief was that a gay player would represent a media circus and thus the ultimate distraction. But despite Sam's unquestionable credentials, his measurables—size, speed, strength, agility, and the like—did not guarantee him a high draft position, especially since he did not really have an NFL positional fit and had a mediocre performance at the meat market that was the February 2014 NFL Scouting Combine. The SEC is by far the best conference in college football, yet every year former SEC stars fail to make teams, never mind excel in the NFL. Thus, while one certainly could suspect that Sam falling out of the draft might have been a sign of bigotry, it also could have been a sign of skepticism about Sam's place in the NFL. Most likely, it would be a combination of both.

Nonetheless, the St. Louis Rams, just two hours from the University of Missouri, made Sam their seventh-round draft pick. In the midst of Sam's emotional celebration, he and his boyfriend, Vito Cammisano, a former Missouri swimmer, drew a great deal of attention—much of it positive, but a lot of it ugly, homophobic, and cruel, and amplified because of the growing power of social media.[32] Sam responded defiantly, "If I want to kiss my boyfriend, I'm gonna kiss him."[33] Draft picks are caught on camera kissing their significant (and sometimes not-so-significant) others all the time, yet this one draw criticism and consternation. One need not dig too deeply to figure out why. Sam fought hard but never made the Rams, and after being cut by them in 2014 he was unable to make the roster of the Dallas Cowboys.

Nonetheless, Sam won a number of honors in 2014 in recognition of his courage and accomplishments, including being named a *GQ* Man of the Year, being named a finalist for the *Sports Illustrated* Sportsperson of the Year Award, and winning the Arthur Ashe Courage Award at the 2014 ESPN ESPY Awards. He eventually appeared in one game for the Montreal Alouettes of the Canadian Football League, a history-making debut in 2015. After taking a hiatus from football, Sam signed on to be a coach for the Barcelona Dragons of the European League of Football in April 2022, but after an injury to a player in camp in early June, he ended up starting at defensive line in their opening game on June 5.

For all of the progress gay male athletes have made, it has been slow and it has been modest. When Carl Nassib, a defensive end for the Las Vegas Raiders, announced that he was gay on June 21, 2021, during Pride Month, he was the only active gay athlete in a major American men's team sport. In his announcement on Instagram he also pledged $100,000 to the Trevor Project, which provides suicide prevention and crisis support for LGBTQ and questioning teenagers.

In his first game after he made his announcement, the Raiders' season opener against the Baltimore Ravens, Nassib had a strip sack of Ravens quarterback Lamar Jackson in overtime. The Raiders recovered and went on to score the winning touchdown. Nassib has more than two dozen quarterback sacks in his NFL career, which continued in 2022 for the Tampa Bay Buccaneers, with whom he signed after being released by the Raiders. He is clearly a talented NFL football player, but he is historically much more important than that. He is a pioneer who has showed enormous courage. In the words of historian John Howard, Nassib "is a gentle giant among mere mortals."[34]

Sam and Nassib operate in the shadows of Dave Kopay, who played as a running back for eight years in the NFL. Mostly a journeyman, Kopay carried the ball 235 times for 876 yards and scored two touchdowns. He played in 111 games, starting 13. He also was an able pass catcher, including four for touchdowns, and returned the occasional kick and punt for five teams. While he remained closeted during his career, which ended in 1972, he came out in 1975 after reading an article in the *Washington Star* about the difficulties gay athletes faced. The article quoted an unnamed former teammate whom Kopay could identify as Jerry Smith, with whom he had shared a sexual encounter, and after reading the report Kopay decided to tell his own story. He hoped that he and Smith could write a book together, but Smith never came out (he died of AIDS in 1987) and Kopay honored Smith's desire for anonymity. He contacted Lynn Rosellini, the author of the *Star* piece, which had received considerable hate mail, including a number maintaining that she had to be lying, that the macho sport of football simply couldn't have any gay players. He went on the record, came out, and became the first American professional athlete to do so. This moment is so vital that *Outsports* named it number one on its list of the one hundred most important moments in LGBT sports history.[35]

Kopay did not receive a lot of hate mail about the story: "Mostly the mail that poured in was amazingly supportive and telling their own stories. There were hundreds of letters forwarded to me." As a result of the article, he wrote his own memoir, *The David Kopay Story: An Extraordinary Self-Revelation*, which came out in 1977, went on to become a best-seller, remains in print, and had a profound impact on athletes from Billie Jean King to anonymous teens who would later thank Kopay for saving their lives.[36] When *Outsports* was putting together its list of the hundred most important moments in LGBT sports history there were lots of debates and disagreements, but according to *Outsports* cofounder Jim Buzinski, "When it came to picking the top moment, though, our experts were unanimous—it was Dave Kopay, the most significant gay athlete in modern history."[37]

After Kopay, only five other former NFL players have come out as gay, with the still-active Nassib the sixth. Roy Simmons, a lineman who played for the New York Giants and Washington Redskins from 1979 to 1983, was the first to follow Kopay, in 1992. Esara Tualo (2002), Wade Davis (2012), Kwame Harris (2013), Ryan O'Callaghan (2017), and

Colton Underwood (2021) have all come out in this century. Indeed, while the number of openly gay athletes remains a trickle, a little perspective is in order: From the origins of American professional sports with the establishment of the National League in 1876 through the year 2000, four men came out as gay, all after the end of their careers. In addition to Glenn Burke and Dave Kopay, there was also former Major League Baseball player Billy Bean, who played for three major league teams from 1987 to 1995, and Simmons. That's it. That is the entire list, and the earliest of them played starting in the late 1960s. And some of Tualo's teammates later admitted that had he come out during his career he almost certainly would have been targeted for injury and other abuse. Any change is thus enormously welcome and important, even if it is too slow in coming. One hopes that more athletes can have the freeing experience Kopay writes about in his autobiography, which closes, "It's a new life for me now—without football, living openly as a homosexual. But I'm facing it with the strength of an honest man. And that's got to be a good beginning."[38]

OF TERFS AND TURF: TRANS ATHLETES IN MODERN SPORT

One of the most treacherous hot-button issues in recent years has been the question of trans athletes competing in sports. This is, by and large, a culture war creation. Thus far it seems that right-wing politicians in states across the country are passing laws aimed to oppress. As of December 2022, eighteen states had passed laws restricting or banning trans girls from competing in a wide range of sports, even though in the vast majority of those states there had been zero cases of such athletes trying to compete.[39] In other words, these were symbolic red meat, anti-trans gestures, not policies aimed at addressing real issues their constituencies faced.

Given the suicide rates and other issues faced by trans teens and young adults, this cruel approach seems especially loathsome, acts of hostility to no particular end other than the hostility itself. For many on the modern right, the cruelty is not an ancillary outcome to their policies—the cruelty is the point. And this is not to say that there are no concerns; just because the modern right is often cruel does not mean concerns about protecting girls' and women's sports for girls and women should be ignored.

The difficulty becomes clear when we consider the fact that there is a history of men competing as women in sports—not as trans athletes, but as cheaters. But the consequences of these few incidents have been rigorous and ugly, sometimes resulting in gender policing in which invasive (and thus abusive) policies have emerged to monitor girls and women.[40] In general, girls and women deserve their own spaces for sport. In general, trans athletes should be able to participate in all aspects of society, including sports. But the space in between "in general" is the issue—and sports science will have to be a major part of the solution. This is especially alarming since sport science has often been the pretext for abuses to begin with. Yet the vast majority of sport science has been a force for good, for better performance but also for better athlete health. So we will need answers to myriad questions. At what point have individuals transitioned enough, through hormone blocking and other efforts, to ensure that they are not just men competing as women? At what age should this happen? What are the possible side effects, especially for adolescent athletes?

Once puberty hits, boys and girls are different physically and athletically, and men and women are definitely different—and when we are talking about high levels of sport in particular, any added advantage to an athlete can be a massive difference maker. What qualifies as a good high school boys shot put, for example, might be elite in women's competition. Yet the overwhelming majority of trans athletes, especially trans girls who want to participate in sports, simply want to have fun, to play, to be part of a team. It is enormously cynical to imagine that any significant number of trans athletes who want to compete are tenting their fingers and scheming in hopes of winning women's Olympic medals. It would be naive to imagine that there won't be some fraction of men attempting to abuse those rules, or that there won't be cynical politicians and others pushing other conservative men to playact as trans to prove a larger political point. But making sweeping laws for bad actors seems cynical at best.

A number of very vocal women, some of them quite famous, have earned the label "trans-exclusionary radical feminists" (TERFs). They have been unremittingly hostile to transgender people, especially trans women. And they have revealed that their demand to protect female spaces is often more derived from anti-trans bigotry than anything else. But the uncomfortable question is, what are female spaces? And the uncomfortable answer has to recognize some number of bad faith actors who are abusing unclear, undefined concepts of transgenderism to do some horrible things—things far worse than simply taking a medal podium spot at a high school track meet. We shouldn't make cruel and symbolic policies at the expense of trans teens, but maybe we should recognize that the biggest threat to women, in America and worldwide, has always been men, and that men acting in bad faith—and more than that, simply bad men—will find, use, and exploit loopholes. We shouldn't confuse outliers for means. We also should not assume that outliers don't exist. In other words, when writing laws and policies, we should not write for the outliers, but we need to take them into account. We do a disservice to the discussion to pretend that there are no debates here, and that all feminists who are skeptical of opening the doors to all self-declared trans athletes are necessarily TERFS—and even if they are, that all of them are always wrong all the time. Pretending that these are easy issues does a disservice to transgender athletes, to women, to girls, and, frankly, to all of us.

Conclusion: Taking a Knee

Sport and Politics in Twenty-First-Century America

OH SAY CAN YOU SEE? FLAG CONTROVERSIES

In many ways, then, we come back to where we began—with the American flag, the national anthem, and the attempt to use sport to define patriotism and to exclude based on those misconceptions of that patriotism. In 1918, during World War I, the playing of "The Star Spangled Banner" was both obviously political and relatively innocuous—"relatively" because that event occurred against a backdrop of an American society where criticism of the war and American involvement in it could get you jailed for sedition and other charges that had the support of the Wilson administration. Thus, in 1918, the intertwining of politics, nationalism, the anthem, and sport began what would become a complicated and usually not especially nuanced relationship, especially inasmuch as sport in the United States deeply reflected the country's segregation, sexism, xenophobia, and homophobia.

The nativist America First backdrop of the 1918 World Series was heightened by the Great War, but those sentiments would never entirely disappear when putative American patriotism intersected with sports. "The playing of the national anthem should be as much a part of every game as the kickoff," NFL Commissioner Elmer Layden asserted in 1945, after the conclusion of World War II. "We must not drop it simply because the war is over, we should never forget what it stands for."[1] This began a custom the NFL maintains to the current day, one that became a league rule in 1978.

Colin Kaepernick thus inherited a long and fraught tradition when he first sat and then later kneeled during the national anthem before football games in 2016 in protest against white supremacy and especially police violence against Black people. He was especially horrified by the death of Mario Woods, who had been shot twenty times by San Francisco police on December 2, 2015. In August 2016, Kaepernick sat on the sidelines during the playing of the national anthem before a preseason game. The first two weeks, no one even noticed—or at least felt the need to point it out. After the August 26 preseason game against the Packers, Jennifer Lee Chan, a beat writer for *Niners Nation*, captured an image of Kaepernick sitting during the anthem and tweeted it to the world. The tweet "went viral, prompting international media attention, and inspiring intense national debates over issues of racial inequality, police brutality, patriotism, and social justice activism's role in sports."[2]

The next week, after consulting with NFL player and former Green Beret Nate Boyer, Kaepernick and star safety Eric Reid kneeled during the playing of the anthem. They continued to kneel, with more and more players across the league joining each week. From there a conflagration raged. Kaepernick initially claimed, "I am not going to stand up to show pride in a flag for a country that oppresses Black people and people of color. To me, this is bigger than football and it would be selfish on my part to look the other way. There are bodies in the street and people . . . getting away with murder."[3]

Reid, writing in the *New York Times*, justified and explained his and Kaepernick's position, and that of increasing numbers of players, a year after the players first engaged in the kneeling gesture. As he watched the numbers of African Americans killed by police, one—the killing of Alton Sterling in Baton Rouge, Reid's hometown—really stood out. When Kaepernick first started sitting for the anthem, "to be honest, I didn't notice at the time, and neither did the media." But once the media did notice, "the backlash against him began." Reid wanted to get involved, and he and Kaepernick "spoke at length about many of the issues that face our community, including systemic oppression against people of color, police brutality and the criminal justice system. We also discussed how we could use our platform, provided to us by being professional athletes in the NFL, to speak for those who are voiceless." At that point, they met with Boyer and "came to the conclusion that we should kneel, rather than sit, the next day during the anthem as a peaceful protest. We chose to kneel because it is a respectful gesture. I remember thinking our posture was like a flag flown at half-mast to mark a tragedy."[4]

It thus "baffle[d]" Reid "that our protest is still being misconstrued as disrespectful to the country, flag and military personnel. We chose it because it's exactly the opposite. It has always been my understanding that the brave men and women who fought and died for our country did so to ensure that we could live in a fair and free society, which included the right to speak out in protest." Far from being anti-American, Reid argued, "It goes without saying that I love my country and I'm proud to be an American. But, to quote James Baldwin, 'exactly for this reason, I insist on the right to criticize her perpetually.'"[5]

But in the United States the very act of criticism, especially when it comes from Black people, is a problem. A lot of people who scream and shout about freedom really mean freedom for them, and not for others. As writer Brit Bennett has put it, "The suddenness of" the anger of those who oppose not only Kaepernick and the kneelers, but anyone who supports them, "always surprised me. Kneeling is, almost universally, considered a gesture of humility and respect. On the football field players take a knee when someone gets injured. In different faiths, kneeling is a common posture of prayer. Servitude even. And yet, kneeling during the anthem inspires rage because the issue, of course, is not the anthem or flag or military. The problem is black disobedience. A kneeling black body becomes dangerous because a disobedient black body is dangerous."[6]

It thus did not matter that Kaepernick added his time and money to his protest. He founded the Know Your Rights Camp initiative and promised that he would protest until the flag "represents what it's supposed to represent." The first of these camps "featured a set of ten fundamental rights: to be free, healthy, brilliant, safe, loved, courageous, alive, trusted, and educated, and to know your rights."[7] Knowing one of the main attack lines of his critics, he asserted, "I'm not anti-American. I love America."[8] Even in the midst of his protest, Kaepernick ultimately "affirm[ed] Black optimism," despite his trenchant critiques of many of America's racial ills.[9]

Kaepernick's self-defenses were all for naught as his attackers ruthlessly fulminated against him on social media, burned his jersey, and engaged in the patriotism-for-show that accompanies these sorts of stories. No matter how earnest Kaepernick was about his outrage and sadness over the deaths of Mario Woods and Oscar Grant, Rekia Boyd and Michael Brown, Tamir Rice and Laquan McDonald, Sandra Bland and Freddie Gray, and so many others, he had become a figure in the culture wars, where reason and rationale have no place—especially when many of the critics are motivated as much by racism as by patriotism.

And the most vocal critic, with the biggest megaphone, was candidate and then president Donald Trump, who throughout his time in office condemned Kaepernick, other players who kneeled, and the league itself for not cracking down with the ruthlessness he hoped to see against the offending players. In August 2016, after Kaepernick's protest first came to light, Trump, by then the Republican nominee for president, said on *The Don Monson Show*, "I think it's a terrible thing, and you know, maybe he should find a country that works better for him. Let him try. It won't happen." By March 2017, Trump hinted that Kaepernick had not been signed as a free agent because NFL owners feared his poisoned tweets. NFL owners "don't want to get a nasty tweet from Donald Trump. Do you believe that?" Protests continued and indeed accelerated in 2017. So did Trump's tone about kneeling players. During a rally in Alabama in September 2017, Trump declared, "Wouldn't you love to see one of these NFL owners, when somebody disrespects our flag, to say, 'Get that son of a bitch off the field right now. Out! He's fired. He's fired.'" In October of that year, Vice President Mike Pence got in on the act. He attended an Indianapolis Colts game at Lucas Oil Stadium and made a big display of leaving the stadium as soon as some players kneeled, in a clearly planned moment. Indeed, on Twitter Trump suggested that he orchestrated Pence's performative display. NFL Commissioner Roger Goodell became a target of Trump when the NFL refused to punish players or force them to stand for the anthem. The same month that Pence cosplayed culture warrior, Trump attacked Goodell and the NFL after the league refused to impose a policy on the players—70 percent of whom, remember, are Black—"Total respect for our great country!" The tweets, often selectively capitalized, continued through 2020. Trump never relented, but the issue largely faded from public consciousness except as an occasional culture war flare-up.[10] Football, by far the country's most popular sport, and the NFL, by far the country's most popular sports league, "had become the most polarizing professional sport in the United States."[11]

NFL players refused to be cowed by Trump's outbursts. The weekend before the Alabama rally where Trump excoriated the kneeling "sons of bitches" in the NFL, six players kneeled during the anthem at NFL games. The weekend after, more than two hundred kneeled or remained in the locker room. Yet, like a toddler throwing a tantrum, Trump got exactly the attention that he wanted—"more proof to his base," as the journalist John Feinstein put it, "that Black athletes were 'unpatriotic,' even though the protests never had anything to do with patriotism."[12]

Kaepernick's protest was not against NFL rules and certainly was not illegal, but that was largely immaterial. He was in the center of the storm, and he did not have enough ballast to keep from getting swept up. The NFL responded in 2018 by creating rules that players had to stand during the anthem or face a fine, though they could stay in the locker room when the anthem played. This splitting of the baby "made no one happy and created its own backlash," and the NFL ultimately did not even enforce it.[13] Kaepernick proved inspirational for the Black Lives Matter (BLM) movement, even as he was blackballed by the NFL. Dave Zirin refers to his outsized influence as "The Kaepernick Effect," explaining that "the masses of athletes who took a knee between 2016 and 2018" represented "the canary in the coal mine, signaling the coming struggle and also laying the groundwork for what we saw in 2020" with the nationwide BLM protests, which, despite conservative misrepresentations, were overwhelmingly peaceful and affirmative.[14] Literally tens of thousands of high school and college athletes followed in Kaepernick's wake and modeled his example. One journalist has characterized Kaepernick and those who followed his example as "football's fearless activists."[15]

Kaepernick was far from the first person to use the anthem as a forum for protest. At the Opening Ceremonies of the 1958 Pan-American

Games in Chicago, Eroseanna "Rose" Robinson, a Black athlete representing the United States in the women's high jump, remained sitting during the national anthem at Soldier Field. She was not impressed by "the bloated displays of American greatness. To her, the anthem and the flag represented war, injustice, and hypocrisy." Robinson, a social worker, had already been deeply involved in civil rights activism with the Congress of Racial Equality (CORE) for years by the time of her decision not to stand for the anthem at the Pan-Am Games. Indeed, the year before, at the height of the Cold War and in the wake of winning the AAU national championship in the high jump, she refused to go on a State Department–sponsored tour of the Soviet Union, declaring, "I don't want to be used as a political pawn."[16] She was well aware that the disproportionately Black track team would return to an America where she and many of her teammates were not allowed to drink at the same water fountains or attend the same universities as their white teammates in large swaths of the country. Robinson would spend the rest of her life active in civil rights and pacifist causes.

At the beginning of the 1995–1996 NBA season, Mahmoud Abdul-Raouf of the Denver Nuggets decided he would no longer stand for the anthem before games. Abdul-Raouf (known as Chris Jackson before he changed his name after converting to Islam) believed the flag was a "symbol of oppression, of tyranny." Instead, he sat on one of the sideline chairs that make up the bench area, stretch on the sidelines, or else remain in the locker room while it played. No one even noticed until March, when a local reporter wrote a small blurb about Abdul-Raouf's anthem protest and that opened up a floodgate of media attention. A nonstory became a local story, which became a national story.[17] Predictably, Abdul-Raouf found himself vilified in the press and by conservative fans. The American Legion declared that he was "treasonous."[18] The NBA suspended Abdul-Raouf for one game but then decided to force him to stand, allowing him to close his eyes and look away from the flag, praying into his hands. He was traded before the next season and within two years was out of the league, coming back for one last season two years later, even though—much like Kaepernick a generation in the future—he was clearly still good enough to still play in the league.

In 2003, on the eve of the U.S. invasion of Iraq by the George W. Bush administration, Toni Smith, the captain of the women's basketball team at Manhattanville College, a Division III school in Purchase, New York, turned her back to the flag during the national anthem before the Valiants' games. At one game, a Vietnam War veteran ran onto the court and held a flag in front of her face. According to historian Marc Ferris, "Smith's stance ignited a debate over her constitutionally protected, free-speech right to protest versus her duty to avoid making waves before every game."[19] But hers was more than a simple protest against the Bush administration's mendacious march to war. "It wasn't an anti-war protest in the sense that I just wanted to be against the war," she later said. "It was an anti-war protest in the sense that the war was emblematic of the ways that the country perpetuates these practices domestically . . . that the way it punishes and kills is always handed out more harshly on Black and Brown communities. It was important to me that people connect the two."[20]

A decade after 9/11, Goshen College, a Mennonite School with an NAIA athletic program, announced that it would replace "The Star Spangled Banner" with "America the Beautiful." The violent nature of the anthem's lyrics clashed with the college's mission, expressed in its slogan, "Healing the world, peace by peace." As the college explained, "Goshen College made a decision in 2011 to play 'America the Beautiful' instead of the 'Star-Spangled Banner' before athletic events because it fits with our national sports tradition and honors this country, while better resonating with our Christ-centered core values (passionate learning, compassionate peacemaking, servant leadership and global citizenship) and respecting the views of our diverse constituencies. We stand by the freedom of all to express their religious faith, love for this country and hopes for change in different ways."[21]

At the Pan-American Games in 2019, gold medal-winning hammer thrower Gwen Berry echoed Rose Robinson's quiet protest from nearly seventy years earlier when she bowed her head and raised a fist during the playing of the anthem. Her image of proud defiance evoked that of Carlos and Smith from Mexico City in 1968. "America can do better," Berry said, and defended her activism by asserting, "Athletes are humans. Just because we decide to dedicate our lives to a sport doesn't mean we don't have an opinion about world issues." As the 2020 Olympics approached (COVID-19 would delay them until 2021), the United States Olympic Committee reprimanded Berry and put her on probation for a year, effectively threatening her career if she protested again and costing her about $50,000 in endorsement deals. She remained unbowed: "When you see something that isn't right, speak out. When you experience something that is inhuman, tell someone. This is how you can begin to sprinkle change onto the issue. It is imperative that you speak up for what is right. We should encourage all we can and speak power and strength to anyone that will listen."[22] After she faced deep, vicious criticism for a similar protest during the U.S. Olympic Trials in 2021, Berry asserted that people placed "patriotism over basic morality" and maintained that in the wake of the way so many feigned interest in the BLM movement that "the commercials, statements, and phony sentiments regarding black lives were just a hoax."[23] In the wake of the protests over George Floyd's murder at the hands of Minneapolis police, the U.S. Olympic and Paralympic Committee (USOPC) issued a statement that it "stands with those who demand equality." Berry found the statement hypocritical and galling. As she tweeted, "I want an apology letter . . . mailed . . . just like you and the IOC MAILED ME WHEN YOU PUT ME ON PROBATION." She later called for a public apology in light of the rampantly self-serving way the USOPC had acted.[24] As with so many Black athletes, Berry was well ahead of the organization she represented and that had earlier called her out.

The NFL similarly backtracked and effectively tried to erase its own mealymouthed history as a result of the Black Lives Matter protests and marches that took place after Floyd's murder. Goodell effectively reversed any league policies and criticism with regard to kneeling in June 2020: "The protests around the country are emblematic of centuries of silence, inequality and oppression of black players, coaches, fans and staff. We are listening. I am listening, and I will be reaching out to players who have raised their voices and others on how we can improve and go forward for a better and more united NFL family." Gutlessly, he never mentioned Kaepernick's name. This caused star defensive back Tyrann

Mathieu to respond on Twitter, "Not to spoil the ending for you, but the pure-hearted win in the end. Remember that."[25] It is thus perhaps not surprising that *Sports Illustrated* gave its 2020 "Sportsperson of the Year" award to "The Activist Athlete."[26]

There is also a long history of fan hypocrisy and general apathy during the anthem performances at sporting events. In 1954, Arthur Ehlers, a World War I veteran and the general manager of the Baltimore Orioles, complained that fans talked, fidgeted, and generally ignored the anthem. He found that behavior "distasteful," but he also made the point that playing it before every game "tends to cheapen the song and lessen the thrill of response," so he decided to eliminate the playing of the anthem before games.[27] This lasted about a month, until the Baltimore City Council weighed in, reminding Ehlers and the Orioles that Francis Scott Key had written the song in response to the flag he saw flying at Fort McHenry, which was also one of the city's main tourist attractions. The council passed a unanimous resolution encouraging the playing of "The Star-Spangled Banner" before all games.

Fans across the country also engage in participatory rituals that certainly are as disrespectful of the anthem as anything any protester has ever done. In Baltimore fans scream out "O" when the song reaches the line "Oh say does that Star Spangled Banner yet wave." Fans of the Washington Capitals yell out "Oh!" and "Red!" over those words in the song. A group of Houston Rockets fans known as "The Red Rowdies" scream "Rockets red glare" during the anthem. In my hometown in New Hampshire, when the anthem is played before Newport Tigers football games, fans and players replace "free" in "Land of the Free" with "Tigers," players raising their helmets as they scream the word. Americans play act as if the anthem is sacred to them—except for all those times when it isn't.

Yet the backdrop for Kaepernick's protest was heightened by an American political context in which, as one historian has written, "patriotism and American professional sports had long ago merged into a strategic alliance, even as its emphasis ebbed and flowed with public sentiment. Since the September 2001 terrorist attacks that felled New York's World Trade Center, football, with its large crowds, pregame pageantry, and extensive television coverage, had become an especially potent stage for increased patriotic fervor."²⁸ And so when players pushed back, reawakened activism, and stood for something beyond sport, there was an ironic backlash—fundamentally conservative professional sports leagues had suddenly become "too woke, too liberal, or too tied to the Democratic party," despite the fact that sports owners donate far more to Republican politicians than to Democrats. Conservative figures from Donald Trump to Sean Hannity to Tucker Carlson railed against the leagues, their players, and the owners who refused to crush them. The fact that these issues are so closely connected to race is no coincidence. In the words of Alex Shephard of the *New Republic*, all accusations aside, "It is really the right . . . that has insisted on pushing politics into professional sports. In its universe, keeping politics out of sports means pretending that a racist voting law doesn't exist; it means insisting that there is no world outside the arena, which has never been true and is itself a political position."²⁹

There were questions as to whether professional sports teams—private entities operating in a private league, to be sure, though many of them playing in taxpayer funded stadiums—could force their players to stand at attention for the anthem. While employers may be able to prohibit protest, can they mandate patriotism? And can they do so in publicly funded stadiums? After all, they could not mandate that a Jehovah's Witness stand for the anthem without running into serious constitutional issues. More importantly, though, sports owners found themselves in an awkward position, as in the NFL and especially the NBA majorities—usually large majorities—of their players are Black and overwhelmingly understand the nature of Kaepernick's critiques whether they chose to kneel or not, and thus the owners and league could not exactly push too far. Players had leverage and knew it, especially as white allies joined the cause.

When the anthem protest movement spread to colleges and then high schools, the debate became more interesting. As far back as 1943, in *West Virginia State Board of Education v. Barnette*, the Supreme Court declared that school districts could not mandate patriotic "rituals." In so doing the court overruled one of its own decisions, *Minersville School District v. Gobitis*, from just three years earlier.³⁰ The Barnettes were Jehovah's

Witnesses whose religion prohibited them from saluting the flag, saying the Pledge of Allegiance, or participating in anthem ceremonies, as their faith proscribes that these activities as acts of worship or idolatry that conflict with their understanding of biblical teachings. As a result of their adherence to these principles, hundreds of Jehovah's Witnesses across the country faced ridicule, harassment, and violence in the World War II era. As Justice Robert Jackson wrote in the 6–3 majority opinion, "If there is any fixed star in our constitutional constellation, it is that no official, high or petty, can prescribe what shall be orthodox in politics, nationalism, religion, or other matters of opinion or force citizens to confess by word or act their faith therein."[31] Protest certainly falls under the protections of this decision. After all, as the majority argued, "the very purpose of a Bill of Rights was to withdraw certain subjects from the vicissitudes of political controversy, to place them beyond the reach of majorities and officials and to establish them as legal principles to be applied by the courts."[32] It is thus significant that *Barnette* "invok[ed] the broad Free Speech Clause of the First Amendment rather than relying primarily on the Religion Clause." In other words, even in a case in which religious freedom was at issue, the court chose to take a more expansive free speech view of the flag controversy.[33]

The Supreme Court has regularly defended the right of students to protest as well, most prominently in *Tinker v. Des Moines Independent Community School District.* In that 1969 decision, the court upheld the right of students to protest the Vietnam War, in this case by wearing black armbands, a gesture the school district tried to ban. In this decision Justice Abe Fortas, writing for the majority, presented his famous dictum that students do not "shed their constitutional rights to freedom of speech or expression at the schoolhouse gate." The case emphasized whether acts of protest caused "substantial disruption," which does not result from students wearing armbands or, say, kneeling silently during the national anthem, both of which fall under the ruling's categories of gestures "akin to pure speech." The court rejected the possibility that such gestures might inspire disruption form others: "In our system undifferentiated fear or apprehension of disturbance is not enough to overcome the right to freedom of expression." Otherwise, of course, all one would need to do to crush free speech would be to, say, start a fight. Furthermore, schools cannot assert that participation in sports or other extracurricular activities is a privilege and not a right. "A student's rights," Fortas wrote, "do not embrace merely the classroom hours. When he is in the cafeteria, or on the playing field, or on the campus during authorized hours, he may express his opinions, even on controversial subjects such as the war in Vietnam, if he does so without materially and substantially interfering with the requirements of appropriate discipline in the operation of the school and without colliding with the rights of others." After all, "the constitutional right at issue is freedom of expression, not that of participation in extracurricular activities."[34] Federal courts have also affirmed that institutions cannot use the end-around of forbidding activities—like kneeling, or the vast majority of expressions on social media—through restrictions in codes of conduct or other rules.[35] In the end, one is reminded of the observation of Justice Oliver Wendell Holmes Jr. that "every American believes in free speech unless it's speech he doesn't agree with," an assertion that more and more seems to apply across the United States and beyond.[36]

Professional, college, and high school athletes are increasingly realizing their power. Football players were instrumental in the resignation in 2015 of University of Missouri president Tim Wolfe, which followed "months of escalating racial tension" on campus, including protests after the killing of Michael Brown in Ferguson, Missouri, in August 2014; swastikas being painted on campus; the student body president being accosted by a group of students who screamed the N-word at him; a play rehearsal being interrupted by a drunk white man yelling racial slurs; and more. There were a number of protest events in response and demands for the feckless Wolfe to resign, but arguably the tipping point came when a group of Black football players threatened to stop participating in football-related activities, including games and practices, which drew the support of white head coach Gary Pinkel and his staff.[37]

Several voices have weighed in advocating for Black students, including athletes, to consider HBCUs to pursue their academic and athletic careers, believing those institutions will care about them as people and not just as enrollment figures that allow them to brag about diversity numbers or as star athletes to juice their sports teams. After all, as journalist Jemele Hill has written, HBCUs "invested in black people when there was no athletic profit to reap."[38] Certainly Hall of Famer Deion Sanders taking the coaching reins for Jackson State for three seasons, drawing unprecedented numbers of five-star recruits and outstanding teams on the field, is an example of this, though Sanders's decision to leave Jackson State in late 2022 to take over head coaching duties at Colorado serves as a reminder of the allure of the big-time programs even as Sanders did enormous amounts of good for the Mississippi-based HBCU and left it in a good position for future success.

And thus when Trump weighed in on Kaepernick's protest, on all kneeling players, and on the NFL itself for not reacting the way he thought Goodell and the league office ought to and more than implying that there ought to be firm and ruthless consequences, it was clear that Trump's (and his supporters') commitment to those principles was always selective at best. To be clear, Trump was not violating the First Amendment per se, but he certainly was using the weight of the presidency to lean on the free speech rights of private individuals. He was not, after all, merely disagreeing with the content of the protests. He was disputing whether they had the right to protest at all.

And one wonders about the nature of a national anthem so fragile that its power is diminished by someone protesting during it. As Jackson wrote in his majority opinion in *Barnette*, "To believe that patriotism will not flourish if patriotic ceremonies are voluntary and spontaneous, instead of a compulsory routine, is to make an unflattering estimate of the appeal of our institutions to free minds."[39] Celebratory patriotism, as historian Ben Railton reminds us, is not the only form of patriotism.[40]

In February 2019, Kaepernick and Reid reached a settlement with the NFL that amounted to an admission that they had been blackballed, likely illegally, for their political activity. Reid had made his way back to the league. Kaepernick never did.

Occasionally a national anthem performance draws attention for something beyond either noteworthy musicianship or the intersection of politics and the song. Before Game 1 of the 2022 World Series, Eric Burton, the lead singer of the band War, forgot the words to the anthem. The

response, though occasionally sanctimonious, was mostly one of bemuse-
ment. There have been other similarly disastrous renditions of a song that
is notoriously hard to sing. Some of them are so bad they simply become
a joke. Legendary track and field athlete Carl Lewis was enlisted to sing
the anthem at the Meadowlands before the New Jersey Nets hosted the
Chicago Bulls on January 21, 1993. The rendition was so horrific that
legendary ESPN *SportsCenter* anchor Charlie Steiner referred to Lewis
as "Francis Scott Off-Key."[41]

On July 25, 1990, Rosanne Barr, always a lightning rod for controversy, did a screeching rendition of the national anthem before a San
Diego Padres game, punctuated by grabbing her crotch and spitting,
imitating a baseball player. The outrage was out of all proportion to the
sin of bad taste she may have been guilty of committing, but in conservative, military-heavy San Diego, Barr became public enemy number one
for far longer than made sense.[42] The *San Diego Tribune* headline the next
day read "Barr-Strangled Banner."[43] President George H. W. Bush, while
riding in Air Force One, called Barr's performance "disgraceful." Conservative wordsmith George Will called her a "slob."[44] Perhaps ironically,
while Barr was specially anathema on the right, by the time of Kaepernick's protest she had become a full-blown Trump acolyte, completing a
180-degree shift in the culture wars.

Sometimes a mangled anthem can be the setting for a nice human
interest story. On April 25, 2003, thirteen-year-old Natalie Gilbert was
singing the anthem before the Portland Trailblazers hosted the Dallas
Mavericks in Game 3 of a playoff series. Then, as the *Sporting News*
recounts, "Gilbert got through 20 seconds of the song, through, 'what
so proudly hailed.' Then she stumbled on the words, dug her head into
the microphone and began looking around as she desperately tried to
remember the words. A 13-year-old kid, lost in front of a crowd of thousands." To the rescue came former NBA point guard and then Portland
head coach Maurice Cheeks: "'Come on, come on,' he told her, putting
his arm around Gilbert as he began to feed her the lines: ' . . . twilight's
last gleaming . . . ' Gilbert recovered, and warbled through the rest of
the anthem. Cheeks moved his hand in circles, in the style of Leonard
Bernstein, and encouraged the crowd to join in and sing as well. By

the time the song was over, Cheeks gave Gilbert a hug and the crowd gave him one of the great anthem ovations in sporting history." Cheeks, who was elected to the Naismith Memorial Basketball Hall of Fame as a player in 2018, received thousands of letters of support for his act of kindness.[45] Maybe we simply take the national anthem—a rote exercise conducted literally thousands of times a year before sporting events, with performances good and bad, conventional and unorthodox, noteworthy and forgettable—far too seriously.

Colin Kaepernick would not play again after the 2016 season. That year was certainly not his best as a professional, but he was still an athlete at his peak, and many, many inferior quarterbacks have played in the NFL since. In that last season—when he was dealing with a series of injuries—he still threw for 16 touchdowns against only 4 interceptions, a ratio that showed he could play at a high level. The 49ers were execrable that season, but that hardly justifies the blackballing that followed. Even All-Pro Eric Reid struggled to find a job in the NFL after his contract expired, but eventually he was re-signed, at least in part because he was unquestionably elite and in part because he played a lower-profile position. Beyond that, Kaepernick had become identified with the kneeling protests more than any other player. He was seen as its originator, its most vocal proponent, and as its leader.

As his friend, teammate, and fellow protester Reid wrote in the *New York Times*, "I can't find words that appropriately express how heartbroken I am to see the constant smears against Colin, a person who helped start the movement with only the best of intentions." After all, Kaepernick had been active on a range of issues, providing a planeload of food and supplies to Somalia when it endured a famine, and he had "invested his time and money into needy communities at home." Kaepernick is "a man I am proud to call my brother, who should be celebrated for his courage to seek change on important issues. Instead, to this day, he is unemployed and portrayed as a radical un-American who wants to divide our country." And to Reid there was little question that Kaepernick was being blackballed because of his political stands: "Anybody who has a basic knowledge of football knows that his unemployment has nothing to do with his performance on the field." After Trump attacked Kaepernick and the other protesters, he was "nevertheless encouraged to see my colleagues and other public figures respond to the president's remarks with solidarity with us. It is paramount that we take control of the story behind our movement, which is that we seek equality for all Americans, no matter their race or gender."[46] Kaepernick became something other than a football player. As Brit Bennett wrote, Kaepernick "has transformed into something else: a hero or a traitor, a martyr or a pariah, depending on who you ask."[47] Former NBA player Etan Thomas, who was outspoken on political issues as a player, has fully embraced the new wave of athlete activism since his retirement from the league, and he has nothing but praise for Kaepernick and the other athletes "who have had the moral courage to withstand the backlash, the criticism, the outrage, the venom, and all of the hate and have used their platform to speak out and bring awareness to an issue that has plagued the country for far too long."[48]

In the end, as Reid wrote, "I refuse to be one of those people who watched injustices and yet do nothing. I want to be a man my children and children's children can be proud of, someone who faced adversity and tried to make a positive impact on the world, a person who, 50 years from now, is remembered for standing for what was right, even though it was not the popular or easy choice."[49]

It is worth noting some final words from Justice Jackson's opinion in *Barnette*: "Struggles to coerce uniformity of sentiment in support of some end thought essential to their time and country have been waged by many good, as well as by evil, men. Those who begin coercive elimination of dissent soon find themselves exterminating dissenters."[50]

* * *

One can imagine a time when the protests of Kaepernick and the thousands who followed in his wake will seem almost quaintly anachronistic, the debate over them silly and mild. In many ways, after all, that is how we think about, say, José Feliciano's anthem and the response to it in 1968. And yet we know that the continuum of American history is one of exclusion, response, and fevered debate. And thus we know that, in the words of Howard Bryant, "to be Black"—but we can also add, to be a woman, to be Hispanic, to be gay—"is to be a dissident."[51]

Indeed, as I write this, WNBA superstar Brittney Griner, arrested in Russia on trumped-up drug charges and handed a draconian sentence, has been released after a prisoner swap for a Russian arms dealer. The social media dialogue (it's the 2020s—is there any other kind?) coming from the right has been predictably appalling—racist and homophobic, full of tough-on-crime palaver and accusations that Griner hates America because, yes, she kneeled and engaged in protest. It is essentially all the ugliness that we've come to expect. Griner was a pawn in a larger geopolitical game, but at the same time, large numbers of her fellow citizens were willing to abandon her to the gulag because of who she is. The fact that many of the critics of the Biden administration's deal for her preferred the release of disgraced (white) former marine Paul Whelan—given a bad conduct discharge for engaging in larceny while he was in the Marines and arrested and convicted of espionage in Russia in 2018—added to the poisonous dialogue. This despite the fact that by all accounts Whelan, facing what for the Russians were much bigger charges—espionage outranking drug possession in their calculation— was not on offer. Griner coming home—something all Americans should have celebrated—became yet another tableau for the unending culture wars in which a Black, gay, politically aware basketball player is not going to fare well among the denizens of the MAGA crowd.

We also know that the next issue is just around the bend, and that issue will once again revive both the spirit of protest and challenge that is at the heart of the American experiment. Those protesters will be condemned: The new verse will be the same as the old verse. And some will be condemned for not singing in the right key, for not knowing the words, or simply for refusing to sing at all.

Notes

Introduction

1. Frank Wilhoit, comment on Henry Farrell, "The Travesty of Liberalism," *Crooked Timber* (blog), March 21, 2018, https://crookedtimber.org/2018/03/21/liberals-against -progressives/#comment-729288.

2. Sigmund Freud, *Civilization and Its Discontents*, trans. Ulrich Baer (New York: Warbler Press, 2022), 45.

Chapter 1

1. On the 1918 baseball season in Boston, see Tom Verducci, "Love, War, Influenza, and the World Series," *Sports Illustrated*, July 2020, 50–77.

2. Estimates range from the 10,274 announced in the *New York Times* to as many as 19,000 fans at Comiskey that day, numbers that would have been disappointingly low no matter which is accurate. Baseball Reference lists the attendance as 19,274, indicating that the *Times* number was a typo or other mistake.

3. Sean Devaney, *The Original Curse: Did the Cubs Throw the 1918 World Series to Babe Ruth's Red Sox and Incite the Black Sox Scandal?* (New York: McGraw-Hill, 2009), 161.

4. See Randy Roberts and Johnny Smith, *War Fever: Boston, Baseball, and America in the Shadow of the Great War* (New York: Basic Books, 2020), xi.

5. *Boston Herald and Journal*, September 4, 1918.

6. Marc Ferris, *Star-Spangled Banner: The Unlikely Story of America's National Anthem* (New York: MJF Books, 2014), 132–33.

7. *Boston Globe*, September 6, 1918.

8. Jim Leeke, *From the Dugouts to the Trenches: Baseball during the Great War* (Lincoln: University of Nebraska Press, 2017), 141.

9. Quoted in Don Babwin, "1918 World Series Started the U.S. Love Affair with National Anthem," *Chicago Tribune*, July 3, 2017, https://www.chicagotribune.com/sports /ct-wrigley-field-national-anthem-20170703-story.html.

10. Quoted in Babwin, "1918 World Series Started the U.S. Love Affair with National Anthem."

11. Luke Cyphers and Ethan Trex, "History of the National Anthem in Sports," ESPN, September 8, 2011, https://www.espn.com/espn/story/_/id/6957582/from-archives-history-national-anthem-sports.

12. Quoted in Babwin, "1918 World Series Started the U.S. Love Affair with National Anthem."

13. *Chicago Tribune*, September 6, 1918.

14. See Babwin, "1918 World Series Started the U.S. Love Affair with National Anthem."

15. Roberts and Smith, *War Fever*, 212.

16. *Boston American*, September 6, 1918.

17. See Gary Waleik, "How 'The Star-Spangled Banner' Became a Pregame Mainstay," WBUR Boston, August 31, 2018, https://www.wbur.org/onlyagame/2018/08/31/star-spangled-banner-national-anthem-1918-world-series.

18. See David Ray, MBE, *From Webb Ellis to World Cup* (Rugby: Webb Ellis Ltd./Rugby Football Museum, 2015), 2.

19. See Ferris, *Star-Spangled Banner*, 77.

20. Ferris, *Star-Spangled Banner*, 77–78.

21. Ferris, *Star-Spangled Banner*, 76–77.

22. Roberts and Smith, *War Fever*, 122.

23. See David Goldblatt, *The Games: A Global History of the Olympics* (New York: W. W. Norton, 2016), 79–81; and Jules Boykoff, *Power Games: A Political History of the Olympics* (London: Verso, 2016), 42–43.

24. There is some speculation that gamblers may have influenced the outcome of the 1918 World Series, a year before the infamous scandal that would rock the baseball world in 1920 when the Chicago White Sox were discovered to have thrown the 1919 World Series. See Devaney, *The Original Curse*.

25. Cyphers and Trex, "History of the National Anthem in Sports."

26. Quoted in Waleik, "How 'The Star-Spangled Banner' Became a Pregame Mainstay."

27. Quoted in Babwin, "1918 World Series Started the U.S. Love Affair with National Anthem."

28. Ben Railton, *Of Thee I Sing: The Contested Nature of American Patriotism* (Lanham, MD: Rowman & Littlefield, 2021), xv. See also Ben Railton, *We the People: The 500-Year Battle over Who Is American* (Lanham, MD: Rowman & Littlefield, 2019).

CHAPTER 2

1. David Goldblatt, *The Games: A Global History of the Olympics* (New York: W. W. Norton, 2016), 109–10.

2. Video highlights of the race are available at https://olympics.com/en/video/amsterdam-1928-radke-lina.

3. Lynne Emery, "An Examination of the 1928 Olympic 800 Meter Race for Women," *Proceedings of the North American Society for Sports History* (1985), 30.

4. Ian Jobling, "The Women's 800 Metres Track Event Post 1928: Quo Vadis?" *Journal of Olympic History* 14, no. 1 (March 2006): 44.

5. Jobling, "The Women's 800 Metres Track Event Post 1928," 44.

6. Goldblatt, *The Games*, 114.

7. Colleen English, "'Not a Very Edifying Spectacle': The Controversial Women's 800-Meter Race in the 1928 Olympics," *Sport in American History* (blog), October 8, 2015, https://ussporthistory.com/2015/10/08/not-a-very-edifying-spectacle-the -controversial-womens-800-meter-race-in-the-1928-olympics/.

8. *The Bulletin*, Sydney, Australia, August 28, 1928.

9. Amby Burfoot, *First Ladies of Running: 22 Inspiring Profiles of the Rebels, Rule Breakers, and Visionaries Who Changed the Sport Forever* (New York: Rodale, 2016), xiv.

10. *Chicago Tribune*, August 3, 1928; quoted in English, "'Not a Very Edifying Spectacle.'"

11. See *Pittsburgh Press*, August 3, 1928; quoted in English, "'Not a Very Edifying Spectacle.'"

12. *New York Times*, August 3, 1928.

13. Jobling, "The Women's 800 Metres Track Event Post 1928," 44.

14. Burfoot, *First Ladies of Running*, 71.

15. Roseanne Montillo, *Fire on the Track: Betty Robinson and the Triumph of the Early Olympic Women* (New York: Crown, 2017), 84.

16. Montillo, *Fire on the Track*, 83.

17. Jobling, "The Women's 800 Metres Track Event Post 1928," 44.

18. Jobling, "The Women's 800 Metres Track Event Post 1928," 46–47, fn. 15.

19. Jules Boykoff, *Power Games: A Political History of the Olympics* (London: Verso, 2016), 54.

20. Jobling, "The Women's 800 Metres Track Event Post 1928," 45.

21. Burfoot, *First Ladies of Running*, 5.

22. Burfoot, *First Ladies of Running*, 229.

23. Susan Ware, *Title IX: A Brief History with Documents* (Long Grove, IL: Waveland Press, 2007), 9.

24. Babe Didrikson Zaharias, *This Life I've Led: My Autobiography* (Cleveland, OH: Barakaldo Books, 2020), Kindle edition, 65.

25. Don Van Natta Jr., *Wonder Girl: The Magnificent Sporting Life of Babe Didrikson Zaharias* (New York: Little, Brown, 2011), 137.

26. Allen Guttmann, *The Olympics: A History of the Modern Games*, 2nd ed. (Champaign: University of Illinois Press, 2002), 51.

27. Boykoff, *Power Games*, 58–59.

28. Boykoff, *Power Games*, 59.

29. Quoted in Goldblatt, *The Games*, 169.

30. *New York Times*, February 8, 1953; quoted in Boykoff, *Power Games*, 60.

31. Quoted in Goldblatt, *The Games*, 168–69.

32. Paul Gallico, *Farewell to Sport* (Lincoln, NE: Bison Books, 2008), 233.

33. See Lindsay Parks Pieper, "Babe Didrikson at the 1932 Olympic Games," in Steven Gietschier, ed. *Replays, Rivalries, and Rumbles: The Most Iconic Moments in American Sports* (Urbana: University of Illinois Press, 2017), 42.

34. Van Natta, *Wonder Girl*, 142–43.

35. Zachary Michael Jack, introduction to Gallico, *Farewell to Sport*, xii.

36. Robert Lipsyte, "Jock Culture: Robert Lipsyte on Paul Gallico's *Farewell to Sport* and the Importance of Destroying Your Illusions," *Columbia Journalism Review* 45, no. 2 (July/August 2006): 52, 54.

37. Van Natta, *Wonder Girl*, 118–19.

38. Zaharias, *This Life I've Led*, 79.

39. Van Natta, *Wonder Girl*, 120.

40. Zaharias, *This Life I've Led*, 79.

41. Van Natta, *Wonder Girl*, 120.

42. Zaharias, *This Life I've Led*, 79.

43. Gallico, *Farewell to Sport*, 239.

44. Gallico, *Farewell to Sport*, 239.

45. Lipsyte, "Jock Culture," 54.

46. Gallico, *Farewell to Sport*, 240.

47. Van Natta, *Wonder Girl*, 145.

48. Pieper, "Babe Didrikson at the 1932 Olympic Games," 50.

49. Quoted in Jack, introduction to *Farewell to Sport*, xiii.

50. Dave Zirin, *A People's History of Sports in the United States* (New York: New Press, 2008), 119–20.

51. Quoted in Goldblatt, *The Games*, 169.

52. *Washington Post and Times Herald*, September 7, 1958.

53. Mary Ellen Pethel, *Title IX, Pat Summitt, and Tennessee's Trailblazers: 50 Years, 50 Stories* (Knoxville: University of Tennessee Press, 2022), 94.

54. See Mark Dyreson, "Icons of Liberty or Objects of Desire? American Women Olympians and the Politics of Consumption," *Journal of Contemporary History* 38, no. 3 (2003): 435–60.

CHAPTER 3

1. James W. Johnson, *The Black Bruins: The Remarkable Lives of UCLA's Jackie Robinson, Woody Strode, Tom Bradley, Kenny Washington, and Ray Bartlett* (Lincoln: University of Nebraska Press, 2017).

2. In the words of his biographer Jules Tygiel, who recounts all these feats, "It is probable that no other athlete, including Jim Thorpe, has ever competed as effectively in as broad a range of sports." Jules Tygiel, *Baseball's Great Experiment: Jackie Robinson and His Legacy*, 25th anniversary edition (New York: Oxford University Press, 2008), 60.

3. Both of these stories will be fleshed out in the next chapter.

4. Tygiel, *Baseball's Great Experiment*, 62.

5. David Falkner, *Great Time Coming: The Life of Jackie Robinson from Baseball to Birmingham* (New York: Touchstone, 1995), 79.

6. Jackie Robinson, *I Never Had It Made: An Autobiography* (New York: HarperCollins, 1995), 18.

7. Falkner, *Great Time Coming*, 78.

8. Robinson, *I Never Had It Made*, 18–19.

9. Arnold Rampersad, *Jackie Robinson: A Biography* (New York: Knopf, 1997), 102.

10. Robinson, *I Never Had It Made*, 19.

11. Major Adam Kama, "The Court Martial of Jackie Robinson," *Army Lawyer* 1 (2020): 70–71.

12. Rampersad, *Jackie Robinson*, 103.

13. Robinson, *I Never Had It Made*, 20.

14. Robinson, *I Never Had It Made*, 20.

15. Robinson, *I Never Had It Made*, 22.

16. Falkner, *Great Time Coming*, 81.

17. Rampersad, *Jackie Robinson*, 104. Kama explains the significance of this call—and how rare it is to have such a documented phone call in the court-martial record—in "The Court-Martial of Jackie Robinson," 72.

18. Robinson, *I Never Had It Made*, 22.

19. Kama, "The Court-Martial of Jackie Robinson," 76.

20. Jules Tygiel, "The Court-Martial of Jackie Robinson," in *The Jackie Robinson Reader: Perspectives on an American Hero* (New York: Plume, 1997), 49.

21. Kama, "The Court-Martial of Jackie Robinson," 76–77.

22. Kama, "The Court-Martial of Jackie Robinson," 77–78.

23. *United States v. 2nd Lieutenant Jack R. Robinson, 0–10315861, Calvary Company C, 758th Tank Battalion.*

24. Robinson, *I Never Had It Made*, 22.

25. Tygiel, "The Court-Martial of Jackie Robinson," 46.

26. Rampersad, *Jackie Robinson*, 109.

27. Robinson, *I Never Had It Made*, 23.

28. Falkner, *Great Time Coming*, 85.

29. Kama, "The Court-Martial of Jackie Robinson," 79.

30. Falkner, *Great Time Coming*, 84.

31. Robinson, *I Never Had It Made*, 23.

32. Rampersad, *Jackie Robinson*, 113.

33. Robinson, *I Never Had It Made*, 23.

34. Robinson, *I Never Had It Made*, 24.

35. Sam Huston College was an HBCU named not after the legendary Texan who gave the city of Houston its name but a similarly named benefactor from Iowa who donated $9,000 in the college's early years, stabilizing an institution that had been forced to close several times because of financial struggles. Huston College merged with Tillotson College in 1952. Negro League legend Rube Foster pitched for Tillotson before moving on to his fame as a player and owner in Black baseball.

36. Johnson, *The Black Bruins*, 13.

37. *Austin American Statesman*, August 24, 2013.

38. Robinson, *I Never Had It Made*, 7.

39. Robinson, *I Never Had It Made*, 8.

40. Robinson, *I Never Had It Made*, 8–9.

41. Johnson, *The Black Bruins*, 136.

42. Rampersad, *Jackie Robinson*, 114.

43. Paul Putz, "Who Was Karl Downs? Exploring the Life and Legacy of Jackie Robinson's Mentor," *Faith & Sports* (blog), March 12, 2021, https://blogs.baylor.edu

/faithsports/2021/03/12/who-was-karl-downs-exploring-the-life-and-legacy-of-jackie
-robinsons-mentor/.

44. Rampersad, *Jackie Robinson*, 114.

45. John R. M. Wilson, *Jackie Robinson and the American Dilemma* (New York: Longman, 2010), 41.

46. Rampersad, *Jackie Robinson*, 114.

47. Rampersad, *Jackie Robinson*, 114.

48. Chase Hoffberger, "Jackie Robinson's Austin," *Austin Chronicle*, February 21, 2014.

49. Jeff Miller, "Jackie Robinson's Forgotten Season as a College Basketball Coach," *Bleacher Report*, April 15, 2014.

50. Hoffberger, "Jackie Robinson's Austin."

51. Miller, "Jackie Robinson's Forgotten Season as a College Basketball Coach."

52. Hoffberger, "Jackie Robinson's Austin."

53. Miller, "Jackie Robinson's Forgotten Season as a College Basketball Coach."

54. Hoffberger, "Jackie Robinson's Austin."

55. Hoffberger, "Jackie Robinson's Austin."

56. Miller, "Jackie Robinson's Forgotten Season as a College Basketball Coach."

57. Jake Harris, "Jackie Robinson once coached basketball at an Austin college," *Austin American Statesman*, March 30, 2016.

58. Miller, "Jackie Robinson's Forgotten Season as a College Basketball Coach."

59. Johnson, *The Black Bruins*, 136.

60. Falkner, *Great Time Coming*, 87.

61. Miller, "Jackie Robinson's Forgotten Season as a College Basketball Coach."

62. Robinson, *I Never Had It Made*, 69–70.

63. Robinson, *I Never Had It Made*, 70.

64. Putz, "Who Was Karl Downs?"

65. Hoffberger, "Jackie Robinson's Austin."

CHAPTER 4

1. Donald McRae, *Heroes without a Country: America's Betrayal of Joe Louis and Jesse Owens* (New York: Ecco, 2002).

2. See Howard Bryant, *The Heritage: Black Athletes, a Divided America, and the Politics of Patriotism* (Boston: Beacon Press, 2018), especially vii–viii.

3. Kyle Swenson, "Red, White, and Bruised," *Longreads*, July 2016. https://longreads.com/2016/07/14/cleveland-gop-convention/.

4. See Nishani Frazier, *Harambee City: The Congress of Racial Equality in Cleveland and the Rise of Black Power Populism* (Fayetteville: University of Arkansas Press, 2017); and James Robenalt, *Ballots and Bullets: Black Power Politics and Urban Guerrilla Warfare in 1968 Cleveland* (Chicago: Lawrence Hill Books, 2018).

5. *The Evening Star*, Washington, DC, March 22, 1946.

6. On the Willis signing, see Gretchen Atwood, *Lost Champions: Four Men, Two Teams, and the Breaking of Pro Football's Color Line* (New York: Bloomsbury, 2016), 44–45.

7. Louis Moore, *We Will Win the Day: The Civil Rights Movement, the Black Athlete, and the Quest for Equality* (Lexington: University Press of Kentucky, 2017), 38.

8. *Miami Times*, October 28, 1950.

9. Moore, *We Will Win the Day*, 38.

10. James W. Johnson, *The Black Bruins: The Remarkable Lives of UCLA's Jackie Robinson, Woody Strode, Tom Bradley, Kenny Washington, and Ray Bartlett* (Lincoln: University of Nebraska Press, 2017), 140–41.

11. Keyshawn Johnson and Bob Glauber, *The Forgotten First: Kenny Washington, Woody Strode, Marion Motley, Bill Willis, and the Breaking of the NFL Color Barrier* (New York: Grand Central Publishing, 2021), xvi.

12. Douglas M. Branson, *Greatness in the Shadows: Larry Doby and the Integration of the American League* (Lincoln: University of Nebraska Press, 2016), x.

13. *Chicago Star*, July 12, 1947.

14. Moore, *We Will Win the Day*, 36.

15. Moore, *We Will Win the Day*, 35.

16. There is a debate about whether Veeck did or did not try to buy the Phillies and fill the roster with Negro League players, or how seriously he tried to do so. For the debate, see Jules Tygiel, "Revisiting Bill Veeck and the 1943 Philllies," *National Pastime: The Baseball Research Journal* 35 (2006): 109–14; this article is in response to David M. Jordan, Larry R. Gerlach, and John P. Rossi. "A Baseball Myth Exploded: The Truth about Bill Veeck and the '43 Phillies," *National Pastime: The Baseball Research Journal* (1998): 3–13.

17. Moore, *We Will Win the Day*, 35.

18. Larry Moffi and Jonathan Kronstadt, *Crossing the Line: Black Major Leaguers 1947–1959* (Lincoln: University of Nebraska Press, 2006), 15.

19. Moore, *We Will Win the Day*, 8.

20. *Chicago Star*, July 12, 1947.

21. Peter Dreier and Robert Elias, *Baseball Rebels: The Players, People, and Social Movements That Shook Up the Game and Changed America* (Lincoln: University of Nebraska Press, 2022), 87.

22. Moore, *We Will Win the Day*, 39.

23. See Luke Epplin, *Our Team: The Epic Story of Four Men and the World Series That Changed Baseball* (New York: Flatiron Books, 2021).

24. William Marshall, *Baseball's Pivotal Era, 1945–1951* (Lexington: University Press of Kentucky, 1999), 221.

25. Branson, *Greatness in the Shadows*, 242.

26. Ron Thomas, *They Cleared the Lane: The NBA's Black Pioneers* (Lincoln: University of Nebraska Press, 2002), 26.

27. Russell T. Wigginton, *The Strange Career of the Black Athlete: African Americans and Sports* (Westport, CT: Praeger, 2006), 21.

28. Thomas, *They Cleared the Lane*, 28.

29. Bill Reynolds, *Rise of a Dynasty: The '57 Celtics, the First Banner, and the Dawning of a New America* (New York: New American Library, 2010); Lew Freedman, *Dynasty: Auerback, Cousy, Havlicek, Russell, and the Rise of the Boston Celtics* (Guilford, CT: Lyons Press, 2008).

30. Bill Russell with Bill McSweeny, *Go Up for Glory* (New York: Penguin, 2020), 102.

31. Bill Russell with Alan Steinberg, *Red and Me: My Coach, My Lifelong Friend* (New York: HarperCollins, 2009), ix.

32. Adam Goudsouzian, *King of the Court: Bill Russell and the Basketball Revolution* (Berkeley: University of California Press, 2010), 4.

33. Russell with McSweeney, *Go Up for Glory*, 102.

34. Russell with McSweeney, *Go Up for Glory*, xv.

35. *New York Times*, June 14, 1987.

36. Russell with McSweeney, *Go Up for Glory*, xv.

37. *New York Times*, June 14, 1987.

38. Dave Zirin, *A People's History of Sports in the United States* (New York: New Press, 2008), 153.

39. Bill Russell and Taylor Branch, *Second Wind: The Memoirs of an Opinionated Man* (New York: Ballantine Books, 1979), 230.

40. Zirin, *A People's History of Sports in the United States*, 153.

41. Russell and Branch, *Second Wind*, 222.

42. Michael Connelly, *Rebound! Basketball, Busing, Larry Bird, and the Rebirth of Boston* (Minneapolis, MN: MVP Books, 2008), 286. Bill Reynolds takes a similarly ill-fated approach to the 1978 Red Sox and one game's role in a "divided city" in *'78: The Boston Red Sox, a Historic Game, and a Divided City* (New York: New American Library, 2009). That game against the hated New York Yankees did unite Boston and all of New England in one way—from that day forward the Yankees' shortstop that day, Russell Earl "Bucky" Dent, would be known as "Bucky Fucking Dent" as a result of the cheap pop fly home run that effectively decided the game.

43. *New York Times*, June 9, 1987.

44. Goudsouzian, *King of the Court*, 4.

45. "Bill Russell's Fight against Racism," *SLAM*, August 1, 2022.

46. Willie O'Ree with Michael McKinley, *Willie: The Game-Changing Story of the NHL's First Black Player* (Toronto: Viking, 2020), 117.

47. O'Ree, *Willie*, 122.

48. O'Ree, *Willie*, 123–24.

49. O'Ree, *Willie*, 135.

50. Wigginton, *The Strange Career of the Black Athlete*, 22.

51. O'Ree, *Willie*, 150.

52. Carnegie uses the phrase a number of times, including in the title of his memoir. Herb Carnegie with Bernice Carnegie, *Fly in a Pail of Milk: The Herb Carnegie Story* (Toronto: ECW Press, 2019).

53. *Minneapolis Spokesman*, January 11, 1952.

54. Jarome Iginla, foreword to O'Ree, *Willie*, 6.

55. See NHL, "The Willie O'Ree Community Hero Award," https://www.nhl.com/fans/willie-oree-community-hero-award.

56. O'Ree, *Willie*, 237.

57. The most famous iteration of the "Curse" story is Dan Shaughnessy, *The Curse of the Bambino* (New York: Penguin, 1991).

58. You, dear reader, could be one of the surpassingly few to read one of the more obscure of the many books written about the triumphant 2004 Red Sox: Derek Catsam, *Bleeding Red: A Red Sox Fan's Diary of the 2004 Season* (Washington, DC: Vellum, 2005). Is it the best of these many books? Who is to say, other than the book-buying public? But it is a book!

59. Though I've long made this argument, two authors made it quite clearly before me: Howard Bryant, *Shut Out: A Story of Race and Baseball in Boston* (New York: Routledge, 2002); and Jerry M. Gutlon, *It Was Never about the Babe: The Red Sox, Racism, Mismanagement, and the Curse of the Bambino* (New York: Skyhorse Publishing, 2009).

60. For a perhaps too generous assessment of whether Yawkey was or was not a racist, see Bill Nowlin, *Tom Yawkey: Patriarch of the Boston Red Sox* (Lincoln: University of Nebraska Press, 2018), 420–42.

61. Bryant, *Shut Out*, 25.

62. For a historical but also personal perspective on Isadore Muchnick, see David M. Muchnick and Frances Muchnick Goldstein, "Principled Politics: Personal & Local," in Bill Nowlin, ed., *Pumpsie & Progress: The Red Sox, Race, and Redemption* (Burlington, MA: Rounder Books, 2010), 110–21.

63. Moore, *We Will Win the Day*, 57; Bryant, *Shut Out*, 33–40.

64. Howard Bryant, who has written the best, most comprehensive history on the Red Sox' woeful history on race, gives his account of the tryout in chapter 3 of *Shut Out*, 23–40. Gutlon's chapter on the tryout is chapter 8, "The Great Scam," in *It Never Was About the Babe*, 91–108. See also Glenn Stout, "Tryout and Fallout: Race, Jackie Robinson, and the Red Sox," 65–91; Nowlin, "From Jackie to Pumpsie: Wendell Smith on Race and the Red Sox," 96–103; and Nowlin, "What Did the 1945 tryout Accomplish?" 104–108, in Nowlin, *Pumpsie & Progress*.

65. Moore, *We Will Win the Day*, 57.

66. See David Nevard with David Marasco, "Who Was Piper Davis?" 134–47; and Nowlin, "A Postscript from Piper," 148–49, in Nowlin, *Pumpsie & Progress*.

67. For a good biographical sketch of Green, see Bill Nowlin, "Pumpsie Green," in Nowlin, *Pumpsie & Progress*, 1–53.

68. Moore, *We Will Win the Day*, 58.

69. Hal Bock, "Red Sox' First Black Player Never Could Relax," *South Coast Today*, March 22, 1997, https://www.southcoasttoday.com/story/sports/1997/03/23/red-sox-first-black-player/50620886007/.

70. Bryant, *Shut Out*, 33.

71. See Charles K. Ross, *Mavericks, Money, and Men: The AFL, Black Players, and the Evolution of Modern Football* (Philadelphia: Temple University Press, 2016).

72. Ross, *Mavericks, Money, and Men*, 18, 22.

73. On Marshall the innovator and showman, see Andrew O'Toole, *Fight for Old DC: George Preston Marshall, the Integration of the Washington Redskins, and the Rise of a New NFL* (Lincoln: University of Nebraska Press, 2016), ix and passim.

74. Alan Levy, *Tackling Jim Crow: Racial Segregation in Professional Football* (Jefferson, NC: McFarland, 2003), 120.

75. Charles K. Ross, *Outside the Lines: African Americans and the Integration of the National Football League* (New York: New York University Press, 1999), 143.

76. Ross, *Outside the Lines*, 150.

77. Levy, *Tackling Jim Crow*, 129. On the Marshall-Udall clash, see also O'Toole, *Fight for Old DC*, 108–42.

CHAPTER 5

1. See David K. Wiggins and Chris Elzey, "Creating Order in Black College Sport: The Lasting Legacy of the Colored Intercollegiate Athletic Association," in Wiggins and Ryan A. Swanson, eds., *Separate Games: African American Sport behind the Walls of Segregation* (Fayetteville: University of Arkansas Press, 2016), 145–64.

2. Rob Fink, *Football at Historically Black Colleges and Universities in Texas* (College Station: Texas A&M University Press, 2019), 3.

3. Derrick E. White, *Blood, Sweat, and Tears: Jake Gaither, Florida A&M, and the History of Black College Football* (Chapel Hill: University of North Carolina Press, 2019), 15.

4. Tom Shanahan, "Overlooked," *Shanahan Report* (blog), September 1, 2020, https://tomshanahan.report/2020/09/timing-right-to-reexamine-bear-bryant-folkore/.

5. Dan Jenkins, "An Upside-Down Game," *Sports Illustrated*, November 28, 1966, 22–27.

6. White, *Blood, Sweat, and Tears*, 53.

7. Donald Spivey, *Bates Must Play! Racism, Activism, and Integrity in College Football* (Durham, NC: Carolina Academic Press, 2021).

8. Spivey, *Bates Must Play!*, 4.

9. Jaime Schultz, *Moments of Impact: Injury, Racialized Memory, and Reconciliation in College Football* (Lincoln: University of Nebraska Press, 2016).

10. White, *Blood, Sweat, and Tears*, 8.

11. Christopher J. Walsh, *Who's #1? 100-Plus Years of Controversial National Champions in College Football* (Lanham, MD: Taylor Trade, 2007); 190–94 (all polls and organizations); 203–207 (AP poll); 221–24 (UPI poll).

12. On Ole Miss and football, see Derek Catsam, "'Sic 'Em White Folks!': Football, Massive Resistance, and the Integration of Ole Miss," *Sport History Review* 40 (2009): 82–98.

13. James Silver, "Mississippi: The Closed Society," address before Southern Historical Association, November 7, 1963, James W. Silver Collection, University of Mississippi University Archives and Special Collections, Speeches and Letters to the Editor, available at https://egrove.olemiss.edu/jws_spch/6/; see also James W. Silver, *Mississippi: The Closed Society*, new enlarged edition (New York: Harcourt, Brace, & World, 1966).

14. Quoted in Michael Dorman, *We Shall Overcome: A Reporter's Eye-Witness Account of the Year of Racial Strife and Triumph* (New York: Dell, 1964), 55–56.

15. See Terry Frei, *Horns, Hogs, and Nixon Coming: Texas vs. Arkansas in Dixie's Last Stand* (New York: Simon & Schuster, 2002).

16. Don Yaeger, with Sam Cunningham and John Papadakis, *Turning of the Tide: How One Game Changed the South* (New York: Center Street, 2006).

17. See Shanahan, "Overlooked."

18. Chad Carlson, "The Integration of College Hoops Came through Many Small Shining Moments," History News Network, April 3, 2022, https://historynewsnetwork.org/article/182850.

19. Kurt Edward Kemper, *Before March Madness: The Wars for the Soul of College Basketball* (Urbana: University of Illinois Press, 2020), 134.

20. Carlson, "The Integration of College Hoops Came through Many Small Shining Moments."

21. Frank Fitzpatrick, "Texas Western's 1966 Title Left Lasting Legacy," ESPN Classic, November 19, 2003, https://www.espn.com/classic/s/013101_texas_western_fitzpatrick.html.

22. Russell J. Henderson, "The 1963 Mississippi State University Basketball Controversy and the Repeal of the Unwritten Law: 'Something More Than the Game Will Be Lost,'" *Journal of Southern History* 63, no. 4 (November 1997): 831–32.

23. See Jason A. Peterson, *Full Court Press: Mississippi State University, the Press, and the Battle to Integrate College Basketball* (Jackson: University Press of Mississippi, 2016), especially 123–70.

24. Henderson, "The 1963 Mississippi State University Basketball Controversy and the Repeal of the Unwritten Law," 843.

25. Douglas Martin, "Leland Mitchell, Who Defied Racism on the Basketball Court, Dies at 72," *New York Times*, July 10, 2013.

26. Henderson, "The 1963 Mississippi State University Basketball Controversy and the Repeal of the Unwritten Law," 843.

27. Martin, "Leland Mitchell, Who Defied Racism on the Basketball Court, Dies at 72."

28. Henderson, "The 1963 Mississippi State University Basketball Controversy and the Repeal of the Unwritten Law," 849.

29. Henderson, "The 1963 Mississippi State University Basketball Controversy and the Repeal of the Unwritten Law," 849–50.

30. Mississippi State University, "'Game of Change' Guard Mitchell Dead at 72," July 9, 2013, http://www.msstate.edu/web/media/announcement.php?id=1709.

31. Martin, "Leland Mitchell, Who Defied Racism on the Basketball Court, Dies at 72."

32. Henderson, "The 1963 Mississippi State University Basketball Controversy and the Repeal of the Unwritten Law," 851.

33. Martin, "Leland Mitchell, Who Defied Racism on the Basketball Court, Dies at 72."

34. Fitzpatrick, "Texas Western's 1966 Title Left Lasting Legacy."

35. Fitzpatrick, "Texas Western's 1966 Title Left Lasting Legacy."

36. Charles H. Martin, *Benching Jim Crow: The Rise and Fall of the Color Line in Southern College Sports, 1890–1980* (Urbana: University of Illinois Press, 2010), 110.

37. James A. Michener, *Sports in America* (New York: Dial Press, 2015), 165.

38. Michener, *Sports in America*, 165–66. The *Sports Illustrated* features on "The Black Athlete" began with the July 1, 1968 issue.

39. Fitzpatrick, "Texas Western's 1966 Title Left Lasting Legacy."

40. Fitzpatrick, "Texas Western's 1966 Title Left Lasting Legacy."
41. Martin, *Benching Jim Crow*, 92.
42. Martin, *Benching Jim Crow*, 93.

CHAPTER 6

1. See Stefan Fatsis, "No Viet Cong Ever Called Me Nigger," *Slate*, June 8, 2016, https://slate.com/culture/2016/06/did-muhammad-ali-ever-say-no-viet-cong-ever-called-me-nigger.html, for an analysis of the partner quotation that often went hand in hand with this one but that Ali likely never said.
2. SI Staff, "The Long, Hard Run," *Sports Illustrated*, August 16, 1994, 59.
3. Edwin Shrake, "Taps for the Champ," *Sports Illustrated*, May 8, 1967, 24.
4. Branson Wright, "Remembering Cleveland's Muhammad Ali Summit, 45 Years Later," *Plain Dealer*, Cleveland, June 3, 2012, https://www.cleveland.com/sports/2012/06/gathering_of_stars.html.
5. SI Staff, "The Activist Minds," *Sports Illustrated*, December 19, 2016, 56.
6. Dave Zirin, *Jim Brown: Last Man Standing* (New York: Blue Rider Press, 2018), 145.
7. SI Staff, "The Activist Minds," 53.
8. Jim Brown with Steve Delsohn, *Out of Bounds: In His Own Words* (New York: Citadel, 2018), 186.
9. See Brown with Delsohn, *Out of Bounds*, 188. On the relationship between Malcolm X and Ali, see Randy Roberts and Johnny Smith, *Blood Brothers: The Fatal Friendship between Muhammad Ali and Malcolm X* (New York: Basic Books, 2016).
10. Adam Goudsouzian, *King of the Court: Bill Russell and the Basketball Revolution* (Berkeley: University of California Press, 2010), xv.
11. "Tribute to U.S. Ambassador Carl B. Stokes," House of Representatives, February 1, 1997, *Congressional Record* 143, no. 17 (February 11, 1997): H412–H413. On Stokes's life and career, see Leonard M. Moore, *Carl B. Stokes and the Rise of Black Political Power* (Urbana: University of Illinois Press, 2003).
12. Leigh Montville, *Sting Like a Bee: Muhammad Ali vs. the United States of America 1966–1971* (New York: Doubleday, 2017), 163.
13. Wright, "Remembering Cleveland's Muhammad Ali Summit, 45 Years Later."
14. Zirin, *Jim Brown*, 147.
15. Wright, "Remembering Cleveland's Muhammad Ali Summit, 45 Years Later."
16. Wright, "Remembering Cleveland's Muhammad Ali Summit, 45 Years Later."
17. Goudsouzian, *King of the Court*, 207.
18. Kyle Swenson, "Red, White, and Bruised," *Longreads*, July 14, 2016, https://longreads.com/2016/07/14/cleveland-gop-convention/; Moore, *Carl B. Stokes and the Rise of Black Political Power*, 45–51; Nishani Frazier, *Harambee City: The Congress of Racial Equality in Cleveland and the Rise of Black Power Populism* (Fayetteville: University of Arkansas Press, 2017), 153–55; James Robenalt, *Ballots and Bullets: Black Power Politics and Urban Guerrilla Warfare in 1968 Cleveland* (Chicago: Lawrence Hill Books, 2018), 110–22.
19. Wright, "Remembering Cleveland's Muhammad Ali Summit, 45 Years Later."
20. SI Staff, "The Activist Minds," 53.

21. SI Staff, "The Long, Hard Run," 60.
22. Zirin, *Jim Brown*, 146–47.
23. Wright, "Remembering Cleveland's Muhammad Ali Summit, 45 Years Later."
24. Wright, "Remembering Cleveland's Muhammad Ali Summit, 45 Years Later."
25. Zirin, *Jim Brown*, 146.
26. "The Activist Minds," *Sports Illustrated*, December 19, 2016.
27. Montville, *Sting Like a Bee*, pp. 162–63.
28. Wright, "Remembering Cleveland's Muhammad Ali Summit, 45 years later."
29. SI Staff, "The Activist Minds," 54.
30. Wright, "Remembering Cleveland's Muhammad Ali Summit, 45 Years Later."
31. Zirin, *Jim Brown*, 148.
32. Jonathan Eig, *Ali: A Life* (Boston: Houghton Mifflin Harcourt, 2017), 247.
33. Brown, *Out of Bounds*, 191.
34. Wright, "Remembering Cleveland's Muhammad Ali Summit, 45 Years Later."
35. Zirin, *Jim Brown*, 149.
36. Eig, *Ali*, 247.
37. Wright, "Remembering Cleveland's Muhammad Ali Summit, 45 Years Later."
38. Zirin, *Jim Brown*, 147.
39. Zirin, *Jim Brown*, 150.
40. SI Staff, "The Activist Minds," 54.
41. SI Staff, "The Activist Minds," 54.
42. Eig, *Ali*, 247.
43. Montville, *Sting Like a Bee*, 163.
44. Eig, *Ali*, 248.
45. Montville, *Sting Like a Bee*, 162.
46. Eig, *Ali*, 245.
47. Zirin, *Jim Brown*, 148.
48. Eig, *Ali*, 245.
49. Eig, *Ali*, 246.
50. Eig, *Ali*, 246.
51. Montville, *Sting Like a Bee*, 162–63.
52. Zirin, *Jim Brown*, 148.
53. Montville, *Sting Like a Bee*, 162.
54. SI Staff, "The Activist Minds," 54.
55. Eig, *Ali*, 248.
56. Zirin, *Jim Brown*, 149.
57. SI Staff, "The Activist Minds," 54.
58. *Sports Illustrated*, June 19, 1967.
59. Thomas Hauser with Muhammad Ali, *Muhammad Ali: His Life and Times* (New York: Simon & Schuster, 1991), 178.
60. Wright, "Remembering Cleveland's Muhammad Ali Summit, 45 Years Later."
61. Zirin, *Jim Brown*, 147.
62. Bill Russell with Tex Maule, "I Am Not Worried about Ali," *Sports Illustrated*, June 19, 1967, 18–21.

63. *Clay v. United States*, 403 US 698 (1971).
64. SI Staff, "The Activist Minds," 56.
65. Wright, "Remembering Cleveland's Muhammad Ali Summit, 45 Years Later."
66. Montville, *Sting Like a Bee*, 164.
67. SI Staff, "The Activist Minds," 56.
68. Wright, "Remembering Cleveland's Muhammad Ali Summit, 45 Years Later."
69. Zirin, *Jim Brown*, 145–46.
70. Hauser with Ali, *Muhammad Ali*, 201.
71. John Miller and Aaron Kendi, eds. *Muhammad Ali: Ringside* (Boston: Little, Brown, 1999), 34.
72. Marc Ferris, *Star-Spangled Banner: The Unlikely Story of America's National Anthem* (New York: MJF Books, 2014), 213.
73. David W. Zang, *Sports Wars: Athletes in the Age of Aquarius* (Fayetteville: University of Arkansas Press, 2001), 3.
74. *New York Times*, October 6, 2017.
75. Mark Clague, *O Say Can You Hear? A Cultural Biography of the Star-Spangled Banner* (New York: W. W. Norton, 2022), 219.
76. Ferris, *Star-Spangled Banner*, 214.
77. Clague, *O Say Can You Hear?*, 220.
78. Ferris, *Star-Spangled Banner*, 214.
79. Clague, *O Say Can You Hear?*, 220.
80. Roger Weber, "The 1968 National Anthem Performance That Changed Jose Feliciano's Life," *Only a Game*, WBUR, April 12, 2019. https://www.wbur.org/onlyagame/2019/04/12/jose-feliciano-susan-tigers-world-series.
81. Zang, *Sports Wars*, 3.
82. The 1968 performance is available at https://www.youtube.com/watch?v=aQkY2UFBUb4.
83. Clague, *O Say Can You Hear?*, 221.
84. Ferris, *Star-Spangled Banner*, 214.
85. Ferris, *Star-Spangled Banner*, 214.
86. Zang, *Sports Wars*, 3.
87. Zang, *Sports Wars*, 3; Clague, *O Say Can You Hear?*, 219; John Florio and Ouisie Shapiro, *One Nation under Baseball: How the 1960s Collided with the National Pastime* (Lincoln: University of Nebraska Press, 2017), 152; Ferris, *Star-Spangled Banner*, 214.
88. Ferris, *Star-Spangled Banner*, 214.
89. Zang, *Sports Wars*, 3.
90. Clague, *O Say Can You Hear?*, 219.
91. Ferris, *Star-Spangled Banner*, 215.
92. Zang, *Sports Wars*, 5.
93. Scott Ferkovich, "October 7, 1968: Jose Feliciano Lights Tigers' Fire," Society for American Baseball Research, https://sabr.org/gamesproj/game/october-7-1968-jose-feliciano-lights-tigers-fire/.
94. Weber, "The 1968 National Anthem Performance That Changed Jose Feliciano's Life."

95. Zang, *Sports Wars*, 7.
96. Clague, *O Say Can You Hear?*, 220–21.
97. *Free Press*, Detroit, October 8, 1967.
98. Zang, *Sports Wars*, 4.
99. Zang, *Sports Wars*, 7.
100. Zang, *Sports Wars*, 8.
101. Zang, *Sports Wars*, 7.
102. Clague, *O Say Can You Hear?*, 220.
103. Zang, *Sports Wars*, 159–60 fn2.
104. Zang, *Sports Wars*, 5.
105. Zang, *Sports Wars*, 7.
106. Weber, "The 1968 National Anthem Performance That Changed Jose Feliciano's Life."
107. Clague, *O Say Can You Hear?*, 222; Ferris, *Star-Spangled Banner*, 216.
108. Zang, *Sports Wars*, 8.
109. Clague, *O Say Can You Hear?*, 222.
110. Florio and Shapiro, *One Nation under Baseball*, 152–53.
111. *Free Press*, Detroit, October 9, 1968.
112. *New York Times*, October 27, 1967.
113. Zang, *Sports Wars*, 7.
114. Clague, *O Say Can You Hear?*, 221.
115. Zang, *Sports Wars*, 8.
116. Ferris, *Star-Spangled Banner*, 220.
117. Clague, *O Say Can You Hear?*, 222.
118. Zang, *Sports Wars*, 25–26.
119. Clague, *O Say Can You Hear?*, 222.
120. Ferris, *Star-Spangled Banner*, 214.
121. Ferris, *Star-Spangled Banner*, 216.
122. Clague, *O Say Can You Hear?*, 222.
123. Zang, *Sports Wars*, 26.
124. Clague, *O Say Can You Hear?*, 223.
125. The 2010 performance is available at https://www.youtube.com/watch?v=3Up_2VO_Vms.
126. Ferris, *Star-Spangled Banner*, 250.
127. The 2013 performance is available at https://www.youtube.com/watch?v=tnGYuPGLux4.
128. The 2018 Washington, D.C. performance is available at https://www.youtube.com/watch?v=5Ng_dXS2doo.
129. Weber, "The 1968 National Anthem Performance That Changed Jose Feliciano's Life."
130. Weber, "The 1968 National Anthem Performance That Changed Jose Feliciano's Life."
131. The 2018 Comerica Park performance is available at https://www.facebook.com/watch/?v=4818047711637861.

132. "Tampa Bay Rays Use All-Latin American Starting Lineup on Roberto Clemente Day," ESPN.com, September 15, 2022, https://www.espn.com/mlb/story/_/id/34600221/tampa-bay-rays-use-all-latin-american-starting-lineup-roberto-clemente-day.

133. Samuel O. Regalado, "Read All About It! The Spanish-Language Press, the Dodgers, and the Giants, 1958–1982," in Jorge Iber and Samuel O. Regalado, eds., *Mexican Americans and Sports: A Reader on Athletics and Barrio Life* (College Station: Texas A&M University Press, 2007), 145.

134. Dave Zirin, *Welcome to the Terrordome: The Pain, Politics, and Promise of Sports* (Chicago: Haymarket Books, 2007), 24–25.

135. Florio and Shapiro, *One Nation under Baseball*, 133–34.

136. David Maraniss, *Clemente: The Passion and Grace of Baseball's Last Hero* (New York: Simon & Schuster, 2006), 70–71.

137. Maraniss, *Clemente*, 173.

138. Jorge Iber, Samuel O. Regalado, José M. Alamillo, and Arnoldo De León, *Latinos in U.S. Sport: A History of Isolation, Cultural Identity, and Acceptance* (Champaign, IL: Human Kinetics, 2011), 164–65.

139. Maraniss, *Clemente*, 172.

140. Bob Nightengale, "'Ashamed of the Game': Baker on Series' Lack of Black Players," *Sports Weekly*, November 2–8, 2022, 3.

CHAPTER 7

1. See Kevin Witherspoon, *Before the Eyes of the World: Mexico and the 1968 Olympic Games* (DeKalb: Northern Illinois University Press, 2009).

2. Jack Olsen, *The Black Athlete: A Shameful Story: The Myth of Integration in American Sport* (N.p.: Crime Rant Books, 2015), 40. This independently published book is a compilation of the five *Sports Illustrated* articles from the 1968 series of the same name.

3. Pete Axthelm, "Boycott Now—Boycott Later?" *Sports Illustrated*, February 28, 1968, 24–26. See also Charles H. Martin, *Benching Jim Crow: The Rise and Fall of the Color Line in Southern College Sports, 1890–1980* (Urbana: University of Illinois Press, 2010), 117–19.

4. Gary James Bergera, "'This Time of Crisis': The Race-Based Anti-BYU Athletic Protests of 1968–1971," *Utah Historical Quarterly* 81, no. 3 (2013): 229.

5. Harry Edwards, *The Revolt of the Black Athlete: 50th Anniversary Edition* (Urbana: University of Illinois Press, 2017).

6. Richard Hoffer, *Something in the Air: American Passion and Defiance in the 1968 Mexico City Olympics* (New York: Free Press, 2009), 101–2.

7. Simon Henderson, *Sidelined: How American Sports Challenged the Black Freedom Struggle* (Lexington: University Press of Kentucky, 2013), 91–92.

8. *Chicago American*, October 19, 1968.

9. Wyomia Tyus and Elizabeth Terzakis, *Tigerbelle: The Wyomia Tyus Story* (Brooklyn, NY: Akashic Books, 2018), 17.

10. Barbara Heilman, "Like Nothing Else in Tennessee," *Sports Illustrated*, November 14, 1960, 52.

11. Cat M. Ariail, *Passing the Baton: Black Women Track Stars and American Identity* (Urbana: University of Illinois Press, 2020), 84.

12. Ariail, *Passing the Baton*, 100.

13. Carroll Van West, "The Tennessee State Tigerbelles: Cold Warriors of the Track," in David K. Wiggins and Ryan A. Swanson, eds., *Separate Games: African American Sport behind the Walls of Segregation* (Fayetteville: University of Arkansas Press, 2016), 71.

14. Quoted in Jennifer H. Lansbury, *A Spectacular Leap: Black Women Athletes in Twentieth-Century America* (Fayetteville: University of Arkansas Press, 2014), 115.

15. Gilbert Rogan, "Flamin' Mamies Bouffant Belles," *Sports Illustrated*, April 20, 1964, 31.

16. Rogan, "Flamin' Mamies Bouffant Belles," 30. In 1963, the Texas Track Club came in twelfth at the national AAU championships—respectable, certainly, but hardly elite.

17. Kit Fox, "How Big Hair Got These Runners on the Cover of Sports Illustrated," *Runner's World*, November 3, 2015, https://www.runnersworld.com/runners-stories/a20856319/how-big-hair-got-these-runners-on-the-cover-of-sports-illustrated/.

18. "19th Hole: The Readers Take Over," *Sports Illustrated*, May 4, 1964, 114.

19. Fox, "How Big Hair Got These Runners on the Cover of Sports Illustrated."

20. Tyus and Terzakis, *Tigerbelle*, 21.

21. Tyus and Terzakis, *Tigerbelle*, 75–76.

22. Rogan, "Flamin' Mamies Bouffant Belles," 31.

23. Rogan, "Flamin' Mamies Bouffant Belles," 32.

24. Van West, "The Tennessee State Tigerbelles," 61.

25. Lansbury, *A Spectacular Leap*, 160.

26. Amy Bass, *Not the Triumph but the Struggle: The 1968 Olympics and the Making of the Black Athlete* (Minneapolis: University of Minnesota Press, 2002), 189.

27. Hoffer, *Something in the Air*, 91.

28. Douglas Hartmann, *Race, Culture, and the Revolt of the Black Athlete: The 1968 Olympics and Their Aftermath* (Chicago: University of Chicago Press, 2003), 125.

29. Edwards, *The Revolt of the Black Athlete*, xxi.

30. Tyus and Terzakis, *Tigerbelle*, 173.

31. Tyus and Terzakis, *Tigerbelle*, 173.

32. Bass, *Not the Triumph but the Struggle*, 266.

33. Tyus and Terzakis, *Tigerbelle*, 173.

34. Tyus and Terzakis, *Tigerbelle*, 173–74.

35. Bass, *Not the Triumph but the Struggle*, 226.

36. Shana Renee, "Track Legend Wyomia Tyus Protested at the '68 Olympics and Hardly Anyone Noticed," ESPN, November 7, 2018, https://www.espn.com/espnw/voices/story/_/id/25211468/track-legend-wyomia-tyus-protested-68-olympics-hardly-anyone-noticed.

37. Tyus and Terzakis, *Tigerbelle*, 175.

38. Tyus and Terzakis, *Tigerbelle*, 175–76.

39. See Jules Boykoff, *Power Games: A Political History of the Olympics* (London: Verso, 2016); and David Goldblatt, *The Games: A Global History of the Olympics* (New York: W. W. Norton, 2016).

40. Tyus and Terzakis, *Tigerbelle*, 176.

41. Tyus and Terzakis, *Tigerbelle*, 177.

42. Renee, "Track Legend Wyomia Tyus Protested at the '68 Olympics and Hardly Anyone Noticed."

43. Tyus and Terzakis, *Tigerbelle*, 177.

44. Tyus and Terzakis, *Tigerbelle*, 176.

45. Renee, "Track Legend Wyomia Tyus Protested at the '68 Olympics and Hardly Anyone Noticed."

46. Tyus and Terzakis, *Tigerbelle*, 18.

47. Amby Burfoot, *First Ladies of Running: 22 Inspiring Profiles of the Rebels, Rule Breakers, and Visionaries Who Changed the Sport Forever* (New York: Rodale, 2016), 89.

48. Lindsay Parks Pieper, *Sex Testing: Gender Policing in Women's Sports* (Urbana: University of Illinois Press, 2016), 109–10.

49. Pieper, *Sex Testing*, 110.

50. Pieper, *Sex Testing*, 128; *Los Angeles Times*, December 29, 1981.

51. Pieper, *Sex Testing*, 128.

52. *New York Times*, April 19, 1984.

53. Burfoot, *First Ladies of Running*, 94–95.

54. Shola Lynch, dir., *IX for IX: Runner* (ESPN Films, 2014).

55. Burfoot, *First Ladies of Running*, 95.

56. Burfoot, *First Ladies of Running*, 95.

57. Lynch, *IX for IX: Runner*.

58. *Sports Illustrated*, December 26, 1983–January 2, 1984.

59. Frank Deford, "Cheer, Cheer, Cheer for the Home Team," *Sports Illustrated*, August 13, 1984, 38.

60. Lynch, *IX for IX: Runner*.

61. Jeff Hollobaugh, *The 100 Greatest Track and Field Battles of the 20th Century* (Dexter, MI: Michtrack Books, 2012), 52.

62. Hollobaugh, *The 100 Greatest Track and Field Battles of the 20th Century*, 52.

63. Among the many works on South African sport and politics, see Robert Archer and Antoine Bouillon, *The South African Game: Sport and Racism* (London: Zed Press, 1982); Douglass Booth, *The Race Game: Sport and Politics in South Africa* (London: Frank Cass, 1998); John Nauright, *Long Run to Freedom: Sport, Cultures, and Identities in South Africa* (Morgantown, WV: Fitness Information Technology, 2010); and Derek Catsam, *Flashpoint: How a Little-Known Sporting Event Fueled America's Anti-Apartheid Movement* (Lanham, MD: Rowman & Littlefield, 2021).

64. See Jason Henderson, *Collision Course: The Olympic Tragedy of Mary Decker and Zola Budd* (Edinburgh: Arena Sport, 2016); Kyle Keiderling, *Olympic Collision: The Story of Mary Decker and Zola Budd* (Lincoln: University of Nebraska Press, 2016); Lynch, *IX for IX: Runner*.

65. Burfoot, *First Ladies of Running*, 98.

66. Lynch, *IX for IX: Runner*.

67. Hollobaugh, *The 100 Greatest Track and Field Battles of the 20th Century*, 52.

68. Keiderling, *Olympic Collision*, 154.

69. Burfoot, *First Ladies of Running*, 98.

70. Pieper, *Sex Testing*, 212, fn81.

71. Lynch, *IX for IX: Runner.*
72. Keiderling, *Olympic Collision,* 154.
73. *Los Angeles Times,* August 11, 1984.
74. *Los Angeles Times,* August 11, 1984.
75. Lynch, *IX for IX: Runner.*
76. Burfoot, *First Ladies of Running,* 99.
77. *Time,* July 29, 1985, 76.
78. *Newsweek,* July 29, 1985, 62. Portentously, on the same page as the story on the rematch was a little paragraph announcing that a Concord, New Hampshire, schoolteacher named Sharon Christa McAuliffe had been selected "to be the first 'citizen passenger' to launched into space."
79. Lynch, *IX for IX: Runner.*
80. For the stats in these races see Henderson, *Collision Course,* 231–32.

CHAPTER 8

1. Title IX of the Education Amendments of 1972 (Public Law No. 92-318, 86 Stat. 235). See also Sherry Boschert, *37 Words: Title IX and Fifty Years of Fighting Sex Discrimination* (New York: New Press, 2022); Susan Ware, *Title IX: A Brief History with Documents* (Long Grove, IL: Waveland Press, 2014).
2. 110 *Congressional Record,* February 8, 1964, 2577.
3. Laura Mogulescu, "How We Told the Ongoing Story of Title IX," History News Network, May 2022, https://historynewsnetwork.org/article/183202.
4. Billie Jean King, Johnette Howard, and Maryanne Vollers, *All In: An Autobiography* (New York: Knopf, 2021), 83–89.
5. King, Howard, and Vollers, *All In,* 210.
6. King, Howard, and Vollers, *All In,* 235.
7. Boscherts, *37 Words,* 116.
8. Mary Ellen Pethel, *Title IX, Pat Summitt, and Tennessee's Trailblazers: 50 Years, 50 Stories* (Knoxville: University of Tennessee Press, 2022), 1.
9. Kate Fagan, "Don't Look Away," *Sports Illustrated,* May 13, 2021, https://www.si.com/wnba/2021/05/13/wnba-25th-season-daily-cover.
10. Megan Rapinoe, *One Life* (New York: Penguin, 2020) 194–95; Caitlin Murray, *The National Team: The Inside Story of the Women Who Changed Soccer* (New York: Abrams Press, 2019), 315–18.
11. *Sports Illustrated,* December 16–23, 2019.
12. *GQ,* December 2019–January 2020.
13. The best history of the USWNT is Murray, *The National Team.*
14. *Cannon v. University of Chicago,* 441 US 677 (1979).
15. *Grove City College v. Bell,* 465 US 555 (1984).
16. *Franklin v. Gwinnett County Public Schools,* 503 US 60 (1992); *Cohen et al. v. Brown University,* 809 F. Supp. 978 (1992).
17. *Gonyo v. Drake University,* 837 F. Supp. 989 (1993); *Favia v. Indiana University of Pennsylvania,* 812 F. Supp. 578 (1993).
18. Mogulescu, "How We Told the Ongoing Story of Title IX."

19. Serena Williams, as told to Rob Haskell, "Serena Williams Says Farewell to Tennis on Her Own Terms—and in Her Own Words," *Vogue*, September 2022, https://www.vogue.com/article/serena-williams-retirement-in-her-own-words.

20. King, Howard, and Vollers, *All In*, 223.

21. David Goldblatt, *The Games: A Global History of the Olympics* (New York: W. W. Norton, 2016), 316.

22. Peter Dreier and Robert Elias, *Baseball Rebels: The Players, People, and Social Movements That Shook Up the Game and Changed America* (Lincoln: University of Nebraska Press, 2022), 212.

23. Dreier and Elias, *Baseball Rebels*, 213.

24. Dreier and Elias, *Baseball Rebels*, 214.

25. Glenn Burke with Erik Sherman, *Out at Home: The True Story of Glenn Burke, Baseball's First Openly Gay Player* (New York: Berkley, 2015).

26. Jim Buzinski, "Moment #15: Former NBA Player John Amaechi Comes Out," *Outsports*, September 18, 2011, https://www.outsports.com/2011/9/18/4051846/moment-15-former-nba-player-john-amaechi-comes-out.

27. Dave Zirin, *Welcome to the Terrordome: The Pain, Politics, and Promise of Sports* (Chicago: Haymarket Books, 2007), 228.

28. John Amaechi, "A Gay Former NBA Player Responds to Kobe Bryant," *Off the Dribble* (blog), April 15, 2011, https://archive.nytimes.com/offthedribble.blogs.nytimes.com/2011/04/15/a-gay-former-player-responds-to-kobe-bryant/.

29. Alex Reimer, "Why Kobe Bryant's Evolution on LGBTQ Issues Was a Really Big Deal," *Outsports*, January 27, 2020, https://www.outsports.com/2020/1/27/21083018/kobe-bryant-lakers-nba-lgbtq-spots-ally-basketball.

30. Cyd Zeigler, "Jason Collins Played It Right with Patience and Hard Work," *Outsports*, February 23, 2014, https://www.outsports.com/2014/2/23/5433726/jason-collins-brooklyn-nets-gay-nba-patience.

31. Out.com Editors, "Watch: OUT + Barefoot Present: One Stride, Many Journeys, Featuring Robbie Rogers and Jason Collins," *Out*, November 1, 2017, https://www.out.com/2017/11/01/watch-out-barefoot-present-one-stride-many-journeys-featuring-robbie-rogers-and-jason-collins. See also Cyd Zeigler, "Robbie Rogers Says LGBT Athletes Coming Out Is 'the Answer.' He's Right," *Outsports*, November 2, 2017, https://www.outsports.com/2017/11/2/16600728/nba-pro-sports-gay-athlete-jason-collins-robbie-rogers.

32. Holly Yan and Dave Alsup, "NFL Draft: Reactions Heat up after Michael Sam Kisses Boyfriend on TV," CNN, May 13, 2014, https://www.cnn.com/2014/05/12/us/michael-sam-nfl-kiss-reaction.

33. Jim Buzinski, "Michael Sam: 'If I want to kiss my boyfriend, I'm gonna kiss him,'" *Outsports*, January 13, 2015, https://www.outsports.com/2015/1/13/7539743/michael-sam-vito-cammisano-kiss-esquire-interview-dave-kopay.

34. John Howard, "Carl Nassib's Coming Out Will Save Lives; How Many Depends on the NFL's Support," History News Network, July 4, 2021, https://historynewsnetwork.org/article/180610.

35. Cyd Zeigler, "Outsports' 100 Most Important Moments in LGBT-Sports History," *Outsports*, July 5, 2011, https://www.outsports.com/2011/7/5/4051478/outsports-100 -most-important-moments-in-lgbt-sports-history.

36. David Kopay with Perry Deane Young, *The David Kopay Story: An Extraordinary Self-Revelation* (New York: Bantam Books, 1977).

37. Jim Buzinski, "Dave Kopay Comes Out as Gay in Newspaper Interview," *Outsports*, October 4, 2011, https://www.outsports.com/2020/10/31/21543248/celebrating-lgbtq -sports-history-dave-kopay-nfl-washington-coming-out.

38. Kopay and Young, *The David Kopay Story*, 242.

39. The latest update on the number of states with such bans can be found at the LGBTQ Movement Enhancement Project, https://www.lgbtmap.org/equality-maps/ sports_participation_bans.

40. See Lindsay Parks Pieper, *Sex Testing: Gender Policing in Women's Sports* (Urbana: University of Illinois Press, 2016).

CONCLUSION

1. Margaret Haerens, *The NFL National Anthem Protests* (Santa Barbara, CA: ABC-CLIO, 2019), 18.

2. Haerens, *The NFL National Anthem Protests*, 1.

3. Mark Clague, *O Say Can You Hear? A Cultural Biography of the Star-Spangled Banner* (New York: W. W. Norton, 2022), 180.

4. Eric Reid, "Why Colin Kaepernick and I Decided to Take a Knee," *New York Times*, September 25, 2017.

5. Reid, "Why Colin Kaepernick and I Decided to Take a Knee."

6. Brit Bennett, "Victory Formation," in Michael Chabon and Ayeley Waldman, eds., *Fight of the Century: Writers Reflect on 100 Years of Landmark ACLU Cases* (New York: Avid Reader Press, 2020), 31.

7. Clague, *O Say Can You Hear?*, 292.

8. Clague, *O Say Can You Hear?*, 181.

9. Stave Marston, "The Revival of Athlete Activism(s): Divergent Black Politics in the 2016 Presidential Election Engagements of LeBron James and Colin Kaepernick," in Frank Jacob, ed., *Sports and Politics* (Berlin: De Gruyter, 2022), 120.

10. Dan Cancian, "Everything Trump Has Said About NFL Kneeling So Far," *Newsweek*, June 8, 2020, https://www.newsweek.com/everything-donald-trump-said-nfl -anthem-protests-1509333.

11. Haerens, *The NFL National Anthem Protests*, 1.

12. John Feinstein, *Raise a Fist, Take a Knee: Race and the Illusion of Progress in Modern Sports* (New York: Little, Brown, 2021), 332.

13. Clague, *O Say Can You Hear?*, 186.

14. Dave Zirin, *The Kaepernick Effect: Taking a Knee, Changing the World* (New York: New Press, 2021), xii.

15. Mike Freeman, *Football's Fearless Activists: How Colin Kaepernick, Eric Reed, Kenny Stills, and Fellow Athletes Stood up to the NFL and President Trump* (New York: Sports Publishing, 2020), 181 and passim.

16. Amira Rose Davis, "Sixty Years Ago She Refused to Stand for the Anthem," *Zora (Medium)*, September 26, 2019, https://zora.medium.com/sixty-years-ago-she-refused-to-stand-for-the-anthem-cf443b4e75c7.

17. Fred Barbash and Travis M. Andrews, "A Brief History of 'The Star-Spangled Banner' Being Played at Games and Getting No Respect," *Washington Post*, August 30, 2016.

18. Quoted in Christopher D. Rounds, "The Policing of Patriotism: African American Athletes and the Expression of Dissent," *Journal of Sport History* 47, no. 2 (2020): 122.

19. Marc Ferris, *Star-Spangled Banner: The Unlikely Story of America's National Anthem* (New York: MJF Books, 2014), 245.

20. Davis, "Sixty Years Ago She Refused to Stand for the Anthem."

21. "National Anthem at Goshen College," Goshen College website, https://www.goshen.edu/news/anthem/.

22. Davis, "Sixty Years Ago She Refused to Stand for the Anthem."

23. Christopher Brito, "Olympic Hammer Thrower Gwen Berry Responds to Backlash after She Turns Her Back on the U.S. Flag during National Anthem," CBS News, June 29, 2021, https://www.cbsnews.com/news/gwen-berry-olympics-national-anthem-flag/.

24. Quoted in an Associated Press story found in *Odessa American*, Texas, June 5, 2020.

25. Nancy Armour, "NFL Had to Change. Players Made Sure It Did," *Sports Weekly*, June 10–16, 2020.

26. *Sports Illustrated*, December 2020.

27. Ferris, *Star-Spangled Banner*, 223.

28. Clague, *O Say Can You Hear?*, 181.

29. Alex Shephard, "Republicans Have Ruined Sports for Republicans," *The Soapbox* (blog), April 19, 2021, https://newrepublic.com/article/162092/republicans-ruined-sports-republicans?utm_source=newsletter&utm_medium=email&utm_campaign=tnr_daily.

30. *Minersville School District v. Gobitis*, 310 US 586 (1940).

31. *West Virginia State Board of Education v. Barnette*, 319 US 624 (1943).

32. *West Virginia State Board of Education v. Barnette*, 319 US 624 (1943).

33. Leo Pfeffer, "*West Virginia State Board of Education v. Barnette*," in Kermit L. Hall, ed., *The Oxford Guide to United States Supreme Court Decisions* (Oxford: Oxford University Press, 1999), 331.

34. *Tinker v. Des Moines Independent Community School District*, 393 U. S. 503 (1969).

35. *T.V. & M.K. v. Smith-Green Community School Corporation*, 807 F. Supp. 2d 767 (N.D. Ind. 2011).

36. Lee Green, "Limits on Schools to Punish Student-Athletes for National Anthem Protests," National Federation of State High School Associations, April 5, 2017, https://www.nfhs.org/articles/limits-on-schools-to-punish-student-athletes-for-national-anthem-protests/.

37. Elahe Izade, "The Incidents That Led to the University of Missouri President's Resignation," *Washington Post*, November 9, 2015.

38. Jemele Hill, "It's Time for Black Athletes to Leave White Colleges," *Atlantic*, October 2019. See also Andrew Perry, "Black Athletes Have a Trump Card They Are Not

Using Enough," *Hechinger Report*, September 10, 2019, https://hechingerreport.org/black
-athletes-have-a-trump-card-they-are-not-using-enough/.

39. *West Virginia State Board of Education v. Barnette*, 319 US 624 (1943).

40. Ben Railton, *Of Thee I Sing: The Contested History of American Patriotism* (Lanham, MD: Rowman & Littlefield, 2021), xii and passim.

41. Ferris, *Star-Spangled Banner*, 243.

42. Clague, *O Say Can You Hear?*, 226–30.

43. *San Diego Tribune*, July 26, 1990.

44. Barbash and Andrews, "A Brief History of 'The Star-Spangled Banner' Being Played at Games and Getting No Respect."

45. Sean Deveney, "Hall of Famer Maurice Cheeks Recalls National Anthem Assist: 'I Didn't Know I Would Do That,'" *Sporting News*, September 7, 2018, https://www
.sportingnews.com/us/nba/news/maurice-mo-cheeks-national-anthem-natalie-gilbert
-video-coach-nba-hall-of-fame-trail-blazers/h749s8eomo4l1gy86ju2g9r26.

46. Reid, "Why Colin Kaepernick and I Decided to Take a Knee."

47. Bennett, "Victory Formation," 32.

48. Etan Thomas, *We Matter: Athletes and Activism* (Brooklyn, NY: Akashic Books, 2018), 71.

49. Reid, "Why Colin Kaepernick and I Decided to Take a Knee."

50. *West Virginia State Board of Education v. Barnette*, 319 US 624 (1943).

51. Howard Bryant, *Full Dissidence: Notes from an Uneven Playing Field* (Boston: Beacon Press, 2020), 1.

Bibliography

Books

Archer, Robert, and Antoine Bouillon. *The South African Game: Sport and Racism.* London: Zed Press, 1982.

Ariail, Cat M. *Passing the Baton: Black Women Track Stars and American Identity.* Urbana: University of Illinois Press, 2020.

Ashe, Arthur R., Jr. *A Hard Road to Glory: A History of the African American Athlete, 1919–1945.* New York: Warner Books, 1988.

Atwood, Gretchen. *Lost Champions: Four Men, Two Teams, and the Breaking of Pro Football's Color Line.* New York: Bloomsbury, 2016.

Auerbach, Red, and John Feinstein. *Let Me Tell You a Story: A Lifetime in the Game.* New York: Little, Brown, 2004.

Babicz, Martin C., and Thomas W. Zeiler. *National Pastime: U.S. History through Baseball.* Lanham, MD: Rowman & Littlefield, 2017.

Balliett, Will, and Thomas Dyja, eds. *The Hard Way: Writing by the Rebels Who Changed Sports.* New York: Thunder's Mouth Press, 1999.

Bass, Amy. *Not the Triumph but the Struggle: The 1968 Olympics and the Making of the Black Athlete.* Minneapolis: University of Minnesota Press, 2002.

Bass, Amy, ed. *In the Game: Race, Identity, and Sports in the Twentieth Century.* New York: Palgrave Macmillan, 2005.

Bell, Andrew McIlwaine. *The Origins of Southern College Football: How an Ivy League Game Became a Dixie Tradition.* Baton Rouge: Louisiana State University Press, 2020.

Beste, Laken, and Rowan Lincoln. *Ballin' during the Black Fives Era: A Forgotten Time to Be Honored and Remembered.* Coppell, TX: Beste & Lincoln, 2021.

Booth, Douglass. *The Race Game: Sport and Politics in South Africa.* London: Frank Cass, 1998.

Boschert, Sherry. *37 Words: Title IX and Fifty Years of Fighting Sex Discrimination.* New York: New Press, 2022.

Boykoff, Jules. *Power Games: A Political History of the Olympics.* London: Verso, 2016.

Branson, Douglas M. *Greatness in the Shadows: Larry Doby and the Integration of the American League.* Lincoln: University of Nebraska Press, 2016.

Brown, Jim, with Steve Delsohn. *Out of Bounds: In His Own Words.* New York: Citadel, 2018.

Bryant, Howard. *Full Dissidence: Notes from an Uneven Playing Field*. Boston: Beacon Press, 2020.

———. *The Heritage: Black Athletes, a Divided America, and the Politics of Patriotism*. Boston: Beacon Press, 2018.

———. *Shut Out: A Story of Race and Baseball in Boston*. New York: Routledge, 2002.

Burfoot, Amby. *First Ladies of Running: 22 Inspiring Profiles of the Rebels, Rule Breakers, and Visionaries Who Changed the Sport Forever*. New York: Rodale, 2016.

Burin, Eric, ed. *Protesting on Bended Knee: Race, Dissent, and Patriotism in 21st-Century America*. Grand Forks: Digital Press at the University of North Dakota, 2019.

Burke, Glenn, with Erik Sherman. *Out at Home: The True Story of Glenn Burke, Baseball's First Openly Gay Player*. New York: Berkley, 2015.

Cagan, Joanna, and Neil deMause. *Field of Schemes: How the Great Stadium Swindle Turns Public Money into Private Profit*. Monroe, ME: Common Courage Press, 1998.

Campbell, Eddie. *The Goat Getters: Jack Johnson, the Fight of the Century, and How a Bunch of Raucous Cartoonists Reinvented Comics*. San Diego, CA: IDW Publishing, 2018.

Carnegie, Herb, with Bernice Carnegie. *A Fly in a Pail of Milk: The Herb Carnegie Story*. Toronto: ECW Press, 2019.

Catsam, Derek. *Bleeding Red: A Red Sox Fan's Diary of the 2004 Season*. Washington, DC: Vellum, 2005.

———. *Flashpoint: How a Little-Known Sporting Event Fueled America's Anti-Apartheid Movement*. Lanham, MD: Rowman & Littlefield, 2021.

Chabon, Michael, and Ayelet Waldman, eds. *Fight of the Century: Writers Reflect on 100 Years of Landmark ACLU Cases*. New York: Avid Reader Press, 2020.

Clague, Mark. *O Say Can You Hear? A Cultural Biography of the Star-Spangled Banner*. New York: W. W. Norton, 2022.

Connelly, Michael. *Rebound! Basketball, Busing, Larry Bird, and the Rebirth of Boston*. Minneapolis, MN: MVP Books, 2008.

Coverdale, Miles, Jr. *The 1960s in Sports: A Decade of Change*. Lanham, MD: Rowman & Littlefield, 2020.

Demas, Lane. *Integrating the Gridiron: Black Civil Rights and American College Football*. New Brunswick, NJ: Rutgers University Press, 2010.

Devaney, Sean. *The Original Curse: Did the Cubs Throw the 1918 World Series to Babe Ruth's Red Sox and Incite the Black Sox Scandal?* New York: McGraw-Hill, 2009.

Dorinson, Joseph, and Joram Warmund. *Jackie Robinson: Race, Sports, and the American Dream*. New York: M. E. Sharpe, 1998.

Dorman, Michael. *We Shall Overcome: A Reporter's Eye-Witness Account of the Year of Racial Strife and Triumph*. New York: Dell, 1964.

Dreier, Peter, and Robert Elias. *Baseball Rebels: The Players, People, and Social Movements That Shook Up the Game and Changed America*. Lincoln: University of Nebraska Press, 2022.

Edwards, Harry. *The Revolt of the Black Athlete: 50th Anniversary Edition*. Urbana: University of Illinois Press, 2017.

Eig, Jonathan. *Ali: A Life*. Boston: Houghton Mifflin Harcourt, 2017.

Elder, Bill. *All Guts and No Glory: An Alabama Coach's Memoir of Desegregating College Athletics.* Montgomery, AL: NewSouth Books, 2007.

Epplin, Luke. *Our Team: The Epic Story of Four Men and the World Series That Changed Baseball.* New York: Flatiron Books, 2021.

Falkner, David. *Great Time Coming: The Life of Jackie Robinson from Baseball to Birmingham.* New York: Touchstone, 1995.

Feinstein, John. *Raise a Fist, Take a Knee: Race and the Illusion of Progress in Modern Sports.* New York: Little, Brown, 2021.

Ferris, Marc. *Star-Spangled Banner: The Unlikely Story of America's National Anthem.* New York: MJF Books, 2014.

Field, Russell, ed. *Playing for a Change: The Continuing Struggle for Sport and Recreation.* Toronto: University of Toronto Press, 2015.

Fields, Sarah K. *Female Gladiators: Gender, Law, and Contact Sport in America.* Chicago: University of Illinois Press, 2005.

Fink, Rob. *Football at Historically Black Colleges and Universities in Texas.* College Station: Texas A&M University Press, 2019.

Florio, John, and Ouisie Shapiro. *One Nation under Baseball: How the 1960s Collided with the National Pastime.* Lincoln: University of Nebraska Press, 2017.

Frazier, Nishani. *Harambee City: The Congress of Racial Equality in Cleveland and the Rise of Black Power Populism.* Fayetteville: University of Arkansas Press, 2017.

Freedman, Lew. *Dynasty: Auerbach, Cousy, Havlicek, Russell, and the Rise of the Boston Celtics.* Guilford, CT: Lyons Press, 2008.

Freedman, Samuel G. *Breaking the Line: The Season in Black College Football That Transformed the Sport and Changed the Course of Civil Rights.* New York: Simon & Schuster, 2013.

Freeman, Mike. *Football's Fearless Activists: How Colin Kaepernick, Eric Reid, Kenny Stills, and Fellow Athletes Stood up to the NFL and President Trump.* New York: Sports Publishing, 2020.

Frei, Terry. *Horns, Hogs, and Nixon Coming: Texas vs. Arkansas in Dixie's Last Stand.* New York: Simon & Schuster, 2002.

Frost, Amanda. *You Are Not American: Citizenship Stripping from Dred Scott to the Dreamers.* Boston: Beacon Press, 2021.

Gallico, Paul. *Farewell to Sport.* Lincoln, NE: Bison Books, 2008.

Gietschier, Steven, ed. *Replays, Rivalries, and Rumbles: The Most Iconic Moments in American Sports.* Urbana: University of Illinois Press, 2017.

Gitlin, Martin. *Powerful Moments in Sports: The Most Significant Sporting Events in American History.* Lanham, MD: Rowman & Littlefield, 2017.

Goldblatt, David. *The Games: A Global History of the Olympics.* New York: W. W. Norton, 2016.

Goudsouzian, Aram. *King of the Court: Bill Russell and the Basketball Revolution.* Berkeley: University of California Press, 2010.

Graham, Tom, and Rachel Graham Cody. *Getting Open: The Unknown Story of Bill Garrett and the Integration of College Basketball.* New York: Atria Books, 2006.

Greenberg, Murray. *Passing Game: Benny Friedman and the Transformation of Football.* New York: Public Affairs, 2008.

Gutlon, Jerry M. *It Was Never about the Babe: The Red Sox, Racism, Mismanagement, and the Curse of the Bambino.* New York: Skyhorse Publishing, 2009.

Guttmann, Allen. *The Olympics: A History of the Modern Games.* 2nd ed. Champaign: University of Illinois Press, 2002.

Haerens, Margaret. *The NFL National Anthem Protests.* Santa Barbara, CA: ABC-CLIO, 2019.

Hagerman, Bonnie. *Skimpy Coverage: Sports Illustrated and the Shaping of the Female Athlete.* Charlottesville: University of Virginia Press. 2023.

Hall, Kermit L., ed. *The Oxford Guide to United States Supreme Court Decisions.* New York: Oxford University Press, 1999.

Hartmann, Douglas. *Race, Culture, and the Revolt of the Black Athlete: The 1968 Olympic Protests and Their Aftermath.* Chicago: University of Chicago Press, 2003.

Hauser, Thomas, with Muhammad Ali. *Muhammad Ali: His Life and Times.* New York: Simon & Schuster, 1991.

Henderson, Jason. *Collision Course: The Olympic Tragedy of Mary Decker and Zola Budd.* Edinburgh: Arena Sport, 2016.

Henderson, Simon. *Sidelined: How American Sports Challenged the Black Freedom Struggle.* Lexington: University Press of Kentucky, 2013.

Hiestand, Emily, and Ande Zellman, eds. *The Good City: Writers Explore 21st-Century Boston.* Boston: Beacon Press, 2004.

Hoffer, Richard. *Something in the Air: American Passion and Defiance in the 1968 Mexico City Olympics.* New York: Free Press, 2009.

Holding, Michael, with Ed Hawkins. *Why We Kneel, How We Rise.* London: Simon & Schuster, 2021.

Hollobaugh, Jeff. *The 100 Greatest Track and Field Battles of the 20th Century.* Dexter, MI: Michtrack Books, 2012.

Iber, Jorge, and Samuel O. Regalado, eds. *Mexican Americans and Sports: A Reader on Athletics and Barrio Life.* College Station: Texas A&M University Press, 2007.

Iber, Jorge, Samuel O. Regalado, José M. Alamillo, and Arnoldo De León. *Latinos in U.S. Sport: A History of Isolation, Cultural Identity, and Acceptance.* Champaign, IL: Human Kinetics, 2011.

Jackson, Robert Scoop. *The Game Is Not a Game: The Power, Protest, and Politics of American Sports.* Chicago: Haymarket Books, 2020.

Jacob, Frank, ed. *Sports and Politics.* Berlin: De Gruyter, 2022.

Jarvie, Grant, ed. *Sport, Racism, and Ethnicity.* London: Falmer Press, 1991.

Jenkins, Sally. *The Real All Americans.* New York: Broadway Books, 2007.

Johnson, Claude. *The Black Fives: The Epic Story of Basketball's Forgotten Era.* New York: Abrams Press, 2021.

Johnson, James W. *The Black Bruins: The Remarkable Lives of UCLA's Jackie Robinson, Woody Strode, Tom Bradley, Kenny Washington, and Ray Bartlett.* Lincoln: University of Nebraska Press, 2017.

Johnson, Keyshawn, and Bob Glauber. *The Forgotten First: Kenny Washington, Woody Strode, Marion Motley, Bill Willis, and the Breaking of the NFL Color Barrier.* New York: Grand Central Publishing, 2021.

Keiderling, Kyle. *Olympic Collision: The Story of Mary Decker and Zola Budd.* Lincoln: University of Nebraska Press, 2016.

Kemper, Kurt Edward. *Before March Madness: The Wars for the Soul of College Basketball.* Urbana: University of Illinois Press, 2020.

King, Billie Jean, Johnette Howard, and Maryanne Vollers. *All In: An Autobiography.* New York: Knopf, 2021.

Kirwin, Bill, ed. *Out of the Shadows: African American Baseball from the Cuban Giants to Jackie Robinson.* Lincoln: University of Nebraska Press, 2005.

Kopay, David, and Perry Deane Young. *The David Kopay Story: An Extraordinary Self-Revelation.* New York: Bantam Books, 1977.

Krieger, Jorg, and Stephan Wassong, eds. *Dark Side of Sport.* Champaign, IL: Common Ground Research Networks, 2019.

Lansbury, Jennifer H. *A Spectacular Leap: Black Women Athletes in Twentieth-Century America.* Fayetteville: University of Arkansas Press, 2014.

Lapchick, Richard. *Broken Promises: Racism in American Sports.* New York: St Martin's/ Marek, 1984.

Leeke, Jim. *From the Dugouts to the Trenches: Baseball during the Great War.* Lincoln: University of Nebraska Press, 2017.

Leonard, David J. *Playing While White: The Privilege and Power On and Off the Field.* Seattle: University of Washington Press, 2017.

Levy, Alan H. *Tackling Jim Crow: Racial Segregation in Professional Football.* Jefferson, NC: McFarland, 2003.

Lock, Carlos A. *Black College Football: The Game That Time Forgot.* Sarasota, FL: Bardolf, 2020.

Long, Michael C., ed. *42 Today: Jackie Robinson and His Legacy.* New York: New York University Press, 2021.

Mailer, Norman. *The Fight.* New York: Random House, 1975.

Maraniss, Andrew. *Strong Inside: Perry Wallace and the Collision of Race and Sports in the South.* Nashville, TN: Vanderbilt University Press, 2014.

Maraniss, David. *Clemente: The Passion and Grace of Baseball's Last Hero.* New York: Simon & Schuster, 2006.

Marshall, William. *Baseball's Pivotal Era 1945–1951.* Lexington: University Press of Kentucky, 1999.

Martin, Charles H. *Benching Jim Crow: The Rise and Fall of the Color Line in Southern College Sports, 1890–1980.* Urbana: University of Illinois Press, 2010.

McRae, Donald. *Dark Trade: Lost in Boxing.* London: Mainstream Publishing, 1996.

———. *Heroes without a Country: America's Betrayal of Joe Louis and Jesse Owens.* New York: Ecco, 2002.

Michener, James A. *Sports in America.* New York: Dial Press, 2015.

Miller, John, and Aaron Kenedi, eds. *Muhammad Ali: Ringside.* Boston: Little, Brown, 1999.

Miller, Patrick B. *The Sporting World of the Modern South*. Chicago: University of Illinois Press, 2002.

Moffi, Larry, and Jonathan Kronstadt. *Crossing the Line: Black Major Leaguers 1947–1959*. Lincoln: University of Nebraska Press, 1994.

Montillo, Roseanne. *Fire on the Track: Betty Robinson and the Triumph of the Early Olympic Women*. New York: Crown, 2017.

Montville, Leigh. *Sting Like a Bee: Muhammad Ali vs. the United States of America 1966–1971*. New York: Doubleday, 2017.

———. *Tall Men, Short Shorts: The 1969 NBA Finals: Wilt, Russ, Lakers, Celtics, and a Very Young Sports Reporter*. New York: Doubleday, 2021.

Moore, Leonard N. *Carl B. Stokes and the Rise of Black Political Power*. Urbana: University of Illinois Press, 2003.

Moore, Louis. *We Will Win the Day: The Civil Rights Movement, the Black Athlete, and the Quest for Equality*. Lexington: University Press of Kentucky, 2021.

Mortillaro, Nicole. *Willie O'Ree: The Story of the First Black Player in the NHL*. Toronto: James Lorimer, 2020.

Murray, Caitlin. *The National Team: The Inside Story of the Women Who Changed Soccer*. New York: Abrams Press, 2019.

Nauright, John. *Long Run to Freedom: Sport, Cultures, and Identities in South Africa*. Morgantown, WV: Fitness Information Technology, 2010.

———, and David K. Wiggins, eds. *Routledge Handbook of Sport, Race, and Ethnicity*. London: Routledge, 2019.

Noll, Roger G., and Andrew Zimbalist, eds. *Sports, Jobs & Taxes: The Economic Impact of Sports Teams and Stadiums*. Washington, DC: Brookings Institution Press, 1997.

Nowlin, Bill. *Tom Yawkey: Patriarch of the Boston Red Sox*. Lincoln: University of Nebraska Press, 2018.

Nowlin, Bill, ed. *Pumpsie & Progress: The Red Sox, Race, and Redemption*. Burlington, MA: Rounder Books, 2010.

Ogden, David C., and Joel Nathan Rosen, eds. *Fame to Infamy: Race, Sports, and the Fall from Grace*. Jackson: University Press of Mississippi, 2010.

Olsen, Jack. *The Black Athlete: A Shameful Story: The Myth of Integration in American Sport*. N.p.: Crime Rant Books, 2015.

O'Ree, Willie, with Michael McKinley. *Willie: The Game-Changing Story of the NHL's First Black Player*. Toronto: Viking, 2020.

O'Toole, Andrew. *Fight for Old DC: George Preston Marshall, the Integration of the Washington Redskins, and the Rise of a New NFL*. Lincoln: University of Nebraska Press, 2016.

Peterson, Jason A. *Full Court Press: Mississippi State University, the Press, and the Battle to Integrate College Basketball*. Jackson: University Press of Mississippi, 2016.

Peterson, Robert W. *Pigskin: The Early Years of Pro Football*. New York: Oxford University Press, 1997.

Pethel, Mary Ellen. *Title IX, Pat Summitt, and Tennessee's Trailblazers: 50 Years, 50 Stories*. Knoxville: University of Tennessee Press, 2022.

Pieper, Lindsay Parks. *Sex Testing: Gender Policing in Women's Sports*. Urbana: University of Illinois Press, 2016.

Plimpton, George. *Shadow Box: An Amateur in the Ring*. Guilford, CT: Lyons Press, 1977.

Railton, Ben. *Of Thee I Sing: The Contested History of American Patriotism*. Lanham, MD: Rowman & Littlefield, 2021.

———. *We the People: The 500-Year Battle over Who Is American*. Lanham, MD: Rowman & Littlefield, 2019.

Rampersad, Arnold. *Jackie Robinson: A Biography*. New York: Knopf, 1997.

Rapinoe, Megan. *One Life*. New York: Penguin, 2020.

Redihan, Erin Elizabeth. *The Olympics and the Cold War, 1948–1968: Sports as Battleground in the U.S.–Soviet Rivalry*. Jefferson, NC: McFarland, 2017.

Reid, Jason. *Rise of the Black Quarterback*. New York: Andscape Books, 2022.

Remnick, David. *King of the World*. New York: Vintage Books, 1998.

Renkl, Margaret. *Graceland, At Last: Notes on Hope and Heartache from the American South*. Minneapolis: Milkweed Editions, 2021.

Reynolds, Bill. *Rise of a Dynasty: The '57 Celtics, the First Banner, and the Dawning of a New America*. New York: New American Library, 2010.

———. *'78: The Boston Red Sox, a Historic Game, and a Divided City*. New York: New American Library, 2009.

Rhoden, William C. *Forty Million Dollar Slaves: The Rise, Fall, and Redemption of the Black Athlete*. New York: Three Rivers Press, 2006.

Ribowsky, Mark. *Don't Look Back: Satchel Paige in the Shadows of Baseball*. New York: Da Capo Press, 1994.

Rider, Toby C. *Cold War Games: Propaganda, the Olympics, and U.S. Foreign Policy*. Chicago: University of Illinois Press, 2016.

Rider, Toby C., and Kevin B. Witherspoon, eds. *Defending the American Way of Life: Sport, Culture, and the Cold War*. Fayetteville: University of Arkansas Press, 2018.

Robenalt, James. *Ballots and Bullets: Black Power Politics and Urban Guerrilla Warfare in 1968 Cleveland*. Chicago: Lawrence Hill Books, 2018.

Roberts, Randy, and Johnny Smith. *Blood Brothers: The Fatal Friendship between Muhammed Ali and Malcolm X*. New York: Basic Books, 2016.

———. *War Fever: Boston, Baseball, and America in the Shadow of the Great War*. New York: Basic Books, 2020.

Robinson, Jackie. *I Never Had it Made: An Autobiography*. New York: HarperCollins, 1995.

Ross, Charles K. *Mavericks, Money, and Men: The AFL, Black Players, and the Evolution of Modern Football*. Philadelphia: Temple University Press, 2016.

———. *Outside the Lines: African Americans and the Integration of the National Football League*. New York: New York University Press, 1999.

Rowley, Christopher. *The Shared Origins of Football, Rugby, and Soccer*. Lanham, MD: Rowman & Littlefield, 2015.

Russell, Bill, and Taylor Branch. *Second Wind: The Memoirs of an Opinionated Man*. New York: Ballantine Books, 1979.

Russell, Bill, with Bill McSweeny. *Go Up for Glory*. New York: Penguin, 2020.

Russell, Bill, with Alan Steinberg. *Red and Me: My Coach, My Lifelong Friend.* New York: HarperCollins, 2009.

Schulian, John, ed. *Football: Great Writing about the National Sport.* New York: Literary Classics of the United States, Inc., 2014.

Schultz, Jaime. *Moments of Impact: Injury, Racialized Memory, and Reconciliation in College Football.* Lincoln: University of Nebraska Press, 2016.

Shaughnessy, Dan. *The Curse of the Bambino.* New York: Penguin, 1990.

———. *Wish it Lasted Forever: Life with the Larry Bird Celtics.* New York: Scribner, 2021.

Silver, James W. *Mississippi: The Closed Society,* new enlarged edition. New York: Harcourt, Brace, & World, 1966.

Snyder, Brad. *Beyond the Shadow of the Senators: The Untold Story of the Homestead Grays and the Integration of Baseball.* New York: McGraw-Hill, 2003.

Spivey, Donald. *Bates Must Play! Racism, Activism, and Integrity in College Football.* Durham, NC: Carolina Academic Press, 2021.

Stout, Glenn, and Richard A. Johnson. *Red Sox Century: One Hundred Years of Red Sox Baseball.* Boston: Houghton Mifflin, 2000.

Taylor, John. *The Rivalry: Bill Russell, Wilt Chamberlain, and the Golden Age of Basketball.* New York: Ballantine Books, 2005.

Thomas, Etan. *We Matter: Athletes and Activism.* Brooklyn, NY: Akashic Books, 2018.

Thomas, Ron. *They Cleared the Lane: The NBA's Black Pioneers.* Lincoln: University of Nebraska Press, 2002.

Tygiel, Jules. *Baseball's Great Experiment: Jackie Robinson and His Legacy.* 25th Anniversary Edition. New York: Oxford University Press, 2008.

Tygiel, Jules, ed. *The Jackie Robinson Reader: Perspectives on an American Hero.* New York: Plume, 1997.

Tyus, Wyomia, and Elizabeth Terzakis. *Tigerbelle: The Wyomia Tyus Story.* Brooklyn, NY: Akashic Books, 2018.

Van Natta, Don, Jr. *Wonder Girl: The Magnificent Sporting Life of Babe Didrikson Zaharias.* New York: Little, Brown, 2011.

Walsh, Christopher J. *Who's #1? 100-Plus Years of Controversial National Champions in College Football.* Lanham, MD: Taylor Trade, 2007.

Ware, Susan. *Title IX: A Brief History with Documents.* Long Grove, IL: Waveland Press, 2017.

Whalen, Thomas J. *Dynasty's End: Bill Russell and the 1968–69 World Champion Boston Celtics.* Boston: Northeastern University Press, 2004.

Wheeler, Lonnie. *The Bona Fide Legend of Cool Papa Bell: Speed, Grace, and the Negro Leagues.* New York: Abrams Press, 2020.

White, Derrick E. *Blood, Sweat, and Tears: Jack Gaither, Florida A&M, and the History of Black College Football.* Chapel Hill: University of North Carolina Press, 2019.

Wiggins, David K. *More Than a Game: A History of the African American Experience in Sport.* Lanham, MD: Rowman & Littlefield, 2018.

Wiggins, David K., ed. *Out of the Shadows: A Biographical History of African American Athletes.* Fayetteville: University of Arkansas Press, 2006.

Wiggins, David K., and Patrick B. Miller. *The Unlevel Playing Field: A Documentary History of the African American Experience in Sport.* Chicago: University of Illinois Press, 2003.

Wiggins, David K., and Ryan A. Swanson, eds. *Separate Games: African American Sport behind the Walls of Segregation.* Fayetteville: University of Arkansas Press, 2016.

Wigginton, Russell T. *The Strange Career of the Black Athlete: African Americans and Sports.* Westport, CT: Praeger, 2006.

Williams, Yohuru, and Michael G. Long. *Call Him Jack: The Story of Jackie Robinson, Black Freedom Fighter.* New York: Farrar Straus Giroux, 2022.

Wilson, John R. M. *Jackie Robinson and the American Dilemma.* New York: Longman, 2010.

Witherspoon, Kevin B. *Before the Eyes of the World: Mexico and the 1968 Olympic Games.* DeKalb: Northern Illinois University Press, 2008.

Yaeger, Don, with Sam Cunningham, and John Papadakis. *Turning of the Tide: How One Game Changed the South.* New York: Center Street, 2006.

Zaharias, Babe Didrikson. *This Life I've Led: My Autobiography.* Cleveland, OH: Barakaldo Books, 2020. Kindle edition.

Zang, David W. *Fleet Walker's Divided Heart: The Life of Baseball's First Black Major Leaguer.* Lincoln: University of Nebraska Press, 1995.

———. *Sports Wars: Athletes in the Age of Aquarius.* Fayetteville: University of Arkansas Press, 2001.

Zirin, Dave. *Game Over: How Politics Has Turned the Sports World Upside Down.* New York: New Press, 2013.

———. *Jim Brown: Last Man Standing.* New York: Blue Rider Press, 2018.

———. *The Kaepernick Effect: Taking a Knee, Changing the World.* New York: New Press, 2021.

———. *A People's History of Sports in the United States.* New York: New Press, 2008.

———. *Welcome to the Terrordome: The Pain, Politics, and Promise of Sports.* Chicago: Haymarket Books, 2007.

———. *What's My Name, Fool? Sports and Resistance in the United States.* Chicago: Haymarket Books, 2005.

JOURNAL ARTICLES

Bergera, Gary James. "This Time of Crisis: The Race-Based Anti-BYU Athletic Protests of 1968–1971." *Utah Historical Quarterly* 81, no. 3 (2013): 204–229.

Bryant, James A., Jr. "Taking a Knee: Colin Kaepernick and America's Forgotten Freedom Fighters." *History Teacher* 53, no. 4 (August 2020): 783–794.

Catsam, Derek. "'Sic 'Em, White Folks!': Football, Massive Resistance, and the Integration of Ole Miss." *Sport History Review* 40 (2009): 82–98.

Drake, Robert. "Joe Louis, the Southern Press, and the 'Fight of the Century.'" *Sport History Review* 43 (2012): 1–17.

Dyreson, Mark. "Icons of Liberty or Objects of Desire? American Women Olympians and the Politics of Consumption." *Journal of Contemporary History* 38, no. 3 (July 2003): 435–60.

Emery, Lynne. "An Examination of the 1928 Olympic 800 Meter Race for Women." *Proceedings of the North American Society for Sports History* (1985): 30.

Fleming, Tyler. "Now the African Reigns Supreme: The Rise of African Boxing on the Witwatersrand, 1924–1959." *International Journal of the History of Sport* 28, no. 1 (2011): 47–62.

Groom, Winston. "Coach Paul 'Bear' Bryant: The Legacy Off the Field." *Alabama Heritage* (Summer 2013): 47–62.

Henderson, Russell J. "The 1963 Mississippi State University Basketball Controversy and the Repeal of the Unwritten Law: 'Something More Than the Game Will Be Lost.'" *Journal of Southern History* 63, no. 4 (November 1997): 827–54.

Jobling, Ian. "The Women's 800 Metres Track Event Post 1928: Quo Vadis?" *Journal of Olympic History* 14, no. 1 (March 2006): 43–47.

Jordan, David M., Larry R. Gerlach, and John P. Rossi. "A Baseball Myth Exploded: The Truth about Bill Veeck and the '43 Phillies." *National Pastime: The Baseball Research Journal* (1998): 3–13.

Kama, Major Adam. "The Court-Martial of Jackie Robinson." *Army Lawyer* 1 (2020): 68–82.

Lipsyte, Robert. "Jock Culture: Robert Lipsyte on Paul Gallico's *Farewell to Sport* and the Importance of Destroying Your Illusions." *Columbia Journalism Review* 45, no. 2 (July/August 2006): 52–54.

O'Kelly, Charlotte G. "Black Newspapers and the Black Protest Movement, 1946–1972." *Phylon* 41, no. 4 (1980): 313–24.

Rounds, Christopher D. "The Policing of Patriotism: African American Athletes and the Expression of Dissent." *Journal of Sports History* 47, no. 2 (2020): 111–27.

Smith, John Matthew. "Breaking the Plane: Integration and Black Protest in Michigan State University Football during the 1960s." *Michigan Historical Review* 33, no. 2 (Fall 2007): 101–29.

Tygiel, Jules. "Revisiting Bill Veeck and the 1943 Phillies." *National Pastime: The Baseball Research Journal* 35 (2006): 109–14.

White, Derrick E. "From Desegregation to Integration; Race, Football, and 'Dixie' at the University of Florida." *Florida Historical Quarterly* 88, no. 4 (Spring 2010): 469–96.

DOCUMENTARIES/VIDEOS

Jackie Robinson. DVD. Directed by Ken Burns, Sarah Burns, and David McMahon. Florentine Films, 2016.

Muhammad Ali: The Greatest Collection. DVD. HBO Home Films. 1999.

Muhammad & Larry. DVD. Directed by Albert Maysles and Bradley Kaplan. ESPN 30 for 30, ESPN Films, 2011.

Muhammad Ali. DVD. Directed by Ken Burns, Sarah Burns, and David McMahon. Florentine Films, 2021.

IX for IX: Runner. DVD. Directed by Shola Lynch. ESPN Films, 2014.

When We Were Kings. DVD. Directed by Leon Gast. Gramercy Pictures, 2005.

Newspapers, Magazines, and Online Publications

Arizona Sun
Arizona Tribune
Associated Press
Atlantic
Austin American Statesman
Austin Chronicle
Austin Daily Texan
Bleacher Report
Bluefield Daily Telegraph
Boston Globe
Boston Herald and Journal
Call and Post
Charlotte Clymer Substack
Chicago American
Chicago Star
Chicago Tribune
Cleveland Plain Dealer
Clovis News Journal
Detroit Tribune
ESPN
Esquire
Evening Star
Faith & Sports
Fergis Falls Daily Journal
Free Press
Good Faith Media
GQ
Hechinger Report
Hillsdale Daily News
History News Network
Huston-Tillotson University
Hutchinson News
Indiana Gazette
Indianapolis Recorder
Longreads
Los Angeles Times
Miami Times
Minneapolis Spokesman
Nashua Telegraph
Newsweek
New Republic
New Tribune
New York Times

NFHS
Oakland Tribune
Odessa American
Ohio Express
Omaha Guide
Outsports
Phoenix Arizona Sun
Port Arthur News
Progressive Populist
Ram Magazine
Rhinelander Daily News
Runner's World
San Diego Tribune
Sport History Review
Sports Illustrated
Sports Weekly
St. Paul Recorder
Time
Times Herald
Twitter
USA Today
US Sports History
Voice
Washington Post
Yuma Sun
Zora

COURT CASES

Cannon v. University of Chicago, 441 U.S. 677 (1979).
Clay v. United States, 403 US 698 (1971).
Cohen et al. v. Brown University, 809 F. Supp. 978 (1992).
Favia v. Indiana University of Pennsylvania, 812 F. Supp. 578 (1993).
Franklin v. Gwinnett County Public Schools, 503 U.S. 60 (1992).
Gonyo v. Drake University, 837 F. Supp. 989 (1993).
Grove City College v. Bell, 465 U.S. 555 (1984).
Minersville School District v. Gobitis, 310 U.S. 586 (1940).
Tinker v. Des Moines Independent Community School District, 393 U.S. 503 (1969).
T.V. & M.K. v. Smith-Green Community School Corporation, 807 F Supp. 2D 767 (N.M.D. Ind. 2011).
West Virginia State Board of Education v. Barnette, 319 U.S. 624 (1943).
United States v. 2nd Lieutenant Jack R. Robinson, 0–10315861, *Calvary Company C, 758th Tank Battalion*.

Index

Christian colleges and universities, 142–44, 177–78, 197
Church of Jesus Christ of Latter-day Saints (LDS), 142, 144
CIAA. *See* Central Intercollegiate Athletic Association
City College of New York (CCNY), 96–97
Civil Rights Act of 1964, 169, 172
Clague, Mark, 124, 132–33
Clarion-Ledger, 99
Clark Griffith Bat and Ball Fund, 5
Clay, Cassius. *See* Ali, Muhammad
Cleaver, June, 29
Clemente, Roberto, 76, 134–38; Roberto Clemente Day, 134
Cleveland, Grover, 74
Cleveland, Ohio: and Ali Summit, 110–13, 118–20; integration in sports teams, 55–61; and racial tension, 53–54
Cleveland Browns, 32, 55–57, 82, 110, 112
Cleveland Call and Post, 59
Cleveland Indians, 48, 58, 60; Chief Wahoo, 61
Cleveland Municipal Stadium, 59
Cleveland Plain Dealer, 60, 117
Cleveland Rams. *See* Los Angeles Rams
Clifton, Sweetwater, 62
Cobbledick, Gordon, 60
Cohen et al. v. Brown University, 177

Coke (Coca-Cola), 180
Cold War, 81, 152, 160; and American patriotism, 123; and athletic competition, 163, 196; and female athletes, 28–29, 149–50, 156–58, 160
Cole Field House, 102
Coleman, Georgia "Gorgeous," 24
College of the Holy Cross, 62
College Park, Maryland, 102
Collins, Eddie, 75, 80
Collins, Jason, 184
Colombia, 134
Colorado, 203
Columbus, Ohio, 89
Colvard, Dean W., 98–100
Congress of Racial Equality (CORE), 196
Cooper, Charles "Chuck," 61–62
Cooperstown, New York, 6, 135
Comerica Park, 133–34
Comisky Park, 3, 6
Congress (United States), 2, 7, 9, 66, 110
Cosell, Howard, 153
Cousy, Bob, 62
Crimson Tide. *See* University of Alabama
Cronin, Joe, 75
Crooked Timber, xiv
Crusinberry, James, 5
Cuba, 134–35
Cubs. *See* Chicago Cubs
Cuniberti, Betty, 165
Cunningham, Sam, 95

Merle Alvey's Detroit Tigers
Dixieland Band, 125
Messerli, Dr. Fr. M., 16
Mexican American, 43, 96
Mexico, 134
Mexico City, Mexico, 22, 141,
144–46, 151, 198
Miami, Florida, 56, 133
Miami Marlins, 133, 176
Michaels, Al, 163
Michigan, 37, 89
Michigan State University
(Spartans), 88
Michener, James, 103–4
Midwest, 20, 90
Millait, Alice, 19
Minersville School District v.
Gobitis, 200–201
Minneapolis, Minnesota, 77–78,
82, 198
Minnesota Supreme Court, 88
Miñoso, Minnie, 61, 76, 135
Minsk, Belarus, 156–57
Misaka, Wat, 96
Mississippi, 76, 86, 92,
98–100, 203
Mississippi State University
(MSU) (Bulldogs), 97–101
Mississippi Supreme Court, 100
Mitchell, Bobby, 82, 110
Mitchell, Leland, 101
Mitts, Billy, 99–100
MLB. *See* Major League Baseball
Moffett, Captain William, 4
Monroe, Marilyn, 29

Montgomery, Alabama, 53
Montgomery, Lou, 89
Montreal, Canada, 158
Montreal Alouettes, 56, 186
Montreal Canadiens, 70
Montreal Daily Star, 14
Montreal Expos, 77
Montreal Royals, 55
Moore, Louis, 58–59, 76
Morris, Garrett, 138
Morrison, Jim, 124
Moscow, Russia, 149, 158
Motley, Marion, 32, 56, 57, 112
Motown, 124
Mowder, Major Thomas O., 38
MSU. *See* Mississippi State
University
Muchnick, Isadore, 74–75
Mucklerath, Ben W., 35, 37
Muhammad Ali Legacy
Award, 121
Muhammad, Elijah, 107–10,
115–16, 119
Muhammad, Jabir Herbert, 107–8,
116–17
Murray, Andy, 179
Murray, Jim, 157
Murray Hill, 54
Musberger, Brent, 145

NAACP. *See* National Association
for the Advancement of
Colored People
NAIA. *See* National Association
of Intercollegiate Athletics

Wright, John, 55
Wrigley Field, 3–4, 9
Wrigley, Phillip, 4, 9

X, Felton. *See* Russell, William
 Felton "Bill"
X, Malcolm, 66, 109

Yankees. *See* New York Yankees
Yawkey, Tom, 74–75
Yeates Drug Store, 44
Young, Whitney, 47

Zaharias, George, 26, 29
Zirin, Dave, 28, 109, 122, 136, 195

About the Author

Derek Charles Catsam is professor of history and the Kathlyn Cosper Dunagan Professor in the Humanities at the University of Texas Permian Basin, and senior research associate at Rhodes University in Grahamstown, South Africa, where he has been the Hugh Le May Fellow in the Humanities. He is the author of *Flashpoint: How a Little-Known Sporting Event Fueled America's Anti-Apartheid Movement* (2021), *Freedom's Main Line: The Journey of Reconciliation and the Freedom Rides* (2009), *Beyond the Pitch: The Spirit, Culture, and Politics of Brazil's 2014 World Cup* (2014), and *Bleeding Red: A Red Sox Fan's Diary of the 2004 Season* (2005). Catsam has contributed columns and articles on American and African politics and sports to many publications. He lives with his wife, Ana, who is also a historian; his nephew, George; and a menagerie of cats in Odessa, Texas. He maintains his lifelong love for Boston sports teams.

Printed in the USA
CPSIA information can be obtained
at www.ICGtesting.com
LVHW041202260923
759276LV00002B/19